Gilded Lili

Gilded Lili

Lili St. Cyr

and the Striptease Mystique

Kelly DiNardo

BACK STAGE BOOKS
An Imprint of Watson-Guptill Publications
New York

Executive Editor: Bob Nirkind
Project Editor: Ross Plotkin
Production Manager: Alyn Evans
Interior Design: Meryl Levavi
Jacket Design: Charles Woods
The principal typefaces used in the composition
of this book were Electra LH and Linoscript.

First published in 2007 by Back Stage Books,
An imprint of Watson-Guptill Publications,
Nielsen Business Media, a division of The Nielsen Company
770 Broadway, New York, NY 10003
www.watsonguptill.com

Library of Congress Control Number: 2007921237

ISBN-13: 978-0-8230-8889-8
ISBN-10: 0-8230-8889-9

Printed in the United States

First printing, 2007

1 2 3 4 5 6 7 8 9 / 14 13 12 11 10 09 08 07

For Josh

Acknowledgments

The process of writing this book has been quite similar to performing a striptease; there's the buildup, the tease, and finally the reveal. Most important, there is a cast and crew working and helping behind the scenes.

I am incredibly grateful to those who took the time to share their memories and stories, particularly Armando Orsini, Andrea Hedrick, Bob Bethia, Patrick Guinness, Ellie Hiatt, Jamee Carangello, Doris Quinn Godfrey, Kash, Coy Giambone, Betty Rowland, and Gloria Zomar. They were all incredibly giving of their time. John Chaplin, Eric Schaefer, Sheila Weller, Alan Hustak, and William Weintraub shared their expertise, resources, and leads. Kara Mae Harris, Laura Herbert, and Jaye Furlonger answered endless questions and helped me contact several dancers and friends of Lili's.

Shauna Redmond at the Pasadena Public Library, Kristine Krueger at the Academy Library, and Nancy Marrelli of Concordia made digging through various records and primary source documents so much easier.

I worked with a variety of assistants who spent hours helping me with research and transcription work, including Sarah Morocco, Katy Graessle, Eleanor Edwards, Alyson Casey, Caitlin Murray, David Andrukonis, Sarah

Wright, and Lisa Sumner. I am particularly appreciative of John C. Buckholz for his research assistance and translation work.

My agent Eric Myers believed in this project and helped bring it to fruition. Anthony Summers and Robbyn Swan taught me an immense amount about writing and researching a biography. They have been generous of spirit, time, and love. And Rachel Shteir, whose own research and book on striptease was invaluable, was an incredible cheerleader, mentor, and friend throughout.

Several friends and colleagues were arm-twisted into reading various chapters and versions of the manuscript including Peter Abrahams, Michele Aranda, Kathy Balog, Geoff Kirsch, Melissa McCart, Amanda McClements, Nycci Nellis, Amber Pfau, and Loredana Sherman. Two men, in particular, worked with me to shape and edit this manuscript: my friend Bart Mills and my editor at Back Stage Books, Bob Nirkind. If, as they say, to write is human; to edit is divine, then Bart and Bob are certainly my red-pen-wielding angels.

Countless friends and family supported me through this in so many ways. My mother, who taught me the word voracious at the age of five, instilled in me such a love of books and reading that becoming a writer seems inevitable. My father, who answered endless legal questions throughout, rooted me on with enthusiasm and love. My sister tolerated living with me through much of this process—not an easy thing. Kitty, Bob, Nancy, Jim, Mary, Andrew, Courtney, Tom, Barb, Thomas J., and Chad—thank you.

Finally, there is no way this book would be complete without Josh Lewis. He supported and inspired me in so many ways. I am eternally grateful for all of his help, guidance, and most of all, his friendship.

Contents

Foreword

$\mathcal{B}$londe and beautiful—though not exactly by the convention of her era—Lili St. Cyr was said to have inspired Marilyn Monroe. She was more carnal and more dirty, perhaps what Marilyn would have been had she been able to be herself. In truth, Lili looked very little like Marilyn, except for their shared love of peroxide blonde—the *couleur de la decade*. Lili was tall. A little too tall. She was slender. A little too slender. This was an era when it was fashionable to be zaftig and petite.

She was more of a cipher than Marilyn, and she lacked Marilyn's air of naiveté and intellectual, highbrow aspirations. In fact, Lili never seemed to have aspirations, other than escaping her past and stripping. She was, of course, a sex symbol. Lili embodied something intangible and captured the hearts of American men in burlesque theaters and swank nightclubs at a time when Americans seesawed between the Cold War and the Rat Pack, and between Lenny Bruce and Catholic reformers. Lili was big time in the small time. Her acts were *tableaux vivants*, posed homages to the great classical women. She was Salome. She was Cleopatra. In a country where Puritanism was king, Lili was a naughty queen. I think of her as the soul of the fifties—rising as striptease was dying, coyly smiling, mincing, prancing, and above all dancing.

The history of striptease can be told as the story of dames and broads—funny girls and sexy women. Gypsy Rose Lee was a dame; Lili St. Cyr a broad. But while Gypsy wisecracked her way across the stage, men seemed to think that Lili, who was silent, was sexier. She was also more modern, more classy, more aristocratic.

I sometimes think of Lili as being a Technicolor stripper in a Technicolor era, by which I mean that though observers might have called her more refined than other strippers, there was something large about her appeal. There is one particularly fetching picture of her where she wears jewel tones and looks like a Bollywood goddess. There could be something regal about her. She gave the impression of being haughty. Some observers said that she wasn't like other strippers, that she had a kind of elegance other strippers lacked. But when you looked at her, it was not her elegance that was striking. It was her carnality and that impenetrable sex appeal. There was something distant about her, something withdrawn. She was a girl Wild One in a time when girls were only just beginning to be wild ones in public. Every era had its stripper who was not just a stripper, but an icon. Lili was the icon of her era.

Lili didn't necessarily make good choices, not where her career was concerned, or when it came to men. She married six times, but I'm not sure whether she ever found love. On the other hand, her life could have been worse. It was for many of her peers. Something, perhaps toughness, or her will, must have been on her side. She had the resilience of a cartoon character or a superhero. In contrast to today's strippers, whose sexuality, in its attempt to be racy, often seems naïve, Lili was anything but innocent. Instead she captured a sophistication that has gone out of fashion.

In *Gilded Lili: Lili St. Cyr and the Striptease Mystique*, Kelly DiNardo brings Lili to life. She has chased down the facts and has gathered them into an animating intelligence that reveals the particulars of Lili and of Lili's era. With great reporting and incisive thinking, Kelly has captured the woman with verve and grace.

—RACHEL SHTEIR

1.

In the Beginning

Audacity is essential to greatness.
— Friedrich Nietzsche

On a stage set to look like a small cottage, a tall woman with blond curls appeared as Cinderella. She began fully clothed in a peasant dress, with a red skirt and black corset top, which perfectly showed off her body's curves. Exaggerating each movement, she moved around the stage—revealing an ankle, a thigh, the hint of a breast. Slowly, to the beat of the music, she took off her high heels, her dress, then her bra. Suddenly a wand appeared, magically floating in the air, and delivered silk thigh-highs, a blue and pink-trimmed satin gown, and glass slippers. With her new clothes, she slowly covered up her long, tan legs and torso, still slowly swiveling her hips and mesmerizing the audience. She ran her hands through her hair and she puckered her glossy red lips. With a red-painted fingertip, she softly traced her neck, letting her hand slide down, down, down. Then she nuzzled a brown fur stole softly across her face, slid it around her body, and admired her new look before her tall, dark-haired prince arrived. She and her prince waltzed across the stage. He leaned in to kiss her, but she coyly turned her face and offered him just her cheek. Then, as the clock perched above her approached midnight, he disappeared. With each passing minute the clock ticked closer to midnight, a crescendo built, and more of her clothing vanished. Tick. She stood in only a blue, ruffled bra and panties. Tock. She appeared in just a G-string and pasties. Tick tock. She stood nearly naked, wrapping her arms around herself so as to hide her breasts. Tick tock. She stared at the clock, and in a flash she returned to her red and black peasant's dress. She looked forlornly at the glass slipper, the only remnants of her enchanted evening.

Cinderella was not Lili St. Cyr's most famous striptease, but often the fictional world she created on stage echoed, predicted, or commented on the real circumstances in her life. And in many ways, she lived a sexier, bawdier Cinderella tale. Instead of an invisible fairy godmother with a magic wand, she used the sexy twirling of her G-string-clad hips to pull herself up from a working-class life to inhabit a real bejeweled, fur-draped world.

In May 1936, as the jacaranda bloomed with clusters of trumpet-shaped purple flowers throughout Pasadena, an 18-year-old Lili St. Cyr, still known as Marie Van Schaack, took the first steps toward that bejeweled, fur-draped world. She left her childhood home and traveled nearly three thousand miles across the country to New York. Standing in the sun, her dirty blonde hair hanging in waves and curling at her chin, Marie watched the crowds wave good-bye as the boat slipped down the Hudson and out to sea on its way to England.

Before the advent of jet travel, the ships that sailed between America and Europe oozed with the aura of opulence. While many passengers suffered below deck in cramped and squalid steerage berths, the carefree indulgence of the first-class passengers imparted a sense of excitement and wonder about the era's idea of ship travel. Travelers with last names like Rockefeller and Carnegie and the onboard exploits of movie stars and Olympic athletes generated headlines and newspaper columns about the steam liners. Moving between two continents, ocean liners could become their own world, magnificent floating palaces.

On her first trip aboard a grand steam liner, Marie reveled in the excitement of this milieu. She felt she had "penetrated to the very heart of a grandiose and marvelous party. Everything made me crazy, excited me, surprised me, enchanted me. Everything happened like the scenes I'd seen in films. . . . I had the realization that life was mine, that it was my own universe."[1] Her journey in 1936 would be a six-day whirlwind of bubbly dinners and illicit moonlit kisses. Three women had shown Marie that the world could be this glamorous adventure—her grandmother

Alice, the European princess Rosemary Blackadder, and Greta Garbo—
and for the rest of her life she strove to live her life as if traveling first-class
on an ocean liner.

Fact and fiction are inextricably interwoven in the story of Alice's life. In
the great American tradition of personal reinvention, Marie's grandmother, a talented seamstress, so artfully stitched the tales together that the
seam between truth and fairy tale is nearly invisible. Various family members have tried to unravel the threads of her tales, but that has proven
almost impossible. Some stories—like Alice's claim to be a descendant of
either a Moroccan prince or a Moorish sea captain, depending on who is
retelling the tale—are clearly fantasy. Others are less obviously false; perhaps she *was* part Sioux Indian.

In reality, Alice was born Mariah Maude Curry on March 21, 1874, in
Port Edwards, Wisconsin, which was a riverside community roughly mid-
way between Milwaukee and Minneapolis. Her parents, a Canadian
named Daniel Curry and his New Yorker wife Emilie, likely moved to the
area in the second half of the nineteenth century, when Wisconsin experienced a population boom. Between 1836 and 1850, the state's population
exploded from 11,000 to over 300,000. A third of the arrivals were foreign-
born immigrants, primarily from Germany, Norway, and Canada.[2] The
new Wisconsinites settled in frontier towns that stretched out from the
lakes and rivers that supported the miners, fur traders, and lumber workers.
Daniel worked along the banks of the Wisconsin River as a foreman in a
lumberyard. Emilie cared for their six daughters.

Little is known about Alice's childhood and teen years, although
Marie later described her as a pioneer. An early settler portrayed the area
in which Alice grew up as "only a small settlement with a trail running
down the river bank."[3] Women, a minority in these small outposts, could
make a decent amount of money doing the demanding domestic work
that they were expected to do for free in more populated areas. Alice's sister Nellie worked as a cook in the mountains, feeding the men who
worked on the logging crews, and it's likely that Alice held similar work—
possibly sewing or cooking, as she was also a gifted cook. "It didn't matter
what was in the house, she could always whip up something terrific,"
explained Coy Giambone, Nellie's granddaughter.[4] The sisters also
enjoyed the advantages of being the scarcer sex outside of work as well.

"They were strong-willed, independent, and man-crazy—they were all married several times and had lots of boyfriends," said Coy. "For women in those years they had a lot of nerve in picking up and leaving a person if things weren't working out well. They were perfectly willing to work very hard on their own to achieve whatever they were looking for."

Through Alice's own adventures, or perhaps through her father's work, she met Francis "Frank" Cedric Peeso, who worked in a paper mill, later owned a restaurant, and then worked as a painter. In 1895, twenty-one-year-old Alice married Frank. Within a year, Alice gave birth to a daughter, Idella Marian Peeso. The young family then moved in with Frank's family in Merrill, Wisconsin. Alice gave birth to a son, William Austin Peeso, before the family packed up and made the 200-mile journey to Minneapolis. At some point after 1910, Alice and Frank's marriage withered and ultimately died; by 1917, Alice had married Ben Klarquist, a carpenter.

While the factual details of Alice's early life remain scant, what is apparent is that she was determined, fiercely independent, incredibly warm-hearted, and apt to display a vivid imagination.[5]

Later, after Alice was widowed, she traveled around the country visiting her sisters, grandchildren, and great-grandchildren. "She would just take off," explained her granddaughter Ellie Hiatt.[6] "It didn't seem to bother her that she was alone. She just loved to sit and talk to people. She was very personable, her house was always open, and there were no pretenses at all. She would get into telling her stories and I imagine she embellished most anything. But that's all right. We loved to hear it. It was always fun to listen to her."

Alice was such fun that Kris Plasch, Ellie's daughter, asked that her sixteenth birthday present be to visit her great-grandmother once a month. "She just seemed to conquer whatever she set out to do," said Plasch.[7] "She overcame a lot of obstacles; she raised some of her grandchildren and even one of her great-grandchildren, who was a real handful. She adapted to whatever the circumstances were. She was just an amazing, remarkable woman."

While Alice spent a lot of time with several of her grandchildren, she raised Marie, the future ocean traveler. In 1916, romance had bloomed between Alice's nineteen-year-old daughter Idella and Edward Van Schaack, the son of a Dutch settler from New York named Frank Van Schaack and an Iowan farm girl named Rebecca Ann Gray. It is unclear whether Idella and

Edward ever married. Regardless, on June 3, 1917, Idella gave birth to Marie Frances Van Schaack at Abbott Hospital in Minneapolis.[8]

Instead of Marie's mother, it was Alice and her new husband who took the newborn home from the hospital and raised her. Years later, Marie's family told her that Alice and Ben took her home because Idella was too sick to care for her and her father simply disappeared.

But in fact Edward hadn't disappeared: he'd been drafted. Two days after Marie's birth, as America mobilized to join World War I, the nation held a "Registration Day," requiring all men between the ages of twenty-one and thirty to register for possible service. In Minneapolis, the day took on the "bearing of an unofficial patriotic holiday,"[9] and saloons and most stores in the city closed. By fall of 1917, almost 19,000 men reported for training at Camp Lewis in Washington State, one of sixteen new Army installations whose ranks eventually swelled to 44,000. The United States entered the war toward the end of the struggle and Edward spent less than a year in the army, serving most of his hitch at Camp Lewis.[10]

The demands of World War I hastened the changes that had slowly been taking hold in the early part of the century. By the early 1920s, Americans flung aside the reticence, prudence, and general restraint of previous generations for a new emphasis on personal gratification. It was an era of confidence, affluence, and flamboyance. During the decade that would later be known as the "Roaring Twenties," industrialization drew people out of rural areas and into cities. The consumer economy boomed. Workers' wages rose faster than ever, and Americans bought cars, radios, and stoves. Women discovered a new purchasing power, and companies offered them vacuum cleaners, refrigerators, and other technologies that promised to ease their domestic burden and give them more time to indulge in other interests. And the cosmetic industry, an entirely new business, helped women look good during their new-found free time.

The 1920s saw a marked change in the nation's beauty standard: the pale, Rubenesque model of bygone days was replaced by a tan, slim new vision. The late-nineteenth-century idea that beauty included a spiritual quality was traded for the idea that beauty was just a stroke of lipstick away. In 1920, five thousand beauty parlors dotted the United States. By 1930, the number of salons multiplied to forty thousand, supported by a nearly 180-million-dollar cosmetic industry.[11] Women powdered their noses, rouged their cheeks, and dyed their hair. Youthful beauty was a matter of will and money.

This new emphasis on personal gratification, on looking good, on spending money, and on having fun spilled into the bedrooms and the backseats of cars across the country. World War I changed the story of boy-meets-girl throughout America and ushered in what many have called the first sexual revolution. During the war, the military tried to protect soldiers from venereal disease by showing the troops propaganda movies warning that sex could kill. But a survey found that nearly two-thirds of the men had sex overseas and veterans often described their off-duty activities as "wine, women, and song."[12] The soldiers returned from war more sexually experienced and permissive.

Stateside, they found their women more independent in the workplace, at home, and in their fashions. The women unhooked their corsets and slipped off their petticoats, leaving their bodies more visible and mobile. After the war, they shortened their skirts, bared their arms, and bobbed their hair in the new flapper style. The New Woman, whether a college girl or a department store employee, was, above all, independent. "The underlying impulse was freedom—from the mores of the past that required women to keep themselves in check, physically and emotionally," wrote *America's Women* author Gail Collins.[13] "The woman of the Twenties . . . was not going to keep the hearth warm while her mate was out carousing. She was out there with him."

Out there, both men and women found a plethora of sexual information. In Margaret Sanger's crusade for the availability and use of birth control, she wrote articles and brochures filled with facts about what every girl should know. Americans flipped through true confession magazines to read salacious first-person accounts. F. Scott Fitzgerald wrote about petting parties. And Sigmund Freud's ideas on sex were so popular that nearly 200 books on his theories had been published in America by 1920. So much was written on Freud that "if the average student's understanding of the subject was shallow, she picked up enough to be convinced that sex was the center of everything for women as well as men."[14]

There was, of course, resistance in this revolution. Censors and purity campaigners railed against the changes. Anthony Comstock, the most successful reformer, battled with Sanger, abortionists, and publishers and inspired a series of eponymous laws. Even so, for the first time sex was something to be discussed and to be displayed. And all of this talk about sex helped sexual expression move beyond the confines of marriage, not as a deviant behavior, but as the norm. Suitors no longer sat under the vigilant eye of parents; rather, young couples went on dates. They kissed, necked, and nearly 50 percent of women who came of age in the twenties engaged in premarital sex.[15] Married couples began to expect companionship and pleasure in their relationship as well. In 1926, Dr. Theodoor Van de Velde wrote *Ideal Marriage,* in which he stressed the importance of foreplay, encouraged oral sex, and included ten sexual positions for couples to try. He even warned that a husband might hurt his wife if he ignored her pleasure. "Every considerable erotic stimulation of their wives that does not terminate in orgasm on the woman's part represents an injury, and repeated injuries of this kind lead to permanent—or very obstinate damage to both body and soul," wrote Van de Velde.[16] Sex was becoming the central adventure in life.

In Minneapolis, Marie's mother Idella seemed to embrace this new attitude. By the time Edward arrived at Camp Lewis, she was involved with another man, Louis "Jack" Cornett. While it is uncertain whether the two ever wed—and descendants of Cornett's doubt it—they did have two children, a daughter, Bettalee, and a son, Louis, also known as Jack. But Idella's relationship with their father did not last. By 1924, she had married Ian (John) Alfred Blackadder, a Scottish immigrant, and was pregnant with their first child, a daughter named Idella Ruth. A year later, a month before she turned thirty, Idella gave birth to her fifth and last child, a daughter Rosemary, named after Ian's sister.

While Marie's young mother started a new family and her father served in the military, she remained with Alice and Ben, believing they were her parents and that Idella was her older sister. And for much of her childhood, she went by the name Marie Klarquist. At some point in the early twenties, Ben was injured in an accident on a construction site. The doctors suggested that country air might help, so he moved with Alice and Marie to a farm in Wisconsin. The change had no effect on Ben's health and the family moved several more times. Marie claimed she attended seventeen schools during this nomadic period.

By 1929, both families—the Klarquists and the Blackadders—reconnected in Pasadena, California. The two families were part of the swarm of migrants charmed by California. They escaped the harsh, cold winters, and sometimes the law, and came for the promise of sunshine, a reprieve from health problems like asthma, and a new life. So many Midwesterners landed in Pasadena that the transplants named the town after a word from the Chippewas, a Native American tribe that lived in the upper Midwest. The new residents considered Chippewa phrases that translated to crown of the valley or key of the valley, and finally settled on Pasadena, which translates simply to "the valley."

Indeed, Pasadena became the crown of the valley, a luxurious resort town and cultural center that catered to the wealthy. The new Californians planted orange trees, eucalyptus, and other exotic plants that thrived in the sun. Men like businessman Henry Huntington, brewmaster Adolphus Busch, and chewing gum magnate William Wrigley built resort hotels and large winter homes. Artists like writer Upton Sinclair helped the city become a thriving cultural community. Such a high concentration of moneyed businessmen and literati populated Pasadena that by the twenties it claimed to be the wealthiest city per capita in the United States.[17]

During these boom years, most of the town's development took part in the western part of the city. The middle-class and working families settled in the eastern part of the city, and it was here, on Oak Avenue, that Marie and her grandparents lived for almost ten years. Their home at 215 South Oak had originally been built as a garage in 1922, but within a year was converted to a small house. By 1929, when Marie and her family moved in, the house had two bedrooms, a bathroom, living room, kitchen, and a screened-in porch.[18]

Idella and her family initially settled around the corner from Marie and her grandparents, but over the next five years the Blackadders moved four times, until they finally settled in a house on North Figueroa in Eagle Rock, about four miles west of Pasadena.

On October 24, 1929, just months after the two families put down roots in Pasadena, the stock market crashed, and the country began its descent into the Depression. Other less affluent towns were hit harder, but Pasadena retained its rich patina. In 1932, journalist Morrow Mayo wrote, "Pasadena is ten miles from Los Angeles as the Rolls-Royces fly." And in 1939, a study rated Pasadena the most desirable American city in which to live. But Pasadena was not immune to the Depression. Tourism slowed, millionaires shuttered their mansions, and people found work where they could.[19] Alice supported her small family by working as a seamstress while

Ian toiled first at a gas station, then as a salesman for Crown City Dairy, then as a private investigator.[20]

During these early years in Pasadena, her family finally explained to Marie that Idella was really her mother, not her sister, and that Alice was her grandmother, not her mother. Marie rarely talked about the admission or its impact on her. As late as 1982, she wrote in her Canadian memoir *Ma Vie de Stripteaseuse*, "Even today, I don't understand perfectly how much this revelation affected me. I did my best *not* to let it affect me."[21]

Despite her best efforts, Marie did not escape unscathed. She continued to live with her grandparents, whom she adored, but she manipulated the situation to her advantage. She would spend a few days living with Alice and a few days with Idella, where she could "pass unnoticed among her four children and . . . act the way I wanted,"[22] which included sneaking around with her boyfriend. Nearly half a century later, when researchers examined such family circumstances they found girls with absent fathers often felt responsible for their father's departure, suffered from a plummeting self-esteem, were more likely to be promiscuous, and first had sex at an earlier age.[23]

Marie's relationship with her father may have been nonexistent, but she also never forged a bond with her mother. If Idella had initially taken up the twenties mantle of passionate freedom, any trace of that young Idella was long gone by the time her eldest daughter spent any significant time with her. The consequences of that sexual freedom in a time when birth control was still hard to obtain left her with four children to raise in the midst of the Depression. Her marriage to Ian was rocky, and at some point she contracted polio. Contrary to popular belief, the polio virus most often causes a minor coldlike infection with symptoms like headache and nausea. The result of the disease can range from stiff joints to total paralysis to death. For Idella, the illness left her with a crippled leg, making movement difficult. It was likely that all of these setbacks made Idella cold, harsh, and cantankerous, as some described her.

Marie viewed Idella with a mixture of frustration and pity. She thought her mother "was a prisoner in a life she didn't accept in a house she couldn't leave because of her leg."[24] Determined not to become trapped like her mother, Marie instead followed in the feisty footsteps of her grandmother. And so, from the beginning, it was the women who shaped her: the mother she wanted to avoid becoming and the grandmother whose spirit she strove to match.

*I*n the early 1930s, another bold woman gave a jolt to Marie's life: Rosemary Blackadder. Marie's stepfather Ian had been born and raised in the Borders area of Scotland, where the Blackadder family lived since the thirteenth century. Ian was one of three children to parents who inherited a significant amount of money and farmland. The Blackadder children grew up in a household where English, French, and German were spoken. Their parents prized art and literature and valued talent astride a horse. However, their circumstances changed somewhat when World War I began, and Ian immigrated to the United States in the twenties. He left behind his family, including his sister, Rosemary.

Rosemary, a bright student, received a scholarship to Girton College, the first British residential college to offer higher education degrees to women. She traveled to Italy to study art and architecture and witnessed Mussolini's march on Rome. Later she studied painting in Paris and shared an apartment with Anna Mahler, the daughter of composer Gustav Mahler. She traveled through Europe and worked as a freelance journalist. "She had become a cosmopolitan and self-sufficient artist with contacts across Europe and many admirers," wrote Rosemary's grandson Patrick Guinness.[25] One of her admirers was a German prince, Albrecht von Urach, her future husband. He was also a talented artist who included Picasso and Dali among his friends.

This cultured, sophisticated princess that came to visit her "favorite sibling"[26] in Pasadena made such an impact on a teenage Marie that she called her "the most magical woman I ever met."[27] To Marie, who was fascinated with the movies, Rosemary seemed like a character right off the big screen. "She was gracious and elegant. She had good manners and she had the most magnificent wardrobe I've ever seen. Everyone treated her with attention that exceeded what was ordinary. Her enormous valises [and] her leather traveling bags . . . were ornamented with stickers from foreign cities: Paris, Venice, Cairo, Shanghai, Hong Kong."[28] But Rosemary wasn't a character from the movies. She was Marie's first indication that the life she wished for was not just a fantasy, but could be a reality. Rosemary gave her hope and a model to strive for. "She was a character who was living the existence I dreamed of," wrote Marie more than fifty years later.[29] "I had the firm intention of becoming as fascinating, as exciting and exotic, and as completely respected as she was."

Rosemary left Pasadena and in many respects lived with the intoxicating élan Marie dreamed about: she traveled through Europe working as a reporter and lived in Japan for several years with her husband and their daughter. But problems bubbled just below the surface. Through various political maneuverings that changed Germany's lines of succession, Albrecht lost his inheritance and could not make a living painting. Rosemary suggested they move to California and make money drawing cartoons for the movies, but Albrecht would have none of it. He eventually got a job as a photo-journalist and through his work the family moved to Japan. In the late thirties, Albrecht traveled extensively, covering the Japanese invasion of China. Perhaps driven by loneliness, Rosemary went to Tokyo to tell the Emperor he was being misled by his generals. She used her diplomatic passport to enter the Palace buildings and made it to the residence before being arrested and deported. The episode separated her from her daughter and embarrassed her husband. She plunged into a deep depression. "She saw herself as an inadequate wife and mother, once so independent, now always dependent on others," Guinness wrote.[30] For the rest of her life, Rosemary battled depression and mental illness. She was sent to a private mental hospital, lobotomized, and spent the rest of her life in a "tragic living death."[31] Considering the stigma of mental illness at the time, it is doubtful Marie ever knew what happened to Rosemary. Rather, she continued to view her as the beautiful, urbane princess she met in Pasadena.

Rosemary's whirlwind visit proved to Marie that it was possible to actually live in the stylish, cultured world of the movies that so captivated her. Throughout her childhood, Marie settled into the plush chairs of the movie theaters, felt the darkness envelop her, and let the flickering images on the screen bewitch her. She was part of the first generation that grew up totally under the spell of the cinema, spending hours studying the glamorous lives that flashed in front of her. But the movies offered more than a vision of a fashionable, opulent, party-going world. In the dark recesses of these movie theaters Americans learned how to romance each other, to look into each other's eyes, hold each other, and kiss. And it is where Marie learned how to use her charm and beauty to become a true seductress.

Sex was a part of twentieth-century entertainment from the very beginning. During the first decades of the century, impresarios like Florenz Ziegfeld and Earl Carroll began staging upscale variety shows that put young, beautiful girls center stage. During the twenties, as hemlines began to rise offstage, the girls in Earl Carroll's Varieties and Ziegfeld's Follies needed to compete. For a start, chorus girls stripped off their stockings. As the decade progressed, they even appeared nude. With a chic setting and expensive tickets, these cabarets were considered legitimate theater, which allowed them to get away with such displays.

Burlesque followed a stricter standard. In 1868, Lydia Thompson and her British Blondes introduced America to burlesque, a combination of comic performances, skits, and risqué dance routines. The troupe, which performed in tights and what were then considered skimpy costumes, scandalized Americans and sold out theaters. For the rest of the nineteenth century, burlesque poked fun at the upper class and showed off women's bodies. But by the early twentieth century, burlesque focused primarily on bawdy jokes and bare legs. Its performers shed their tights years before their chorus girl counterparts. But with its lewd humor and working-class audience, burlesque was not deigned legitimate theater and regularly battled censors and vice groups.

These live shows lured urban Americans with the promise of sex, but they weren't available everywhere. Movies and their enticements became ubiquitous, magnifying the attractions of sex to gargantuan proportions in the apparent privacy of darkness. When Theda Bara, one of movies' first sirens, starred in the 1916 film *A Fool There Was*, a story of a woman who seduces a married man, destroys his family life, and abandons him in an alcoholic ruin, audiences were fascinated. Bara taunted audiences with her sexuality in more than forty movies in three years. At one point it was estimated that 400,000 people saw a Theda Bara movie every day.[32] The movies gripped audiences with a visceral power that live performances could not match.

But stage performers tried, growing far more provocative in an effort to compete. In the twenties, long before the name Lili St. Cyr lit up the marquee, another name was beginning to alter the teasing face of burlesque: Minsky. The four Minsky brothers—Abe, Billy, Mort, and Herbert—opened several burlesque theaters in New York, where they upgraded burlesque by stealing the best of Ziegfeld, Broadway, and vaudeville and offering it at a much cheaper ticket price, albeit with a lot more sass and a lot less clothing. The Minskys bumped things up a notch, advancing burlesque's leg show to striptease. They added a runway to the stage so that women could strut and shimmy closer to the audience. Down Minsky's runway paraded the queens of burlesque. Carrie Finnell was the girl with the $100,000 legs. Mae Dix snapped bananas off her hips as she sang. Gypsy Rose Lee recited poems while slowly undressing. By the mid-twenties, fully acknowledging burlesque's draw, the Minskys put the stripteasers' names above the comics' on the marquee. "By this time there was no question that the way to sell tickets in burlesque was with sex," Mort Minsky wrote in his memoir.33 "Comics were what people loved once they were in the theater, but it was sex on the marquee that pulled them in."

As the women wore less, the censors pushed harder. And as Minsky literally moved burlesque uptown, competing more openly with shows like Ziegfeld's, Broadway producers and impresarios increased the pressure to rein in burlesque. Of course, they also stole right back from Minsky, making their shows more erotic as well. But what was acceptable in the legitimate theater was not so in burlesque. Minsky and other burlesque producers spent much of the 1920s and early 1930s battling various civic organizations and politicians that crusaded against what they viewed as objectionable entertainment.

In many respects the twenties was a decade of contrasts: Minsky and the censors, Margaret Sanger and Anthony Comstock, bootleg whiskey and Prohibition. But overall, Americans wanted to play. And so Babe Ruth swung for the fences, Mae West sashayed across the stage, Louis Armstrong blew his horn, and Greta Garbo shimmered on the silver screen.

More than any other movie star, Marie was completely spellbound by Garbo, about whom film critic Kenneth Tynan wrote: "[Entranced] by the ecstasy of existing, she gives to each onlooker what he needs." 34 Arriving in Hollywood from Sweden in 1925, Garbo quickly played signature roles like the sophisticated socialite Irene in *The Kiss* and an exotic Russian spy Tania in *The Mysterious Lady*. Her celluloid image personified sex and intrigue and let millions escape into a more glamorous world. When she made her talking picture debut in 1930, two words sufficed: "Garbo Talks." By the early thirties she was Hollywood's highest paid actress, making $250,000 to $300,000 per picture. Other actresses, society ladies, and even shop girls studied and imitated her. She was, in the words of Alistair Cooke, "every man's harmless, fantasy mistress. . . . [and] she gives you the feeling that if your imagination has to sin, it can at least congratulate itself on its impeccable taste."35 For women, Garbo was "divinely untouchable, often unworldly, [and her] allure lay in [the] denial of the humdrum destiny reserved for a woman," wrote Marjorie Rosen in *Popcorn Venus*.36

"Rarely did [she] see or want love, perhaps because it would be [her] ruin or demystification."

The impact on Marie was so great it did not seem to matter that Garbo's characters were punished by disgrace (*The Temptress*) or death (*Flesh and the Devil, The Love, A Woman of Affairs*) for being too audacious, too exciting. In fact, the movies—and Greta Garbo in particular—so wholly fashioned whom Marie would become, that more than fifty years later, describing her escapades on that first transatlantic voyage she noted that Garbo would have been proud. Marie wrote, "I wanted to be nothing other than the mysterious and fascinating characters that she played on screen. . . . I couldn't stop myself from thinking that the golden life of the silver screen was life as it should be lived. And life as I thought I would live it one day."[37]

While Marie certainly inherited a sense of adventure and free spirit from her grandmother Alice, her later sophistication was self-taught, modeled after Garbo and emboldened by the reality that Rosemary presented. The three women showed her that life could be an uninhibited, elegant adventure. And her champagne-filled journey aboard the SS *Manhattan* was the first time she actually lived in the world they opened to her. What transported the teenager from Pasadena to the SS *Manhattan* to mingle with the rich or merely well-heeled travelers was a marriage proposal. She was en route to England to marry American motorcycle racer Cordy Milne.

The champion motorcycle racer whom Marie later compared to James Dean moved to Pasadena from Detroit during the winter of 1922 at nine years of age. Cordy's father James had worked as a maintenance man with Ford, but grew tired of the bitter Michigan winters. Looking for better opportunities, James, his wife Pearl, and their five children moved to Pasadena and settled on Winona Street. James worked as a gardener, but "financial stress"[38] eventually forced both Cordy and his older brother Jack to drop out of school. The two brothers began working as bicycle messengers for Western Union, but quickly traded in their bikes for motorcycles because they could "deliver more telegrams faster and make more money," said Jane Milne Lopez, Jack's daughter.[39]

In the early thirties, when short-track motorcycle racing became popular in Los Angeles, Cordy, "a wiry 130-pounder standing 5 feet 7 inches,"[40] and his taller brother became fixtures on the oval dirt track. The motorcycles of the time were very basic, the only controls being a clutch and a throttle—no brakes. A rider used his body to maneuver and to stop his bike. He skidded his left foot encased in a leather boot with a steel, sandal-like contraption on the heel, across the loose surface of the track for balance. The danger of the sport—Jack later lost a thumb in a racing accident—contributed to the sport's growing popularity. Skillful riders, as both Milne boys were, could earn fifty dollars to seventy-five dollars a night. Cordy and Jack were soon competing on the California circuit, which traveled between San Diego and San Francisco.[41]

During this time Cordy and Marie started dating. Little is known about their first encounter—she said they met at a Chinese restaurant where she worked—but by 1933, fifteen-year-old Marie sat in the stands while her nineteen-year-old boyfriend raised dust on the track below. Her mother, who hoped she would marry well, was rarely pleased with the boys her daughter dated, but since Marie bounced between her mother's and grandmother's houses, she had more freedom than she might have had otherwise. Marie's mother's reproach likely fueled her attraction to Cordy and she later admitted she was always drawn to "forbidden fruit." Cordy's popularity furthered his appeal. Years later, she described Cordy as a "spectacular racer": "The attraction that drew me to him came from . . . his breakneck reputation on the racetrack . . . which . . . made him a local celebrity."[42]

While Marie fell for Cordy as he rode circles around his opponents, it was difficult not to notice the tectonic shifts the turmoil outside of the track was causing. In January of that year, Adolf Hitler began his ascent to power as chancellor of Germany. Within three years of the stock market crash, unemployment tripled in Europe and the United States, leaving much of the world mired in an economic depression.[43] At home, the Jazz Age bleated a final sour note, thousands of farmers destroyed by drought began migrating to California, and Franklin D. Roosevelt marked the start of his presidency with a whirlwind of activity aimed at stopping the nation's slide into financial chaos.

Seemingly immune to the unrest in the world around her, Marie remained more interested in Cordy as a celebrity than as a racer. She attended many of his races, but she gave little notice to the excitement on the track below her. Far more interested in fashion than sport, she sat in the stands examining the latest issue of *Vogue*. The magazine has always been "about the best of everything—the best clothes, the best parties, the 'best people,'" wrote former editor Grace Mirabella.[44] For Mirabella, "fashion is about women. It's about what their lives are like and what they are striving to be." And Marie, who was close enough to see the good life, but far from wealthy enough to live it, escaped through studying the upper-crust glamour of *Vogue*. It defined a life that was "all delight, fabulousness, wealth and beauty"[45] as irresistibly as Hollywood.

Marie remained spellbound by the movies. The advent of sound and the Depression changed the women on the screen. Greta Garbo made her talkie debut as a prostitute in *Anna Christie*. She followed that up as a spy who uses sex to complete her missions (*Mata Hari*) and an alcoholic nightclub singer who has a live-in boyfriend and regularly picks up men (*As You Desire Me*). "Besides Garbo a number of women stars portrayed prostitutes or kept women, among them Marlene Dietrich in *Blonde Venus*, Jean Harlow in *Red Dust*, Irene Dunne in *Black Street*," wrote film historian Robert Sklar.[46] "These movies [implied] that there was no room in the marketplace for women other than on stage or in bed."

In Hollywood, actresses like Greta Garbo and Jean Harlow may have been playing characters who used sex to get the better of men, but a few miles north in Pasadena, Marie, who later claimed to have already lost her virginity and to have had an abortion, denied sex to Cordy, or so she later maintained.

"'Doing it' was the great topic of conversation among the [motorcycle] boys. Whatever name they gave it, the act of making love was for them a rapid and brutal gesture," she wrote later.[47] "Not at all the idea that I had of it. I think that the lovemaking act should be done in a favorable ambiance, an act accomplished without haste, and with lots of tenderness."

Whatever happened between Marie and Cordy, the Depression once again changed the country's sexual attitudes. By the early thirties, both the marriage and divorce rates slowed, as couples could no longer afford to set up house for the first time or separately after a divorce. But the hardships of the Depression also encouraged a more relaxed outlook when it came to birth control, as people could not afford another mouth to feed. In fact, a 1936 Gallup Poll found that 70 percent of Americans favored legalizing the distribution of birth control information.[48]

Cordy continued to excel outside of the bedroom and back on the track, winning the American National Championship in 1933 and 1935.[49] In fact, Cordy and his brother Jack had become such good racers they were prohibited from competing on the same part of the California race circuit; if one raced the northern circuit, the other raced the southern.[50] At the end of 1935, the brothers were invited to race in England, where the sport was much more popular. When Cordy accepted the invitation, Marie was "mad as a hatter . . . not because he was leaving, but because I was staying."[51]

Cordy and Jack left for England, but Cordy did not forget Marie. He invited her to join him, not just in England, but also as his wife. The promise and romance of a cruise to England quickly wiped away whatever reservations she might have held regarding Cordy. While Cordy sent enough money for her travel and new clothing, she wanted more. "Nothing could ever be enough if I was going to live the way I intended. I had to have everything, and whatever amount I possessed, it was never enough."[52] With style guidance from *Vogue* and sewing help from Alice, a skilled seamstress, Marie prepared a wardrobe that made her look more affluent than she was. On her first voyage across the ocean, she planned on living the extravagant life to which she aspired. A flurry of preparations began, with Marie developing a clothing strategy based on successively more magnificent gowns for each night's dinner.

While Marie and Cordy never traveled together, their radically different attitudes toward travel portended their later troubles when their dissimilar outlooks clashed. The "young, crazy guy" and his motorcycle pals would stay up late drinking and playing cards. On one trip, the gong that called guests to breakfast kept annoying Cordy, tired from late-night carousing, and so he threw the bell overboard.[53] Meanwhile, the young, beautiful Marie seemed to demand the attention of her fellow travelers in a less rambunctious way.

During Marie's first dinner on board the SS *Manhattan*, she grabbed the attention of twenty-one-year-old British furrier Maxwell Croft. She never told him she was engaged and the two danced, strolled the ship's deck, and, inevitably, kissed. On the sixth and last evening of her elegant maiden voyage, she caused a sensation by wearing a gossamer gown with layers of tulle in a rainbow of colors. At the end of the evening, she and Maxwell consummated their shipboard romance. Reflecting on the affair nearly fifty years later, Marie took a starry-eyed, cinema-inspired view and wrote, "The two heroes came together at the bosom and the image faded out . . . I no longer had any doubt in my mind, but I was crazily in love with Maxwell."[54]

Whatever Marie's feelings for Maxwell were at the time, it was Cordy she had traveled to England to marry. "I hadn't had the intention of causing Cordy pain," she wrote. "He'd offered me an exit. I had taken advantage of it, assuming the whole time that I'd find an elegant way of not marrying him."

Either Marie did not find a way to break off her engagement to Cordy or she didn't truly want to. In the two months between her arrival in England and their wedding, Marie was pictured in several London newspaper stories as the happy fiancée who raced across the United States and then the ocean to marry the American speedway star. And on July 25, 1936, wearing a black dress with short, puffy sleeves and a hat with a small net veil, nineteen-year-old Marie married twenty-three-year-old Cordy Milne. While a crowd of fans waited outside the Stoke Newington Registrar's Office, fellow racer Dicky Case and his wife Kathleen witnessed the wedding.

However, it seems, marriage to Cordy did not keep Marie apart from Maxwell Croft. Although she claimed Maxwell never knew about Cordy or her marriage, their relationship made headlines in both London and California. Regardless, Marie and Maxwell carried on their affair. Later in life, she maintained she refused to have sex with Cordy and even baited him into sleeping with other women so he would leave her alone. According to Marie, on one occasion when Cordy brought a woman home, she served the lovers breakfast in bed in an attempt to shame them out of the apartment in time for her own tryst with Maxwell.

"Women were flocking to [Cordy] from all over and he wasn't a great one for saying no," said Sandy Hicks, Cordy's daughter from a later marriage."[55] While Cordy's daughter called him a "playboy," it is impossible to know if Marie's saucy tales are true or part of the persona she later developed. It is clear that Marie and Cordy's marriage was no bower of bliss. Two months after their wedding, on September 30, 1936, she sailed on the *Ile de France* for New York. Cordy went to Australia for its racing season while she returned to Pasadena. Once there, Marie talked to her grandmother about her marriage. Alice encouraged Marie to get a divorce, telling her that life was too short to stay with someone you don't really love. "They married too young and wanted different things," said Jane Milne Lopez, Cordy's niece.[56] "She wanted to be a star. He wanted to be a motorcycle racer with a wife who would follow him around."

Although she listed her occupation as an actress in a 1938 Pasadena city directory, Marie always claimed an accidental start in show business.

But she admitted she and Cordy wanted incongruent things. "He wanted to live calmly and peacefully in a little house with lots of kids. I wanted a dramatic life . . . with black limos that would transport me to new adventures."[57]

Their different approaches to life may not have been enough to break up the marriage, but their relationship had been built on superficialities. Cordy's celebrity status initially attracted her to him, but Marie realized in England that being married to a star did not guarantee her the glamorous life she craved. Later, when asked why she thought most marriages fail, she said, "[because] a woman becomes disillusioned and a man doesn't care."[58] But thirty years later Marie fully recognized that her own short-comings helped kill her marriage. Acknowledging that she married Cordy to escape from Pasadena, she wrote, "In those days I had no conscience about marrying a man whom I didn't love just because he was my way to . . . freedom. . . . But it was hopeless. We had nothing in common. I could see only empty years ahead."[59] Infidelity, conflicting goals in life, Cordy's seeming indifference to Marie's needs, and Marie's callous use of Cordy's proposal as an escape doomed the marriage. It took nearly two years after their initial separation, but on December 8, 1938, the state of California granted the couple a divorce.

In the early forties, Cordy returned to Pasadena from Australia, where he and his second wife Verna proceeded to have three daughters. He continued to race in the United States, winning the U.S. championship in 1946. With Jack he opened a motorcycle shop and became a successful businessman. Despite earlier strains, Cordy and Marie remained friendly. During the fifties, when she had become Lili St. Cyr, Cordy, his siblings, and their spouses would go to see her perform at Ciro's, a swanky Los Angeles nightclub. And when Mike Brown, a local high school student who worked at the Milne shop and became close to the Milne family, traveled to New York, Cordy sent him to see her at a small nightclub there.

"I was about eighteen or nineteen and it was a thrill to meet Lili St. Cyr," explained Brown.[60] "She was very gracious and cordial to me. She was just accommodating Cordy's request, but it was very flattering to me. Cordy always showed her the utmost respect and I think she did the same."

But back in the late 1930s, long before she was Lili St. Cyr, Marie's main interest was her old shipmate Maxwell Croft. Despite another transoceanic fling aboard the *Ile de France* with a German ballet dancer named Otto Struller, she still juggled a relationship with Croft. Maxwell, tall and slender with an aquiline nose and inviting smile, wanted to marry her. He traveled to the States for that purpose, but after her breakup with Cordy, Marie was uninterested in remarrying. "I had begun to realize that I didn't want to live with a man who considered me his property," she wrote.[61] "I had the intention of belonging only to myself. Life with [Maxwell] began to resemble life with any other man . . . and that's just what I wanted to avoid."

But Marie remained fascinated by life at sea. Later she even claimed she spent the years between her marriage to Cordy and World War II persuading rich men to pay for her exploits on ocean liners. And indeed, passenger manifests indicate she traveled between England and the United States in October 1936 and August 1937. She was also still entangled with Maxwell and it is likely that the prospect of another free transatlantic voyage with him convinced her to accept him at last. On April 3, 1939, the couple sailed from New York to Liverpool on the *Ile de France.*

Marie later claimed that after landing in England she tried to break off the engagement. Berated by Maxwell's family, she locked herself in a bathroom and refused to come out until they left. When they finally departed, she canceled the wedding. She demanded return passage to the States and, in an instance of cruel chicanery, claimed she took the diamond out of the ring and replaced it with a fake before giving it back. Just ten days after arriving in England, Marie indeed set sail for New York on the *Deutschland.*[62]

Maxwell's family, however, heard a very different version of the affair. "My father told me Maxwell wired him to meet them in Southampton [where the ships dock] and to bring a ring," said Giles Croft, Maxwell's nephew.[63] "The idea was that they were going to pretend they'd gotten married so they could live together. Later, Maxwell had to pretend to get a divorce."

In whatever way the relationship ended, Marie made a lasting impact on Maxwell. More than fifty years later, Maxwell, well into his seventies, showed his son Edward a photo of Marie leaning on her arm. The cream-colored card was signed with a little note.

"He told me they met on board a ship," said Edward Croft.[64] "He said, 'I was very young and I was quite naïve and I nearly married this girl.' I got the impression that he was quite in love with her, but it didn't end too well for him I think. And I don't think he had a clue as to who she became."

2.

Shedding
Marie

*The strength of the feminine is that of
seduction.*

—Jean Baudrillard

After leaving Maxwell Croft behind in England on April 13, 1939, Marie Frances Van Schaack returned to California and slowly started to erase the vestiges of her former life and begin her makeover into Lili St. Cyr, America's best-known postwar striptease artist.

Marie began her transformation where so much fantasy is created: Los Angeles, California. Long before the movie industry established itself there, Los Angeles was a dream factory. The Gold Rush lured prospectors to the area in the mid-nineteenth century. Nearly thirty years later the completion of the Southern Pacific railroad made it easier for thousands of Midwesterners tempted by the Southern California sun and the Pacific waves to emigrate. During this population boom an Ohio man named Horace Wilcox and his wife moved to Los Angeles. Wilcox had made his fortunes in Kansas real estate, and upon his arrival developed a neighborhood his wife named Hollywood. The area, which changed hands in the early twentieth century, maintained a small-town feel until Los Angeles gobbled it up in 1910.[1] The movie industry quickly started to take over the region.

As movies began to define the city, a new mythology developed, one that rivaled the great Greek sagas: the Hollywood story. It was the lore of the glamorous characters that loomed large on screens across the country and the real-life gods and goddesses who portrayed them. It was the suggestion that in Hollywood, unknown soda jerks or shop clerks could become these very gods and goddesses. By the 1920s, the idea took such hold of the country that the aspiring writers, directors, and actors moving to Los Angeles caused yet another population surge and permanently altered the city's image. "They came in droves," wrote Jeffrey Feinman in his insiders' tome *Hollywood Confidential*.[2] "The Gopher Prairies and Grover's Corners of the nation were emptying out. The small-town cuties and drugstore cowboys were heading West, where fame and fortune waited for a pretty face or a big bosom. The mecca of mazuma, the capital of kitsch beckoned." Even through the thirties the ethereal celebrities remained protected from the Depression. And to the rest of the country, Hollywood remained a heavenly Olympus to dream about while waiting in line for the dole.

The Hollywood fantasy continued to be a pleasant diversion as the worry over the Depression gave way to concerns over the looming war in Europe. Two years before the United States would join World War II, another war, one that had ended a lifetime before, seized the country's attention and provided a great distraction. The epic novel about the Civil War, *Gone With the Wind*, was released in 1936 and in December 1939 debuted as one of the first real blockbuster films, grossing more than one billion in today's dollars.[3]

"The message of *Gone with the Wind* . . . was that True Womanhood could no longer hold its own against the emergencies of the modern world," wrote author Gail Collins in her book *America's Women*.[4] "Melanie Wilkes, the yin to Scarlett's yang, was a strong and practical and very, very good woman, but she was stuck in the traditional American pattern. Melanie understood as well as anybody that it would take a new model, a Scarlett, to bring everyone safely through the war and violent social upheaval."

Scarlett was a self-involved woman who used her beauty and sex appeal to manipulate men and get what she wanted, but she was also independent, strong, and cunning. And for audiences in the 1930s, she symbolized the rising number of women who tossed aside the frail, chaste ideal for a self-reliant, shrewd, sometimes conniving model unafraid of using beauty and sexuality to survive and thrive. In fact, by the mid-thirties

Los Angeles was so thick with Midwestern beauty queens confident in what their good looks could acquire that columnist Harry Carr called the hopefuls, "expectant Cinderellas waiting on one foot for the prince and glass slipper."[5]

While waiting for Prince Charming, the transplanted beauties served as an important part of the Hollywood economy. Feinman explained that "waiting for the big break, they waited on tables, washed the cars, cut the hair, and walked the dogs."[6] Some of the luckier ones worked at one of the many Los Angeles nightclubs. The echelons of the L.A. night scene ranged from seedy burlesque clubs to swanky, star-studded playgrounds. Hollywood's Sunset Strip, several blocks of the meandering twenty-seven-mile Sunset Boulevard, was dotted with posh nightspots like the Trocadero, the Mocambo, and Ciro's, where the stars danced and dined. At these chic clubs, performers like Judy Garland and Lena Horne entertained while would-be starlets snapped pictures, worked the coat check, or sold cigarettes to Hollywood's high society. A few blocks away, at the slightly less ritzy Earl Carroll Theater and the Florentine Gardens other hopefuls high-kicked their gorgeous gams in the chorus lines. The Earl Carroll Theater and the Florentine Gardens were run by former New York impresarios who had made names for themselves staging refined burlesque shows back East. Legal trouble from New York censors brought both to Hollywood in the late 1930s.

Earl Carroll, who advertised that through the portals of his club "pass the most beautiful girls in the world," became famous as a connoisseur of female beauty. With rival Florenz Ziegfeld, he set the beauty standard of the day and helped establish the idea that beauty is essential to female worth. Badly stating the attitude of the period, he wrote, "Girls are a commodity the same as bananas, pork chops, or a lot in a suburban development. They are the most fundamental of all commodities."[7] In Hollywood, Carroll opened his eponymous theater in a colossal space that featured lavish revues with comedians, musical acts and, of course, a multitude of leggy beauties.

A Swedish-born character named Nils Thor Granlund staged the Florentine Gardens' equally shapely shows. Granlund, known as N.T.G. in show business and as Granny to his friends, began his career as a publicist for Loew's Theaters. During Prohibition he worked as a radio announcer and claimed he unwittingly helped gangster pals smuggle alcohol by heeding their request to recite poetry on air. The mobsters used the poems as code to let their offshore rum-runners know if the coast was clear for their illicit cargo.[8]

N.T.G. also gravitated to nightclubs, where he produced floor shows that were "quick-fire entertainment, with a sledgehammer approach designed to permeate even the most drunken patron."[9] As *The New York Daily Mirror*'s nightclub columnist Lee Mortimer put it, N.T.G. was "the conceiver, inventor and creator of modern night life."[10] He alleged to have given actress Yvonne DeCarlo and dancer Gwen Verdon their starts. And he truly relished his role as an "ever sagacious 'picker' of talent."[11] It's unknown whether N.T.G. was prescient enough to see some spark in Marie or whether all he saw was another tall beauty for his chorus line, but under his tutelage Marie Van Schaack became a Vegas-style showgirl.

The stories vary as to how Marie and N.T.G. crossed paths. She herself provided differing versions. One acknowledged her own ambitions, saying she responded when N.T.G. "advertised for tall girls for a show at the Florentine Gardens."[12] But in her more frequently told account, she claimed a more accidental show biz start brought on by a bit of luck and her half-sister Idella Ruth's friend Shirley Patterson. In August 1940, Shirley, a seventeen-year-old blonde, was crowned Miss California at a Venice Mardi Gras competition.[13] As part of her winnings, the Eagle Rock High School senior won a week's stage show appearance. On August 15, N.T.G. opened a new show on the Paramount Theater stage preceding the Buster Keaton film spoof *The Villain Still Pursued Her*, which featured fan dancer Faith Bacon and Shirley Patterson.[14] Marie later claimed the beauty pageant winner and future actress was "scared of being alone backstage"[15] and asked Idella to accompany her. As she told it, her mother sent her to chaperone the two girls and she happened to meet N.T.G., who hired her on the spot.

N.T.G. told a completely different story of the girls' foray into life at the Florentine Gardens. In his version, Marie's half-sisters Idella Ruth and Rosemary Blackadder showed up at the club one day asking for a start in show business. N.T.G. hired the "two tall, gorgeous, willowy girls, a blonde and a brunette." According to N.T.G., a few days later during rehearsal their mother came to the club with pictures of Marie. "The pictures showed a long-haired blonde with a sparkling smile and a lovely figure. The pictures showed her almost in the nude, so I had no doubt of her excellent proportions. I thought she was about as perfect as anything I had ever seen."[16]

However it happened, a few months after N.T.G.'s Florentine Gardens debut in March 1940, Idella Ruth and Marie were dancing in the chorus line in one of Los Angeles' hottest night spots. At the Florentine Gardens, round, white-clothed tables spilled down the multi-tiered dining room toward the stage. During the shows, nubile women in headdresses strolled across stage and other lusciously long-limbed ladies danced in pasties and G-strings. In between the leg show, comics or acrobats amused the audience in the usually packed 500-seat club.

As a combination of producer and master of ceremonies, N.T.G. oversaw the whole ensemble to mixed reviews. "He was a little off-color and took advantage of making fun of people from offstage," said dancer Jean Forray, who admitted she nicknamed him Not Too Good.[17] Yvonne DeCarlo, who danced at the Florentine Gardens long before her turn as Lily Munster, explained that "as master of ceremonies, N.T.G. communicated with the regular Joe more successfully than with café society. His jokes were raunchy, and his double entendres tended toward the obvious. . . . He was rough-cut, but gentle, and I never knew him to hurt a living soul. . . . Nothing pleased him more than a good dirty joke; he was forever picking up dinner tabs, and helping anyone who needed it."[18]

Not nearly as magnanimous of N.T.G.'s rough-hewn nature, critics often skewered him. One *Variety* reporter called his revue "a conglomeration of misdirected effort" and put the full blame on N.T.G. "Principals and chorines try their best to make something out of the evening's misfitted mélange but his constant interruptions and bellowing from uninvited tables makes only for chaos and disorder. His action in slapping derrieres and incessant chatter about this or that doll while embraced might be considered cute and elicit such comment as 'ain't he a card,' but hardly in Hollywood. Such crudities belong in the joints with long bars or deep in the alfalfa belt, but it's no go with the home guard. It's much too corny and as dated as burlesque."[19]

Burlesque was anything but dated. In fact, burlesque's boom during the thirties is what allowed striptease to shimmy its way into clubs like Ciro's and the Florentine Gardens. Burlesque thrived during the Depression's economic slump as a cheap entertainment. "Where else could the Depression-weary man in the street get four hours of entertainment with comics, sex, and a few movies thrown in for a quarter?" asked Morton Minsky in his memoir *Minsky's Burlesque*.[20]

More than the bawdy jokes and flickering images on the big screen, the disrobing dames drew the crowds. "Burlesque has been enjoying a sizable business increase," wrote one *Variety* reporter toward the end of the decade.[21] "With stripping still the basis of all burlesque layouts, business was best where conditions and the attitude of the authorities permitted more stripping. Where there was no stripping, there was no business, and usually no burlesque." But striptease wasn't just bumping and grinding in burlesque theaters.

The 1933 Chicago World's Fair featured a midget village, an imitation Mayan temple, and alligator wrestlers. But the crowds really came to ogle fan dancer Sally Rand, who danced naked behind ostrich plumes and a giant opaque balloon, and was by far the biggest attraction. When the government repealed Prohibition the same year, nightclubs began hiring striptease dancers to help fill the clubs. As striptease swiveled its hips into other venues, newspapers, and trade magazines began to review the acts— both in burlesque theaters and nightclubs—giving striptease a little legitimacy in the theatrical world. "Nudity it seems, was the symbol of progress," wrote James Petersen in *The Century of Sex*.[23] "Titillation, the power to divert public attention away from the unthinkable, would become a national resource."

Striptease certainly excited and stimulated, but it also acknowledged women's own sexuality and erotic interest. The dancer's ability to share this interest and connect with an audience added to the perceived threat. And that audience was less and less lower class. As uptown patrons slummed at the burlesque theaters and as striptease infiltrated sophisticated nightclubs, onstage undressing became more and more ubiquitous.

Of course, the snob factor was still prevalent. Burlesque spent much of the thirties battling the censors. But despite several headline-making setbacks such as New York Mayor Fiorello LaGuardia's 1937 crackdown, upscale nightclubs, Broadway, Sally Rand, and Gypsy Rose Lee made sure that striptease would always be taunting and tantalizing American audiences. "Nudity is no longer considered indecent in uptown nightclubs where men and women pay from ten dollars to twenty dollars for seats and similar performances are given," wrote one reporter in *Billboard*. Georgia Sothern could perform as a "red hot, red-headed temptress tossing her hips in fantastic abandon to the wild music of the band"[24] without recourse at Billy Rose's Casino de Paree, but the same abandon at a burly house might draw the ire of the censors. In fact, throughout the thirties many of the top dancers—Georgia Sothern, Ann Corio, and Margie Hart—would alternate weeks at a burlesque theater with weeks at a "legitimate" nitery. By the end of the decade, even *New York Times* critic Brooks Atkinson, who thought burlesque theaters were "dull, ugly, and dirty," admitted that, "The striptease is as much a part of American culture as the hot dog and hamburger. The American sense of humor has handled the striptease more intelligently than the moralists. Ann Corio and Margie Hart are as much a part of show business as the circus. And Gypsy Rose Lee, who can strip from the inside out, as she did at the World's Fair, is a national figure in more ways than one, admired for her wit and intelligence as much as her stage hocus-pocus."[25]

Gypsy Rose Lee and her very brief flashes of flesh really teased the strip out of the burly houses and carnivals. In the late twenties, after a childhood career in vaudeville, Gypsy turned to burlesque and striptease. By 1931, she starred at Billy Minsky's Republic. And by the mid-thirties she wowed fans in the Ziegfeld Follies and circulated in a crowd that included journalist and ambassador Clare Booth Luce, theater critic George Jean Nathan, and actress Tallulah Bankhead.

Gypsy could bounce between burlesque and Broadway with such ease because she completely understood her audience. She knew the literary types sprinkled among the seats wanted to understand what a stripper was thinking. She read with a voracious appetite so as to educate herself and appeal to that erudite audience. At the same time she poked fun at the crowd, snarkily referencing Vincent van Gogh and Oscar Wilde. Tongue firmly in cheek, Gypsy could send up the American aristocracy onstage while clinking champagne glasses with them offstage. She capitalized on the American desire for glamour while she simultaneously laughed at those same aspirations. In the process she appealed to both a working-class audience and the educated elite. Eventually she shucked a career of removing her clothes, traded in on her reputation as the "Literary Stripper," and wrote several books. But more than any other stripteaser she challenged the idea that a woman who disrobed in public was an idiot and bridged the gap between burlesque and upscale nightclub. By the end of the thirties Mayor LaGuardia helped ban burlesque from New York's stage, but Gypsy made certain the strip was just illuminated under a different spotlight.

One acceptable way for the clubs to show off beautiful naked women was in tableaux vivants. In these living pictures, women would portray a great work of art, like the armless Venus DeMilo, or a storied event, like Adam and Eve in the Garden of Eden. Laws in many cities allowed women to be nude on stage as long as they remained completely still.

According to N.T.G., Marie once depicted a Chinese queen in such a scene. She "was borne across the floor on a platform carried by the other girls." One night, with Marie wearing only a bunch of peach blossoms in her lap, one of the girls stumbled and the platform wobbled. Marie "lost her balance, but not her aplomb. She stepped gracefully off the platform and walked offstage wearing nothing but the peach blossoms."[26]

By December 1940, fully entrenched in life at the Florentine Gardens, Marie and her half-sister Idella Ruth, a tall, platinum blonde who took the stage name Barbara Moffett, began to get noticed—not least of all by the frequent celebrity guests. Gossip columns linked Barbara to suave leading man Franchot Tone. Marie reportedly dabbled with Orson Welles and the actor Anthony Quinn.[27] Marie later wrote that during this time she realized "whatever I was going to have in life, I had to get it myself or else marry to obtain it." While many chorus girls simply bided their time until they got their big break or ensnared a wealthy supporter, Marie "knew already that I didn't want to play that game."[28] But her aversion to depending on a husband did not stop her from getting married. When Florentine Gardens' waiter Dick Hubert proposed, she agreed. "I hadn't met anyone I really liked for a long time and Dick filled a vacuum," she admitted later.[29] "I was lonely . . . [and] about this time I was starting to evolve the philosophy [that] if it doesn't work out, there's always divorce."

The couple married in Tijuana, but the marriage didn't stand a chance. While Marie liked the way Dick looked and dressed, she knew they didn't have anything in common. "Our love was superficial," she wrote in her autobiography *And Men My Fuel*.[30] "It depended upon appearances and not much else . . . What should have been a brief, weekend affair had foolishly been spread out over a year—a year that couldn't stand up with what we had to offer." Interestingly, the relationship's shallow basis had little to do with Dick's job as a waiter or the fact that he couldn't compete with rich businessmen or celebrities. Years later, Marie told Walter Winchell, "I'd rather be married to a bellhop or bartender because they know how to treat women, having so much experience."[31] While Dick was the only waiter she married, none of her husbands were particularly wealthy or renowned. However, while her men lacked fame and fortune, they fulfilled other immediate needs—an escape from Pasadena or distraction from her loneliness or help with her choreography. Not wholly cold or exploitive, Marie cared for the men in her life, often passionately, but with a sometimes selfish need for instant gratification she rarely gave much thought to long-term consequences. She also kept men at bay emotionally, never allowing herself to become truly beholden to anyone and making it easier to detach.

Marie may have trifled with matters of the heart, but her attention to business was completely sincere. Backstage, in what Yvonne DeCarlo described as a "kaleidoscope of false eyelashes, makeup [and] mesh stockings,"[32] Marie studied costumes, makeup, and lighting. Years later, producers and club owners would note that while many headliners gave little thought to things like lighting, Lili St. Cyr often gave detailed notes to the crew when it came to these specifics.

In a city teeming with aspiring actresses, many of the girls at the Florentine Gardens and Earl Carroll's club dreamed of big screen success. For most, the dreams faded. "The migration to Hollywood . . . is peopled almost exclusively with pilgrims who did not succeed," wrote Jeffrey Feinman.[33] "For some, failure meant using the return half of the bus ticket home. Others found a way of life that pleased them in the land of illusion, and they settled into steady jobs and a split-level in Ventura." But despite her fascination with Greta Garbo, Marie was blasé about a film career. "When I'd decided to make my career in show business, I'd automatically tossed aside the possibility of doing films," she wrote later. "I couldn't memorize a text . . . [and] you had to wake up early in the morning. Forget it! That [wasn't] a romantic schedule."[34] But like the women Garbo portrayed, Marie rejected the "humdrum destiny reserved for a woman"[35] and remained disinterested in a split-level in Ventura. So Marie shed both the nightclub and her husband in pursuit of a cabaret career and fled to San Francisco.

In San Francisco, Marie joined the chorus of the Music Box, a cabaret-style nightclub she later described as one of the prettiest in which she ever performed. Vivian and Rosetta Duncan, sisters who became famous in the twenties with a vaudeville routine called "Topsy and Eva," staged the show. The act, which featured Rosetta in blackface and a blonde Vivian in her natural peaches-and-cream complexion, remained so popular the sisters portrayed the two characters until the end of their careers in the late fifties.[36]

As part of the revue, Marie was celebrated as the club's "Girl of the Hour." Introduced early in the evening wearing a chic evening gown, jewels, and a fur coat, she slowly paraded around the club, letting the audience drink her in. Each hour, she reappeared wearing less and less until, by the end of the evening, she wore only what the law required. Marie never mingled with the audience or consorted with the men, choosing to maintain a mysterious distance.

"The idea was to keep the men in the club longer, those last ones hoping to see a little more of the 'girl of the hour' each time," she wrote.[37] "My attitude created a kind of aura that pushed the audience to admire me and desire me, but it also created a sort of invisible barrier between the public and me. In the eyes of men, I was a vision of admirable, but untouchable, beauty."

In the eyes of Ivan Fehnova, the Music Box's choreographer, Marie still needed a lot of guidance. According to Fehnova, he was in a pinch and Marie lied about her dance experience. Her first show was a disaster. "Omigod, it was brutal," he said years later.[38] "She didn't even know how to walk. How I worked with that girl. I walked her until I thought she would drop." Fehnova saw fast improvements in his new charge. "It was like working with putty or clay," he remarked. "Every time she practiced I would see improvement." And while Fehnova thought she needed a lot of work, he also recognized a presence and refinement in his young ingenue. "From the beginning she had a natural grace and poise that many ballet dancers work years to get," he said later. "She radiated personality."

Marie always credited Fehnova with smoothing out her stage presence, developing her dance skills, and most importantly, changing her name. Shedding Van Schaack, she chose Fehnova as her surname. For her first name, she adopted Lili. "Lili was a name that evoked mystery and intrigue," she said.[39] "There had already been Lillie Langtry and Diamond Lil."

Beyond their beguiling appeal, both of her inspirations also embraced their sexuality and used their feminine wiles to garner fame, fortune, and independence. At the end of the nineteenth century, Lillie Langtry became a professional beauty after she made a splash at a London party.

She was, as one writer described, "a creature who provoked men to scatter rose petals before her and women to stand on chairs at parties to snatch a better look." Langtry, a married woman, was openly wooed and adored by painters, writers, and royalty. Artists lined up to paint her portrait. Oscar Wilde brought her a lily each day, slept in her doorway on more than one occasion, and wrote *Lady Windermere's Fan* for her. For years she served as the mistress to Edward, Prince of Wales and future King of England. She was reportedly unsure which of her lovers fathered her daughter. After her daughter's birth, her star status lost some of its sheen. She reinvented herself and took to the stage, not for any love of or talent for acting, but as a means of support. Regardless of her interest or aptitude she became a celebrated actress in both England and the United States. After a tour through the States, Langtry returned to England and began racing horses under the name Mr. Jersey so she could gain membership to the all-male racing club. The stunt was not unusual; Lillie Langtry often challenged the era's Victorian ideas. Far more than just a pretty face, George Bernard Shaw said of Langtry that, "she has no right to be intelligent, daring, and independent as well as lovely."[40]

Equally bold, but far removed from the upper class circles Lillie Langtry frequented, the real-life Diamond Lil stole the hearts of men throughout the Bowery of New York at the turn of the century. She was "a hardened woman [and] she valued only diamonds provided by smitten suitors. Without remorse, she betrayed her lovers, broke up marriages, and even murdered a woman."[40] Impressed by Diamond Lil's strength and clever charm, Mae West wrote and starred in a play about her, making the outrageous Lil a heroine in the late twenties. *Diamond Lil* received mixed critical reviews, but was a huge success with audiences—both male and female. In fact, West claimed to have written the play with women in mind. The show focused on relationships between men and women, with Lil rejecting the traditional male-dominated model and using her sexuality as currency. Brazenly resisting male authority, she was a confident and self-reliant woman with a hedonistic lust for life.

The success of *Diamond Lil* led to a 1933 film version. To deal with the disapproval of the Hays Office, Hollywood's censorship board, West changed the title to *She Done Him Wrong* and altered some of the story's details, but reviewers and fans knew they were watching the story of Diamond Lil on the big screen. A tremendous hit, the film grossed over two million dollars by the summer of 1933.[41] Celebrated as an icon, West portrayed characters that both women and men reveled in, making sex part of the public discourse and providing a sexually liberated female role model. Diamond Lil became a part of American mythology, remaining so popular that West revived the play in the late forties and early fifties. As Mae West biographer Jill Watts points out, "she blazed on as a symbol of independent womanhood . . . she refused to be a mother or wife, making it clear that the kind of cooking she was interested in did not happen in the kitchen."[42]

So with a nod, or perhaps a flick of the hip, to Mae West and Lillie Langtry, Marie became Lili Fehnova. But the Music Box's girl of the hour did not stay long. On December 7, 1941, the Japanese attacked Pearl Harbor, and the United States officially entered World War II. California was closest to the enemy, and the bombing resulted in a mixture of fear and vulnerability that officials tried to quell even as they prepared for war. In San Francisco, Mayor Angelo Rossi declared a state of emergency, which included putting the San Francisco–Oakland Bay Bridge and the Golden Gate Bridge under twenty-four-hour guard, searching all baggage at the airport, and readying the reserve fire equipment. Thirty-five police patrolled the Japanese quarter, and San Francisco Hospital dismissed Japanese interns who were not citizens.[43]

Despite the scare, the theaters remained open. One newspaper blurb reassured potential patrons, "only the marquee lights are out. The show must go on—blackout or no blackout. Keep up your morale. Go to the movies and to the other theaters. Nobody wants you to sit at home and brood. Let's go to a show tonight!"[44]

The Duncan sisters did not sit at home and brood, and they did not remain in San Francisco. A little over a month after Pearl Harbor, the Duncans transplanted the entire cast—including Lili Fehnova as the "Girl of the Hour"—to the River House in Lawton Springs, just west of Reno, Nevada.

Lili stayed at the River House through February. She later claimed to have left when the bartender she had a crush on turned out to be a pimp and suggested she become one of his call girls. He told her she was "worth a thousand dollars a pound." Offended and suffering a seriously bruised ego, Lili headed back to Los Angeles. Years later she wrote that as she returned to Los Angeles she thought, "I didn't have as much class as I'd thought . . . [The] proposition had been a big blow to my pride."[45]

Lili resurfaced at the Hollywood Theater in San Diego, a 400-seat theater that once played Mexican musicals. With the arrival of owner Bob Johnston in the late twenties it became a burlesque hall focused almost wholly on the female form. "After an opening parade, the shows usually proceeded in predictable order, with a dance specialty, a production number, a comic scene, the first stripper, a novelty number, another comic turn, the second stripper, the twenty-minute 'picture number,' another comic scene, the featured stripper and the finale," wrote theater critic Welton Jones.[46]

The Hollywood Theater, a family operation run by Johnston and his wife Fanny, faced financial difficulty until the lead-up to the war brought an influx of sailors to the area. "Sure, its primary clientele was sailors," wrote Jones, who explained that during World War II the Hollywood put on as many as seven sold-out shows a day.[47] "But the sailors were joined by the colorful downtown underworld of the day, a mix of prizefighters, gamblers, hustlers, undercover cops, and thrill-seekers . . . [Johnston] knew who he was and what he did, and he knew his customer, too."

And Johnston knew his customers came to see the girls. "If she looked good and she could walk we'd teach her how to dance," he said.[48] "If she couldn't dance, we'd let her stand back there; she was just as good as anything. She could just stand still or wiggle or something like that."

Unlike the typically short and zaftig burlesque stars of the day, Lili was tall and slender, yet still curvy. Her curly and increasingly blonde hair perfectly framed her face with its high cheekbones, eyebrows tweezed into a precise arch and full lips, usually painted a bright red. Her stunningly good looks, more than her dance moves, won her a $25-a-week job at the Hollywood Theater.[49] In fact, Katherine Flores, who performed at the Hollywood as Zena Rae, thought she was a bit clumsy. "She was gorgeous, but she was a klutz," said Flores, who was the chorus line captain.[50] "Fanny looked at her and asked me, 'What do you think?' and I said, 'Just put some costumes on her and let her walk around for God's sake. She's gorgeous.'"

It was at the Hollywood Theater that Lili first began performing what is now the classic burlesque striptease. The strip, now such an unshakeable part of American entertainment, developed a format: the dancer paraded onto the stage, offered a first flash of skin, used the removed bits of her costume or the curtain to prolong the tease and gave an inviting bump and grind of her hips before removing the last bits of clothing. What those last bits might be depended on the performer, city, and whether or not censors or police were in the audience. All of this, as *Striptease: From Gaslight to Spotlight* author Jessica Glasscock pointed out, was "the synthesis of all the influences that had fed into the striptease since the nineteenth century. The parade went back to the earliest chorus girls, and had been perfected by Ziegfeld's showgirls. The flash and the protective curtain were elements of the old tableaux vivants. The bumps and grinds were the confluence of belly dance, modern dance, and the jazz shimmy into one rhythm-punctuated full-body writhe. And the clothing gimmicks were pure vaudeville."[51]

There was also a timing to the striptease. "Usually in the first chorus they would maybe take off a glove," explained Flores.[52] "The second chorus would be a little bit jazzier, and then on the third chorus they'd strip to their net bras and underwear." Either nervous or unaware of the striptease's design, Lili's boss cut her first attempt short. "In the first chorus she had everything just about off," said Flores. "She didn't know. When she was out there, stripping to her skin, Fanny almost died. She went and stopped the second chorus. My God, Lili had just about everything off by the first part. I'll never get over that."

But despite a faulty start, Lili clearly possessed something special. "She was graceful; she didn't have to be taught grace or charm," explained Janne Kane, who danced at the Hollywood as Jan "Irish" Cafara.[53] Katherine Flores agreed. Outside of the chorus line, Flores thought Lili was a good dancer and, much later, a truly imaginative stripteaser.

After her gig at the Hollywood Theater, Lili returned to Los Angeles to find Hollywood marching to the beating war drums. Many leading men signed up to serve: Jimmy Stewart in the Air Force, Robert Mitchum in the Army, and Glenn Ford in the Marine Corps.[54] By October of 1942, roughly 2,700 members of the Hollywood community, or 12 percent of those employed in the movie business, joined the armed forces.[55] For those celebrities who enlisted, their service was often greater off the battlefield. Whether or not they joined the service, a star's value to the war effort more often involved making propaganda films, entertaining troops, and selling war bonds: Gene Kelly was stationed in Washington, D.C., and made several Navy movies, Hedy Lamarr offered to kiss any man who would buy $25,000 worth of bonds, and Lana Turner charged $50,000 a buss.[56] Meanwhile, Lili aided the war effort in her own way — raising troop morale in theaters up and down the California coast.

While she was pleased with the name Lili, she remained uncertain about a surname. "Most girls in pictures change their cognomens for luck, or because they resemble an established star's or [it's] too difficult to remember or pronounce," wrote columnist Lee Mortimer.57 "But Marie Van Schaack was a babe who liked to travel—up and down the West Coast—so she forsook pictures and went into the cabarets. Unique among all was her reason for scrambling her tag. She had gotten a geographical complex . . . which made it necessary for her to be known differently in every town she worked." As a result, she was known as Lili Fehnova in San Francisco, Lili LaRue in Las Vegas, and Lili LaBang in San Diego. But then, after reading about the St. Cyr military academy in France and pondering the success of millionaire Rex St. Cyr, she finally settled on the moniker that would light up marquees: Lili St. Cyr.

Away from the stage lights and the world's bedlam, Lili's family struggled with a more personal chaos: Idella and Ian's marriage was ending very publicly. When Idella and Ian met in Minneapolis, she told him her first husband, Edward Van Schaack, died during World War I. It may have been what she told her daughter as well, for when Lili married Cordy Milne, she listed her father as deceased on their marriage license.

In May 1943, Ian, who now ran a detective agency, received a letter from Edward, who had not died during the war but rather was living in Spokane. Ian and Idella's marriage had already crumbled, but Ian used Edward's surprise emergence to counter the divorce suit his wife filed and ask for an annulment. Judge Roy Rhodes ruled that while the letter did not mention Edward and Idella's marriage—and it's possible they never legally married—the letter clearly showed that Edward was very much alive when Ian and Idella married in 1923. Ian won an annulment of his nineteen-year marriage to Idella.

Lili was strangely absent during the whole matter, but her two half-sisters were not. Ian and Idella's daughters went to court and asked that their father be granted custody of them. The judge agreed and emphasized that under California law, the annulment did not affect the legitimacy of the children. The whole affair, resembling a movie plot, made headlines in Los Angeles. Both girls—Idella Ruth, who performed with Lili in N.T.G.'s revue at the Florentine Gardens as Barbara Moffett, and

Rosemary, who spent the early forties as a comedienne and fill-in for Beryl Wallace, an Earl Carroll beauty—were pictured with their father.[58]

Lili and her half-sisters were just a few of the women who found that a career on the stage offered unique freedom. They among all their sex could achieve fame and financial independence while living outside traditional social constraints. When it got down to striptease it wasn't just offstage that the dancers could veer away from the status quo. Onstage their movements acknowledged that women not only thought about sex, but also fantasized about it. However, many, including the dancers themselves, viewed their time on stage as a temporary phase before settling down to a more traditional life. It was all part of the stripper myth, a bawdier pull-yourself-up-by-your-bra straps American ideology in which a poor woman with no other recourse takes to stripping to survive. In the club she meets a wealthy businessman or rich celebrity, gets married, and retires to live in the house behind a white picket fence. But "in general, striptease sugar daddies were more likely to be low-level bootleggers, racketeers, bellhops, small merchants, policemen, firemen, federal agents, men looking for adventure, taxi drivers, writers, aspiring artists, sailors, and bookies than titled aristocrats," explained Rachel Shteir, author of *Striptease: The Untold History of the Girlie Show*.[59] "If they were not all, as [dancer] Sherry Britton complained, 'leeches and pimps and jerks: degenerates,' they were certainly not all well-off."

Lili discarded the stripper myth early on. "They operate on the theory that it is always open season on strippers," she wrote of the stage door Johnnies, the men that loitered at the backstage entrance.[60] "So after the last 'bump and grind' has been bumped and ground, there is usually one character in the audience who gets the mistaken notion that the entertainer is fair game. Merely dangling a net bra on stage has the same effect on him as waving a red flag has on a bull. . . . The amateur wolf will send a note backstage telling the girl he's crazy to meet her. . . . And usually when he suggests they share a steak and champagne, what he really means is hot dogs and beer."

Whether or not a dancer bought into the stripper myth, most talked about striptease as being something they did out of financial necessity, a last chance before prostitution or destitution. "Besides prostitution, striptease was one of the only ways out of the grueling demands of housework and the toil of the sweatshop," wrote Shteir.[61] "Time and time again, asked what made them turn to taking off their clothes in public, strippers answered that it was easier than crouching behind a cosmetics counter, wielding a broom, or sweating over a conveyor belt."

During the forties most women sweat over a conveyor belt or hunched over a typewriter. The ideal female employee of the era was not the lithe showgirl, but the muscular Rosie the Riveter. Despite the popular notion that Rosie called women to work, trumpeting the entrance of women into the workforce, most unmarried women had always worked. What changed during World War II were the number of married, middle-class women who joined the workplace, the overall acceptability of working women, and the types of jobs available. Rosie and the propagandists summoned roughly six million women to join the "14 million who had already been working and doing everything from paving roads to operating cranes," explained *America's Women* author Gail Collins.[62]

For the attractive and willing, striptease was far easier and seemingly more glamorous than paving roads or hocking wares. "Working in burlesque isn't so awful for a girl," showgirl Lilly Berg told Joseph Mitchell, a reporter who wrote for *The New York Herald Tribune*, *The World-Telegram*, and *The New Yorker*.[63] "I used to work in one of the biggest department stores in this city, and I prefer this. I make more dough, and I'm not so exhausted at night. You can't even sit down in a department store. . . . In a store a cranky old woman can come in and get fresh, and you have to stand there and take it. But if a customer gets fresh here he gets a sock on the puss." And while marrying up often persisted as just stripper myth, dancing gave many a chance to realize the American dream. Many did, in a sense, pull themselves up by the bra strap or G-string to overcome working class origins, with the luckiest and the smartest using their career in burlesque as a building block to some other business opportunity, like opening a bar or nightclub.

For Lili, striptease was also easier than being dependent on a man, easier than having children. Seeing her mother trapped by domesticity, she decided early to snip the apron strings from her twenty-four-inch waist and focus on getting what she wanted from her career, not from her husband. "I wouldn't want to give up my work on the stage, ever," she told one reporter.[64] "As long as I have that I won't have to be dependent on anybody." Of course, her career in fact relied on countless men who were turned on by her taking it off

𝒜s the experienced dancers told Gypsy Rose Lee in the musical based on her life, to really turn men on you've got to get a gimmick. Gypsy shed her clothes while reading literature and poems onstage. Sally Rand and Faith Bacon were famous for their fan work. Others, like the incredibly busty Tempest Storm or six-foot tall Lois DeFee, who billed herself as the Eiffel Eyeful, used their natural attributes. And some, like Blaze Starr, who worked with a panther, or Rosita Royce, who danced with doves, used animals.

In the beginning of her career, Lili and her friend and choreographer Ivan Fehnova put together a routine known as the Flying G. For her finale, she attached fishing line to her G-string, which the lighting and backdrop made invisible. Just as the lights went out, a stagehand in the balcony would reel off the scanty under-thing. According to Fehnova, the first time they tried the Flying G the stagehand didn't properly reel off Lili's undies. On the second try, the line wasn't hooked properly. The G-string didn't shoot into the balcony, but flipped into the air and landed in a customer's martini. On the third try, the routine and the G-string came off smoothly.[65]

During these years, Lili toiled to learn the business. "I knew my limits," she wrote later.[66] "I wasn't made to sing or to be an actress, but I was a very good dancer . . . [and] it was possible to make a debut in burlesque without being terribly talented . . . burlesque merely constituted a step and, what's more important, it paid the rent. I quickly tried to get out of this world, but in the meantime, I had to learn."

Lili learned at the Old Howard, a legendary burlesque theater in Boston. She ground out invitations with her pelvis at Lou Walters' Latin Quarter in Miami. And she undulated up and down Fifty-second Street in New York in small clubs like Leon and Eddie's and the Samoa. The strip of New York's Fifty-second Street between Fifth and Sixth Avenues was once the incubator for jazz singers and small bands. As the epicenter of the jazz world, the area featured artists like Charlie Parker, Miles Davis, Billie Holiday, and Ella Fitzgerald experimenting and performing in the small clubs. It was, as one reporter described, "the cauldron on the wizard's workshop, where sweat, booze, and cigarette smoke provided the background for high art."[67] The performances of the jazz geniuses were generously interspersed with the gyrations of up-and-coming stripteasers perfecting the peel. In fact, by 1945, Fifty-second Street had earned several nicknames, such as 'Stripty-Second Street,' which tipped a hat to those who took it off.[68] Fifty-second Street became a melting pot where high and low art, hot-cha singers and cool beats, romantic interludes and seamy one-notes all came together. It is where musicians, Ivy League students, and limo-driven businessmen mingled. And it is where Lili fully realized she could make money offstage as well as on.

At the time, the small nightclubs of the era, both on Fifty-second Street and outside of New York, insisted the dancers mingle with the audience between shows and encourage the men to drink more. Bar girls, or B-girls as they were known, got a commission based on the number of cocktails they persuaded customers to buy. Unwitting customers often bought drinks for their beautiful companions that wound up spilled or spit out. Honey Bruce, who performed as Hot Honey Harlow and later married comedian Lenny Bruce, described the first time she ever played the champagne game: "My 'date' was perfect for the situation: a big, burly, beer-bellied monument to Budweiser. As soon as I sat down, he gave my thigh a reassuring squeeze and yelled for a waiter. . . . The waiter popped the cork and poured the bubbly. A full glass for my friend bully and equal amounts discreetly poured into my glass and the champagne bucket [for me]. I had to drink a little and it tasted like brake fluid. But I held on, through the first bottle and a second. Every time his aggressive hand started squeezing my flesh I'd giggle, pour him some more champagne, and keep my mind on the [money] I was going to get."[69]

Lili excelled at convincing men to buy her drinks and refused to even come to a table unless a bottle of champagne waited for her there. Later she claimed that she'd been nicknamed the Queen of Champagne on Fifty-second Street and that during each of her visits sales of champagne quadrupled.

It was also on Fifty-second Street that Lili began charging men to take her out for a meal. "I worked in the nightclubs until four in the morning . . . [and] despite the fact that I never drank too much from the same bottle [of champagne], by the end of the night I'd had quite a bit," she explained later.[70] "I [would wake] up with a severe hangover and I didn't want to see anyone. People who invited me to lunch or dinner were often offended if I refused the invitation. I just said to myself: if I have to go to lunch, I'll have to wake up, put on makeup, do my hair, dress and I will have to go to lunch even though it doesn't really do much for me and I'll have to have the air of being amused. It was like a show and I was paid to do shows, so I didn't see why I shouldn't make my hosts pay."

The earlier Lili needed to wake up, the more expensive her fee. Of course, the fact that she charged men $150 for breakfast, $125 for lunch, and $100 for dinner was a tasty tidbit that quickly worked its way into the gossip columns. The coverage made her task much easier, but it is also likely that stunts like this helped link striptease with prostitution. One gentleman involved in burlesque told researchers, "I never met a stripper who would pass up a chance to turn a couple of easy tricks. It is good money . . . besides it is a lonely business."[71]

Women in theater had long been linked to prostitution. During the early part of the nineteenth century, prostitutes and their customers governed the third tier of the theater. Then, when women finally appeared onstage, it was such a rarity that their very presence "became part of a commercial exchange by which she sold her 'self' for the delectation of male spectators," wrote Robert C. Allen, author of *Horrible Prettiness: Burlesque and American Culture*.[72] "The step from selling one's body onstage to selling it offstage was seen as a short one by many men." The association between the two was further strengthened by certain similarities: both the stripper and the prostitute use their sexuality to earn a living, working jobs outside the status quo. And both "often share the same area of town, the 'tenderloin,' and it is easy to think that they are after the same market, the lonely horny male," wrote David A. Scott in his book *Behind the G-String*.[73] "In both, the conflicting realms of sex and work converge." With the association between the theater and prostitution already lurking in the American psyche, it was seemingly inevitable that the disrobing women of burlesque would further connect the strip with the hook.

But the connection between striptease and prostitution may be overblown, a way to demean and dismiss the dancers. Many former burlesque dancers deny that it was a large part of the field. "You're not going to be doing four shows a day and be hooking on the side," said Betty Rowland, a pint-sized dancer who during the forties earned the moniker the Ball of Fire because of her flaming red hair and hot dance routines.[74] "And if you do, it gets around and you're not going to be in the business because they don't want those kinds of people in the business." Liz Renay, who stripped during the fifties, had a slightly different outlook, claiming that "prostitution is a gray area; people prostitute themselves in all sorts of ways."[75] Lili acknowledged that some dancers also prostituted themselves on the side, but like Liz Renay believed prostitution was hardly a black-

and-white issue. "I believe nine out of ten women who marry practice a kind of prostitution," she wrote.[76] "They marry to insure being supported and dole out their sex charms carefully so they'll continue to be supported. Many women care little about who they marry so long as he has money. Isn't that a form of prostitution?"

Lili certainly denied that she herself ever turned tricks, making it clear that a meal together was all anyone had the right to buy. "With me, the motto was, 'Time costs money but sex is free,'" she wrote later.[77]

But sex wasn't really free either. "Men were put on earth to give gifts to women," wrote Zorita, a stripteaser famous for dancing with a live snake during the forties.[78] "That's what makes them happy. . . . And I believe in making them happy. Sometimes that meant making sacrifices. Nobody wants to read that we were virgins or saints or that we just did good deeds for everyone. However, we were not trash either."

Lili may have turned up her nose at the stage door Johnnies, but she always lit up an inviting smile for the wealthy businessmen who came to her door. She grew accustomed to extravagant presents of furs and jewelry from her suitors. "A woman who can attract gifts of diamonds is a true artist and really feminine," she wrote.[79] "This ability separates the girls from the women. I see nothing wrong in a girl making a real effort to get jewelry presents from admiring friends. Men get pleasure from giving jewelry as gifts. Jewelry is personal, expensive and draws men closer."

While "raising the blood pressure . . . with her slow grinds and decorous bumps"[80] at Leon and Eddie's on Fifty-second Street, Lili met Pedro Serramalera, a wealthy Argentinean playboy with slicked back, jet black hair, a round face, and an easy-going, inviting smile. At twenty-one, Pedro inherited a substantial sum of money and spent several years gallivanting around the world as an international polo player, thoroughbred owner, and high-rolling gambler. While he wandered the world, he also dated many beautiful women, explained his son, also named Pedro Serramalera. So it is no surprise that the striking Lili St. Cyr caught his eye in the mid-forties. She later said that he propositioned her in a "grand manner" and "kept me in style in my own hotel suite."[81] Their fling even made a brief splash in the local gossip columns.

Years later, Lili said their affair ended because of his jealousy. "Trouble is, he was terribly jealous, even to the point where he'd look in my closets and under the bed when he entered my suite," she explained.[82]

"He suspected me of cheating. It was crazy!" She claimed Pedro left the country, but that he paid her rent and expenses for six months, confident she would stay with him because he was rich and handsome. Lili maintained she ditched him within a month. But a letter she wrote the day he left in March indicates she was completely smitten and even hoped to get a gig in Rio to see him. "I didn't talk very much when you left today, Baby—I knew if I did I would start to cry, and you hate that—but you must know how I felt," she wrote on stationary from the Ambassador Hotel in New York and signed not just with her name, but also a cherry-red lipstick kiss mark. "It's like I told you one night, Honey—I would do *anything* just to be with you—when you're not here I'm so darned unhappy—Darling please get on the airplane and come back—I love you so much." And in a subsequent letter Lili even admitted her own jealousy. "I guess it's silly to feel this way when you only *like* me—but I can't help it, Baby—you are nicer than any one I've ever known, maybe that's why (also your cute nose!)," she wrote. "I hope you don't go out with that girl in the pictures any more Honey—I guess I'm jealous or something but I only want you to go out with me. I love you so much. I wish I could see you every minute. Well, enough of this nonsense."[83]

By May, various gossip columns reported Pedro and Lili were engaged, with one reporter describing Pedro as "a romantic gaucho who, it seems, is up to his armpits in moolah . . . [and who] bombarded [Lili] with amorous missives and proposals—plus more tangible things such as checks."[84] It is unclear whether the twosome were truly engaged or if it was merely a publicity stunt, but Lili made it apparent she was not going to stop performing. "Please don't say I'm going to settle down with anyone," she asked one reporter when discussing the relationship.[85] "At least not for the next five years. I've got my career ahead of me."

Regardless of how Lili felt or how the relationship ended, Pedro was hardly your typical stage door Johnny. And he was just one of the many wealthy businessmen, actors, and international playboys that deluged her with attention and gifts. She never married these suitors, but her involvement with men like real estate entrepreneur Charles B. G. Murphy, *The King and I* actor Yul Brynner, and South African millionaire Derek Goodman was regularly whispered about and slyly written about in gossip columns. "What she did was very classy and it drew that type of person," said her friend Kiva, who sewed costumes for Lili in the fifties.[86] "But as soon as they wanted something from her, that was when she got rid of them. She was very choosy."

While Lili's offstage machinations certainly kept her comfortable, her onstage manipulations were not yet bringing in top dollar. She danced with the idea that a beautiful girl was a commodity, but she learned simply bumping and grinding wouldn't earn her the fortune she desired. Perhaps it was at Lou Walters' Latin Quarter in Miami where Lili realized her routines lacked the element of sophistication that would bring her the most money. In January 1944, a *Variety* review, using the newly popular mode of comparing women's sexuality to weapons with terms like bombshell, wrote of the show, "As usual Walters is relying on visual appeal and breakneck pacing to supply the come-on, but this year in addition is making a strong play for the military by building his revue around Lili St. Cyr, a long-stemmed stripper who is one of the hottest items to appear in a local class room. Gal is as streamlined as a P-38 and equipped with almost as much fire-power, but is almost certain to offend many as her routine carries beyond the border-line of good taste. She leaves nothing to the imagination."[87]

Aiming higher than "bananas or pork chops," Lili wanted to be a luxury commodity and soon began sashaying back toward the line of good taste by turning her routines into miniature plays. Just two months later, in March 1944, at the age of twenty-six, she began her reign over Montreal.

At the Gayety Theater in Montreal, she would perform routines with titles like "Manhattan Humors" or "Bird of Love." In her act she borrowed themes from fantasy, history, literature, and religion. In one of her early shows she used a gold Buddha placed on an altar inside a Chinese pavilion. To soft Asian-inspired music, her movements told the story of a young bride whose husband imprisoned her in a chastity belt before he went off to war. The bride pleaded to Buddha to free her from the belt so she could be with her true love. As Lili begged Buddha for her sexual liberation, the music beat faster and her clothes seemed to fly off. In the end Buddha released her and with the turn of a key, she removed the chastity belt just as the lights went down.

During her sojourn in Montreal, Lili learned to package titillation for sophisticated tastes. Whereas burlesque was rough and lusty, unbridled and raw, Lili St. Cyr was glamorous and sensual, refined and elegant. She presented imagined romance and the intoxicating suggestion of sex, all while pirouetting along the subtle line of desire and lust, good taste and vulgarity. She chose the name earlier, but it was in Montreal, where "legions of bug-eyed fans" watched as "she became Montreal's most famous woman, simply by stripping with such exotic panache" that she truly became Lili St. Cyr.

3.

An Epidemic
of Striptacoccus

When Lili St. Cyr arrived in the spring of 1944, Montreal was a potent cocktail of British traditions and French *joie de vivre*, a strange paradox of Catholic rules and the uninhibited pursuit of pleasure. Long controlled by the priests, nuns, and laymen who ran the schools and dispensed many of the city's social services, Montreal didn't loosen its clerical collar until the twenties, when Prohibition in the United States made Montreal one of the few places in North America where liquor could be legally imbibed. American mobsters moved to the city to take control of the burgeoning bootlegging industry, and soon any illicit pleasure could be purchased. Flesh was bought and sold in the city's brothels. Gambling, especially barbotte, the craps-like dice game, rolled along. And bars and nightclubs kept right on pouring.

Even after Prohibition was repealed in the United States in 1933, Montreal remained a swaggering, raucous, and even salacious city, a playground for Runyon-esque characters. By the mid-1940s Montreal had a 100-million-dollar gambling industry and perhaps a hundred brothels. Some of the more popular spots employed a dozen women who ground away in two or three shifts around the clock. The city, often called the Paris of North America, was also branded the continent's "capital of gambling, booze, and broads."[1] In 1944, just seven months after Lili arrived, writer Jim Coleman wrote in *MacLean's* magazine, "Montreal is a bountiful oasis in a land of rationing. Demon rum may be rationed in other sections of the country, but there is enough medicinal spirits in Montreal to float the entire Atlantic fleet up St. Catherine Street. . . . The entertainment business in Montreal is booming as never before. Hockey games, wrestling matches [and] theatres are besieged by eager customers with money to spend. Restaurants and the taverns are packed. . . . From dusk until the milkman starts on his morning rounds, the town sputters and fizzes like a Roman candle."[2]

It wasn't just that bawdy fun and boisterous unruliness were the order of the day, but that the law of abandon flowed from the top politicians to the lowliest policeman. Public officials promised reform, but any real crackdown involved a well-choreographed, almost comic routine. Raids usually resulted in an employee, never the real owner or manager, volunteering to be arrested, pleading guilty, paying a fine, and returning to work to be highly compensated for his or her trouble. An officer once said that on arresting one prostitute for the fiftieth time he treated the occasion like a fiftieth anniversary. If a judge ordered a door of a brothel or gambling joint to be locked, police locked side entrances, closets, and fake doors. Everyone was on the take and Montreal was "a picture of mink-coated $30,000-a-year bawdy-house madams driving Cadillacs, gambling joints raking in fortunes under the eyes of corrupt police officers, and city councilors pretending they knew nothing about conditions that were common knowledge."[3]

Lili joined the party in March 1944, and easily settled into the pulsating rhythms of Montreal: performing at the Gayety Theater, dining afterward at El Morocco or one of the other nightclubs, and greeting dawn at one of the city's many "blind pigs," or after-hours haunts. Her arrival caused an immediate sensation. With numbers like the "Chinese Virgin" and "Bird of Love," where she danced with a live bird that undressed her, her shows at the Gayety were met with wild applause and utter adoration. The Gayety may have been what journalist Jim Coleman had in mind when he described the "atmosphere places" of Montreal; nightclubs where "the cigarette smoke has no means of escape and the customers spend the evening squinting at each other through a fog, which billows only when the gyrations of the performers become particularly vigorous."[4] Lili thought the theater "gave the impression of being about to collapse,

[but] really loved it despite everything."[5]

Lili attracted such heavy crowds that the Gayety was in no danger of ruin. In fact, the theater on the corner of St. Catherine and St. Urbain streets became known as "The House that Lili Built." Those curious about the moniker should have tried buying a ticket when she lit up the marquee, explained *The (Montreal) Herald*'s nightlife columnist Al Palmer.[6] "It is not considered an unusual occurrence if traffic is blocked by eager patrons of the arts milling around the box office trying to buy tickets [and] the gambling gentry will lay you terrific odds that she will outdraw any attraction that plays the city."

Lili drew such crowds, in part, because of her routines. "In all my numbers, I created little scenes where it was normal for me to undress," she wrote later.[7] "My numbers were composed of little plays where I expressed, by dancing, romantic visions. I created characters of women who were torn by passion and sexual desire."

These inventive shows always told a story, often with themes from history, literature, and even religion. In one act, Lili appeared in full Indian headdress with feathers pluming down the front of her body. One reviewer noted that the routine "will leave you convinced that if Lili was around when Manhattan Island was sold, the Indians would have managed a far better deal than thirty-two dollars and a bottle of whoopee water."[8] And what once inspired classic artists now inspired her. One of her earliest story-based acts included an interpretation of Leda and the Swan, a mythological tale of a Spartan queen seduced by the god Zeus, who appeared in the guise of a swan. The erotic tale that stirred artists like Leonardo da Vinci and poets like William Butler Yeats now moved the countless fans who slavered over Lili's interpretation.

Another part of Lili's appeal came from the one word most often used to describe her: class. "Everybody in Montreal saw her show because she had class," explained musical prodigy Vic Vogel, who began playing in Montreal nightclubs and blind pigs before he was a teenager.[9] "It wasn't like the old American striptease style, with the throwing and flinging the gloves and the bras in the air. She created this vixen aura, an 'I'm going home with you tonight' situation. When she danced, you thought she was dancing for you. It was personal. It was subtle and it had more meaning. She was such a statuesque woman. You couldn't imagine her going to the bathroom. It's impossible. She was a goddess."

"This was no vulgar, corny stripper," said choreographer Brian MacDonald, who worked with Lili on her dance steps.[10] "This was a very high-class stripper. She managed to keep her audience at a distance and was never particularly vulgar. She was more flamboyant than vulgar. It was, 'Have a good look, boys, 'cause this is all you're gonna see.'"

The subtle tease left much to the imagination and quickened pulses far more than the typical bumps and grinds. "She was a beautiful woman, and everyone was there anticipating that *maybe* she would take off her bra," said Joe Mancini, a waiter who met Lili at one of the city's nightclubs.[11] "*Maybe* she would become nude. The anticipation. That's what attracted people."

"For a young boy like me, it was ridiculous," admits Vogel.[12] "My father had to change the sheets every night. He didn't know what was going on."

By now, Lili's earlier studies in putting on a show were paying off. She knew lighting, settings, costuming, and music. "She was already getting more involved with Latin rhythms, which were more exotic and a little more risqué," said Vogel.[13] "It was rare in those days because everybody was into the big band era."

And she could dance. "It's hard to explain to someone who hasn't studied dancing, but a lot of dancing is linear," explained MacDonald.[14] "For instance, an arabesque in classical ballet is standing on one leg with the other up behind you. That's a certain line. If that leg that's stuck out behind is turned in or droopy or the foot's not stretched or anything like that it looks terrible. But that never happened to her. She had wonderful lines. It sounds corny to say, all these years later, but she could hit a kind of classical attitude that was perfect. She just looked like a goddess. She looked like a statue. She was a very graceful dancer."

But it wasn't just the spine-tingling divinity this heavenly creature seemed to impart onstage that created such a stir when Lili St. Cyr came to Montreal. "She loved the role of being outrageously sexy," said MacDonald.[15] "She played it to the hilt. There was a whole number that went on just when she went down to the theater. She would walk down the main street in Montreal in a huge fur coat with her blonde hair piled on top of her head. The Red Sea parted on the way. And if she stopped at a red light, she'd pull back part of the fur coat, put her hand on her hip and smile at the taxi driver. If it was raining she'd walk down the street with big, colorful umbrellas. She knew that she could stop traffic. She was a very theatrical lady. And, of course, it sold out the theater."

Years later, Lili wrote about these excursions to the Gayety. "Little legends surrounding my personality have been created. It's been said that I walked in an arrogant manner with my mink coat draped carelessly across my shoulders [and] I was preceded by two Husky dogs. All that, of course, is pure invention, but it's nice to think that a legend's been started about me."[16]

Lili's love life contributed to her outrageously sexy image as well. Early on she got involved with Maurice Bresciano, the brother-in-law and employee of Vic Cotroni, a street thug who in the early fifties became Mafioso Joe Bonanno's right-hand man in Montreal. "It was enough to look at Maurice to know that 'he wasn't the type of man to go out with,'" she later wrote.[17] "But that was part of his charm. He discharged a sort of brutal magnetism."

Despite threats from Bresciano's wife and mistress, Lili continued to date Maurice, claiming that "as a general rule, I avoid going out with married men, but . . . Maurice's marriage was already one of those that didn't respect the established rules."[18] But in the end, Bresciano was more brutal than compelling: Lili left him, claiming he beat her in a jealous, drunken rage. Despite severely bruised ribs, she "got lots of satisfaction out of being implicated with him. I let the world know that I had the intention of living according to my laws, and my laws only . . . [and it] gave me a reputation as a femme fatale."[19]

Bresciano wasn't Lili's only fling. "If you had money and you wanted to be seen, she was the person to be seen with," said Vogel.[20] "That was the thing to do. She was it. She was seen with everybody."

"First of all, it was her looks and then it was her name," said Mancini.[21] "But I would say it was mostly that she was like they say, a trophy on a man's arms. And she took advantage of it by flaunting herself, by having the best of everything. It was nothing but champagne and the high life."

In many ways, Montreal felt like living on the grand steam liners again. But as Lili quickly pointed out, if she'd had as many flings as people claimed, "I wouldn't have had time to do anything but walk from one bed to another. I probably caused more scandals than I deserved. It wasn't uncommon that the wicked Lili St. Cyr was accused of breaking up a marriage that hadn't worked."[22]

Her intoxicating performances, jaw-dropping excursions, and rumor-filled love life were enough to make "La Belle Lili" the toast of the town. Journalists reported on her everyday habits, including her pre-show rituals. "Before coming onstage, Lili likes to relax in a chaise lounge, and she takes advantage of this rest to swallow two or three sips of a beverage made to her specifications. The liquor-based drink contains, it seems, certain vitamins which are necessary for Lili to find the energy for her number." All of which, as the same writer demonstrated, raised the opportunity to praise her lithe movements. "It is said that Lili is obliged to supply a considerable effort, and that this effort is never suspected by the audience, because no dancer succeeds like her in presenting a number seemingly consisting of only sweet and delicate movements."[23]

Much more effusive were the town's columnists. Al Palmer, Montreal's own Walter Winchell and Lili's good friend, wrote that Lili "spreads an epidemic of striptacoccus"[24] every time she appears. Another enamored writer referred glancingly to her supporting act, singer Dean Martin, and focused on the headliner, "Montreal's favourite entertainer, Lili St. Cyr, the Grable-bodied dance enchantress whose genuine and inspired artistry always elicits tumultuous applause from audiences. Lili St. Cyr is the most stunningly and strikingly beautiful blonde dancer yet to appear at the Gayety and her terpsichorean evolutions are described as electric."[25]

Women clamored to imitate her. One strange trend began when Lili dyed her hair the "most startling beautiful tint known as 'Blue Mink.'" Apparently, "the peculiar shade . . . started something of a fad in Montreal with several hairdressers reporting customers . . . seeking information regarding the process in an increasing number."[26]

While for many Montrealers day dawned simply as a prelude to night, it was, after all, wartime, and Canada had been fighting in World War II two years longer than America. Families devoured war correspondents' vivid accounts of the battles for news of sons and husbands serving overseas. Suspected fascists, anti-war protesters, and others perceived as threats, including Montreal mayor Camillien Houde, spent years in internment camps. Everything from sugar to fabric was rationed. Lights and neon signs were dimmed to save energy.

But even the war could not dull Lili's bright shine. In the fall of 1942, British scientists working on the atomic bomb moved their operation to Montreal, where the threat of spies seemed lower and where they would be closer to the American effort. By the time she arrived in Montreal in 1944, the British and Canadian scientists enmeshed in the dark pursuits of atomic power delighted in the anatomic distraction Lili provided. To honor their tempting diversion, the young researchers named a shoebox-sized device used to detect and measure levels of radiation, "The Lili." The portable surface ionization detector was heavy and difficult to use, but the next generation apparatus, named the "Super-Lili," was much lighter and more manageable.[27]

"As we improved the instruments, we named them Super-Lili, Super-Lili 1, Super-Lili 2, and so forth," said Kim Krenz, who was a researcher in the lab at the time, but was too busy to catch Lili's act.[28] "I was already married by then, but the other guys in the lab had been to see her. We all agreed that the instruments should be named after her. She was the toast of Montreal at that time."

As the war was ending, the scientists moved to a newly built plant, the Chalk River Nuclear Laboratories, two hours west of Montreal. The Super-Lili eventually moved to the Canadian Science and Technology Museum in Ottawa, where it still resides in the Canadian Innovations exhibit.

In the spring of 1945, Germany surrendered. Montreal, like so many other cities, erupted. "The news went up on the big bulletin board outside the *Montreal Star* offices on St. James Street, in the heart of the financial district, and within minutes stockbrokers and stenographers were running out of their offices to read it," wrote *City Unique* author William Weintraub.[29] "Streetcars coming down the street stopped in front of the bulletin board and passengers jumped out to stare at it. By now horns and whistles could be heard from ships in the harbour, and sirens were sounding. . . . Ticker tape showered down into the canyon of St. James Street, onto singing, cheering crowds. All work came to an end and people hurried out to the street to join the surging mob. . . . Uptown, stores, offices and schools closed for the day and thousands headed for the corner of Peel and St. Catherine Streets, the focal point of the pandemonium. The crowds there, and in other parts of the city, were so thick that cars could barely get through. People were waving flags, marching, shouting, dancing and kissing one another."

Lili, in town performing in a "Latin Quarter Revue," joined in the revelry of the city that now felt like home. "Montreal took me into its heart and vice versa," she wrote. "When I came there, my gypsy spirit felt at home."[30]

Lili's friend Al Palmer was not surprised. Montreal, he wrote, "is not so much a city as a state of mind. To live there is to love it. Those of us who were fortunate enough to be born there consider it the nearest approach to Heaven we know without leaving the ground."[31]

While Montreal took Lili into its heart, other cities also lusted for the strip. World War II boosted the tease as scantily-clad women—from the busty pinups to the undressing dancers—were considered a diversion and morale booster for the soldier. After the war, the soldiers who had graced their barrack walls with pinups returned to find a booming business of men's magazines. The yen for striptease also continued with more and more nightclubs around the United States getting into the act. And Lili, one of the magazine's more popular subjects, struck poses on the covers and in inside pictorials, increasing her popularity even more. So while Lili spent much of the forties making frequent and lengthy trips to Montreal, she also continued to dance her way between Boston and Los Angeles.

Clearly Canadians were not alone in appreciating Lili's rhythmic undulations; wherever she appeared she headlined the show, garnered more coverage for covering less of her body, and slowly becoming a crowd-pleasing favorite. By the mid-forties she even snagged the attention of cartoonist Al Capp, who modeled the buxom, man-eating, marriage-eschewing Wolf Gal character in his Li'l Abner comic after Lili. Wolf Gal eventually earned her own two-volume comic book. In the first, Dogpatch townsfolk are upset because their daughters have all gone wild copying Wolf Gal, "a wile, savage, bootiful critter, wif th' heart of a wolf."[32] To solve the problem, the women try to tame Wolf Gal by marrying her off to a man who keeps her in a cage. In the end, she escapes, devours her husband, and returns to the woods. In the second, Wolf Gal goes in search of love in order to break a curse. She turns to an elegant actress and forces her to give Wolf Gal "the veneer of a lady."[33] Having trouble with the transformation, Wolf Gal learns from the actress that most girls look like ladies on the outside, but feel like she-wolves on the inside. Despite the makeover, Wolf Gal fails to find lasting love, but is changed by the experience, explaining that, "knowin' 'bout love has change me fum a she-wolf into a she, an' a she like me needs a he."[34]

Despite her previous marital flops and the fear of being caged in by marriage, Lili responded to the societal pressure expressed in the Wolf Gal comic that a *she* needed a *he*. This time, the *he* was dancer and actor Paul Valentine, a handsome man who managed to have a "dancer's natural grace [while being] built like a towering bear."[35]

Prone to exaggeration, Paul Valentine choreographed his life story, regularly changing steps and adding flourishes. He was born William Daixel in March 1919, in Manhattan's Lower East Side, and studied dance, spending less than three months in the mid-thirties with the then-new School of American Ballet. At some point he changed his name to Val Valentinoff. It is unclear whether his claims of joining the acclaimed Ballets Russes when he was fourteen, traveling with the troupe for twenty-five dollars a week, and throwing stink bombs on the stage during a Mexico City performance were true.[36] With hopes of more commercial, Hollywood success, he again changed his name to Paul Valentine.

Lili met Paul in the mid-forties during one of her performance stops in New York. Beyond his thick black hair, chiseled face, smooth voice, and dance talent, she also liked his "beauty and energy. . . . He was animated with unparalleled vigor, and always full of projects and dreams."[37] In December 1946, she and Paul married in Tijuana, Mexico.

The newlyweds began working together almost immediately. Lili included Paul in her act or had him added to the bill for his own performance. He helped choreograph her routines and staged a musical revue at L.A.'s Mayan Theater where his bride was the star attraction. In tandem they developed "The Wolf Woman" routine, which capitalized on her connection with Wolf Gal.

During the early, heady days of her romance with Paul, Lili earned her first arrest. In December 1947, she was arrested at the Follies Theater in Los Angeles over a performance about the lonely wife of a sultan who commits adultery with a slave. During a two-day hearing in April, a police officer claimed that only Lili's hands kept her from being nude. Lili said the act was art and an interpretive dance of love. The judge disagreed and she received a $350 fine.[38] The whole thing hardly seemed to register with her.

In the beginning, Lili was excited about working with Paul, wanting to believe they could rival the famous husband-and-wife acting team Alfred Lunt and Lynn Fontanne. She always remained generous in crediting her husband with improving her act. And whether Valentine served as a mentor and director or simply smoothed out her performances, while married to him she developed some of her more interesting routines. For instance, she began to do a take-off on Chrysis, a character in Pierre Louys' 1895 *Aphrodite: Moeurs Antiques*. The erotic novel tells the story of a beautiful courtesan who meets the Queen's lover and convinces him to steal and murder before getting her own comeuppance and being condemned to death by drinking hemlock. Lili also staged a short dance based on Oscar Wilde's *Salome*, a tale of the woman who dances to encourage King Herod to behead John the Baptist. One reviewer described the performance as a "barbaric portrayal [that] shows her gloating over the head of the prophet and [ending] in a wild, frenzied dance."[39] She even staged performances of Cleopatra's death, created a routine based on Oscar Wilde's novel *The Picture of Dorian Gray*, and invented original productions like "Mannequins on Display," which featured her as a mannequin that comes to life.

During this inventive time Marilyn Monroe first saw Lili perform, according to Ted Jordan, who became Lili's fifth husband in the midfifties. In his book *Norma Jean*, Jordan claimed he dated Monroe in the forties when she was still Norma Jean. He wrote that when he and Monroe went to see Lili perform, "It was just about the sexiest thing I had ever seen. St. Cyr never took her clothes off, but in a skimpy costume that highlighted the best features of her statuesque body, she moved with unbelievable grace through a series of ballet-like sketches. There was the parrot sketch, featuring [a] bird making love to her in time with the music . . . Not once did St. Cyr ever touch any part of her body, yet the effect was electric."[40] According to Jordan, Monroe was wildly impressed with how sexy Lili could be without being dirty. In his telling, Monroe became obsessed, and patterned herself after the stripteaser. While Jordan has been widely discredited by those who knew both Marilyn and Lili and other authors, his claim that the twentieth century's greatest sex symbol modeled herself after Lili St. Cyr is not his most outrageous assertion and is quite plausible.

"I don't think it would have been unusual," said Gloria Romanoff, who with her husband ran the legendary Hollywood eatery Romanoff's and was friendly with Monroe.[41] "She was interested in anything that would have built her career. If someone had suggested she see Lili St. Cyr perform, she would have."

Bruno Bernard, a photographer known as Bruno of Hollywood, also witnessed Marilyn's study of Lili. Bernard photographed Monroe,

Elizabeth Taylor, Lili St. Cyr, and hundreds of busty women for the era's popular pinup photos. "Lili's classy sex demonstration was studied religiously by Norma Jean," Bernard wrote in his book *Requiem for Marilyn*.[42] "She caught Lili's show several times. When Norma Jean came to my studio the next time, she asked to see my proof sheets of the photo sessions with Lili St. Cyr. Her curiosity was strictly of a professional nature as she apparently wanted to refine the waddling walk which had earned her the moniker 'Miss Swivelhips.' . . . Marilyn was an expert mimic . . . [and] her study of Lili St. Cyr put her in good stead."

Monroe's scrutiny of Lili came during her transformation from Norma Jean to Marilyn Monroe, from foster child to movie star, from brunette girl next door to blonde sultry siren. By the time Monroe appeared in the 1949 movie *Love Happy* with Lili's then-husband Paul Valentine the makeover was evident.

Marilyn Monroe's friend, photographer James Haspiel, acknowledged Monroe's interest in other performers and believed Monroe "would have a natural interest" in seeing Lili perform. Haspiel also pointed out, "when you hear this kind of thing it's always multiplied and exaggerated. Marilyn is the easiest mark in the world because she's just so revered."[43] Of course, it is just as likely that studio executives found it easier to raise Monroe up as a Hollywood goddess for fans to worship because she lacked the striptease stigma. Jordan's claims are clearly hyperbolic, but it is equally clear Monroe had a professional appreciation for Lili.

Lili's own husband wanted for that same appreciation. As a review of Lili and Paul's performance at the Florentine Gardens indicated, the couple, after less than two years of marriage, was clearly not in sync. "In her interpretation of Bodin's 'Polovetzkian Dances,' Lili is accompanied by 'Guest Star' Paul Valentine," wrote *L.A. Times* critic Philip Scheuer.[44] "Mostly they interpret independently, Lili reclining on the floor and waving her long, languid legs or rising to sway . . . while Valentine spins and leaps elsewhere. Occasionally they grapple briefly; then go their separate ways."

The word grapple was an apt choice, as the two began to fight personally and professionally. "The pleasure of working with Paul tapered quickly," Lili wrote later.[45] "He was a very demanding perfectionist because of his training as a ballet dancer. I was wise enough to know that wasn't my discipline, but Paul didn't see a difference . . . Paul and I had never really been partners; he was a dictator and I was supposed to accept his orders without stumbling." Unable to bear the pressure, Lili had her agent schedule her for performances in Montreal. She escaped to the city she loved, the city that was more than a state of mind, more than a home for her nomadic soul. "Montreal was, above all, Jimmy Orlando."[46]

By the time Lili met Jimmy Orlando in the mid-forties, the tall Italian with black, wavy hair was a popular nightclub owner and local celebrity. But Jimmy grew up worlds away from his small jazz club, in a poor, tough section of Montreal known as Goose Village.

Officially known as Victoriatown, the neighborhood began as a home for the immigrant workers who built Victoria Bridge, which spans the St. Lawrence River. Nicknamed Goose Village because of the wild geese that inhabited the marshy area, the neighborhood was "just half a dozen streets, wedged in between the coal yards and the abattoirs, where many of the residents worked," wrote *City Unique* author William Weintraub.[47] "People in cars driving past the Village, on their way to the bridge, wondered how anyone could live amid the foul stench of the animal wastes being burned at the slaughter houses, but the Villagers were used to it, and to the coal dust that sometimes blew across the coal yards to begrime the washing that was drying on clotheslines."

Jimmy and his seven siblings grew up in Goose Village, amid the coal yards and slaughter houses. And Jimmy bought his first pair of hockey skates to escape the poverty and stench of the area.

"When he was a kid, his father thought skating was like polo, because they were poor Italians and it was the Depression," said Doris Quinn Godfrey, Jimmy's third wife.[48] "So Jimmy was going by a pawn shop and there were these skates in there. They were two or three sizes too big. But he bought them, shoved socks in the toes and wore them. He wanted to skate so badly because he knew that that was his way out of being another poor Italian in Montreal."

The purchase paid off. Jimmy worked his way up through the minor leagues and by 1936, when he was twenty years old, he was skating with the National Hockey League's Detroit Red Wings. Jimmy played defenseman for the Red Wings, which won the Stanley Cup twice during his six-year tenure. "Known as the 'Bad Man on Ice,' Orlando was fiery, exciting, and as tough as they came," wrote Paul Greenland in *The History of the Detroit Red Wings*.[49] "He not only mixed it up with many an opponent, but with fans as well. Easy-going off of the ice, he was considered by many players to be the game's hardest hitting defenseman." Jimmy's most famous brawl landed him on the cover of *Life* magazine, a photo showing him coming off the ice with blood dripping from his face.

"Yeah, I must be a ba-a-a-ad boy," Jimmy once said about his reputation.[50] "But I never hit a guy with my stick—the dukes are good enough for me, especially that left hook. I never looked for a fight in my life, but I've never dodged one. It brings me lots of trouble."

Off the ice, Jimmy earned a reputation as a well-dressed, congenial ladies man. After retiring from hockey, he managed the El Morocco nightclub in Montreal and then opened his own place, Aldo's. "If you were writing of his hockey career it would be necessary to type with boxing gloves on because the Orlando on ice is not the quiet, soft-spoken youngster he is when you visit [him at] his bistro," wrote Al Palmer.[51] "Orlando's career in the NHL is mostly written in liniment. He managed to get into more brawls, bump more opponents on their posteriors, and in general, create more havoc than any other four players in the league . . . But that is not the Jimmy Orlando you'll meet at Aldo's. Here, in his nitery, he is the soul of gentleness and does his best to uphold the high ideals which his fan club . . . credit him."

Aldo's was particularly popular with local gangsters and musicians. The small club was "*the* place," said saxophonist Frank Costi.[52] "If you weren't seen at Aldo's there was something wrong. . . . *Everything* went on there."

Lili likely met Jimmy at El Morocco or Aldo's. It's even more likely that she was drawn to the blend of his tough-guy reputation, immense popularity, and model good looks. "I was so taken with Jimmy that I couldn't resist his virile charm or his smile," Lili wrote later.[53] "He had a magnetism that made him irresistible in the eyes of women, and even men. I was crazily in love."

"It was a very torrid romance," recalled Jamee Carangello, Jimmy's daughter with another woman.[54] "It wasn't just an overnight thing. I think that they were really taken with each other. It was pretty intense."

"She wanted to marry him or move in with him," said a former showgirl who later married Jimmy.[55] "She would do anything for him. In fact, she used to send towels and china and all kinds of gifts to him."

As often as Lili used men for financial gain, she could also be unbelievably generous. "When I fall in love the object of my complete affection can have everything," she wrote later.[56] "My man is king and he is worth—or so I believe—all my time and attention. Men have cost me a fortune, but I don't regret it."

"Every time Lili would come over to have supper, she would bring a gift," said Carangello.[57] "My aunt remembers getting bath salts from her. She still has the bottle of it in her bedroom. My aunt and uncle were very impressed with her."

Lili and Jimmy's relationship was passionate, but it was also tumultuous. "Jimmy Orlando was one of her lovers and, presumably, her favorite," said William Weintraub.[58] "But he was not particularly faithful." Neither was Lili. "When Lili was out of town, Jimmy would do what he had to do, and she would do what she had to do," said Joe Mancini.[59] "She never caused any problems going from one man to another. A man took it as it came."

One man Lili was linked with, though somewhat surreptitiously, was Eddie Quinn, a stocky man with a broad face, wide nose and wave of brown hair brushed off his forehead. Born in Boston, Eddie and his family moved to Montreal during the Depression. A small-time wrestling and boxing promoter, he began promoting matches at the Forum in Montreal. He transformed the city's wrestling scene and became "the king of grunt and groan."[60]

Eddie and Jimmy met at the Forum when Jimmy still played hockey. Eddie gave Jimmy his start in the nightclub business, making Jimmy the manager of his club El Morocco. Always the promoter, when Eddie heard Montreal buzzing about Lili St. Cyr he showed up at the Gayety to invite her to El Morocco. "He gave off a certain abrasive but irresistible charm," Lili wrote of Eddie, admitting that she and he "were more than friends."[61]

Years later, one "old-time insider" even claimed that Jimmy was simply a beard, or diversion, for Lili's real affair with the married Eddie Quinn, who reportedly would "sneak into her chambers after wifey was asleep." And supposedly Eddie even engaged in a tryst with Lili while on a cruise with his wife.[62]

"That's not true," said Doris Quinn Godfrey, Eddie's daughter.[63] "I think there was a liaison, but I think it was casual. It was not long-standing. And I think my mother may have known, but it wasn't discussed over the dinner table and my mother and father remained happily married a long time."

"I don't doubt that Eddie Quinn has made some mistakes . . . just as all of us have at times which accounts for the many confessionals which abound in the Roman Catholic churches in the City of Montreal," wrote the managing director of the Canadian Arena Company after Eddie found himself in some trouble with the Athletic Commission.[64] It's a paragraph Doris "especially likes," but it's not an attitude often applied to Lili.

"She was certainly a beautiful lady and had a lot of class onstage," said one showgirl who worked with Lili in Montreal.[65] "Everybody knew if you were young and good looking you could go in her dressing room, have a bottle of booze with her, and she would jump in bed. And then after, they all talked about her and all the things she did in bed. I don't know if you call that a lot of class. I mean, I was in show business but I certainly wasn't falling in and out of bed with everybody."

"She did sleep with practically everybody she met," Doris said of Lili.[66] "I know she slept with one of Jimmy's brothers. I'm not saying this out of jealousy or anything, because there is no need for that. But it's like with Marilyn Monroe. Everybody claims they've slept with her. Even if only half of the people who claim it are telling the truth, it's still a lot of people. She was passed around, as they would say."

The association between nudity and sex is so entangled, many "just assume that here is a woman who simply exults in being naughty," explained David A. Scott in his book *Behind the G-String*.[67] "[The audience] expects to see the revelation of a woman's sexual self. . . . We think the stripper's performance must be congruent with her feelings. We don't think of her as playing a role or wearing a mask. After all, she's naked—what can she hide?" And so, the general public's impression of striptease dancers is often that they are social deviants with little character, intelligence, or moral compass. *New York World-Telegram* reporter H. Allen Smith once wrote of Lili's peers Margie Hart and Sally Rand that "it is a rare thing, indeed, to find a stripper who has more intelligence than a backing-off lathe. If they have any sense before they come into the trade it goes away. Generally speaking, these girls are hard, tough-talking babes, with the social consciousness of the black widow spider."[68]

Such broad-sweeping descriptions of striptease dancers as stupid, tough, deviant, amoral, or loose help degrade women who embrace the sexual power of their onstage role or who are simply making the best of their circumstances. Regardless, it is impossible to know how many men

Lili slept with, and whether she was passed around or was satisfying her own sexual desires.

Considering the view so many had of striptease dancers and the potential lingering emotional conflict of having been involved with the same man, it is understandable that Jimmy's wives would view Lili in such a way while completely ignoring his own indiscretions. It wasn't just Lili who was rendezvousing with others. When she was performing in other cities, Jimmy would take up with various girls.

"When I was eighteen or nineteen he took me out a couple of times," said Doris, who married Jimmy nearly twenty-five years later.[69] "We were eyeing each other. We had this mini-romance, and then my father cut that off. And I moved to New York to do some modeling."

Jimmy also dallied with an American chorus girl who worked with Lili in Montreal. She claimed "he started asking me out for dates and everything, but I figured with so many girls after him . . . I didn't really want to get involved because I figured it's another one-night stand. At that time I knew that Lili St. Cyr was coming in to visit him and wanted to give him the world. But I guess I finally fell in love with him and he felt that I would be the one to stay with him and not be flitting around with other men."

It was upon returning to Montreal, when Lili found Jimmy still entangled with the showgirl, that Lili took up with his younger brother Frankie, a younger replica of Jimmy with the same shock of black hair, bushy eyebrows, long nose, and warm grin.

"[Frankie] had a marvelous smile that . . . could illuminate a room as well as my heart," wrote Lili.[70] "He was nice, attentive and . . . always gallant, he escorted me [and was] very indulgent to my mood swings and my caprices."

Jimmy's showgirl at the time thought Lili's interest in Frankie was more conniving. "I think she was trying to make Jimmy jealous. And I think the brother really fell for her, but she still had Jimmy in mind. I think Frankie was very flattered that she went for him, but I think that was just her way of trying to make Jimmy jealous, you know, trying to still get him."

In the end, Lili didn't get Jimmy. He married the showgirl and promptly insisted she stop working. "Well, he was Italian. He wouldn't let me work. He believed the wife stays home," she said years later in an interview.[71]

"I think she missed her career," said Jamee Carangello, their daughter.[72] "She met my dad and was smitten like everyone else. I guess she thought she was going to have this super exciting life, but it didn't really turn out that way. My dad was in the club business so he wouldn't be home at night. She'd be home with the kids. It probably didn't turn out the way she wanted."

Lili continued to reject the notion of a life at home with the kids. Years later she claimed to have had as many as eleven abortions and to "despise children." In fact, she wrote, "the thought of having any has always petrified me with shivering fear."[73]

Instead of marrying Jimmy, Lili remained one of Montreal's favorite and most notorious celebrities. But Jimmy's marriage wasn't the end of Lili's romance with him. Rather, it was just another pause in an on-again, off-again relationship that would last almost twenty years.

Of course, during the early stage of her relationship with Orlando, Lili was still married to Paul Valentine. When she returned to the United States to perform in August 1949, Paul met her in New York and confronted her about her infidelity. The two quarreled, Valentine stormed out and, after a fight on the phone with Jimmy, Lili attempted suicide. "I was totally empty," she later explained.[74] "I sat on my bed, wrote a little note, and swallowed as many sleeping pills as I could find." Paul found Lili, rushed her to the hospital, and managed to keep his wife's suicide attempt out of the papers. But the marriage was still over. On their return to Los Angeles the two separated. Lili moved out of the house she had bought and into a hotel. Paul remained in her Hollywood Hills home while the two sorted out their dissolving marriage.

In Los Angeles, Lili returned to the Follies, a burlesque theater on Main Street. At the Follies, she met Walter Kane, Howard Hughes' right-hand man. Lili was taken with his energy and manners. "I was never really in love with him, but he personified grace and elegance," she explained.[75] "He evoked a very special world that I wanted to be part of." The romance was fleeting. Still in a fragile state, she again attempted suicide and was again rescued by Paul.

Admitting that the only intimacy the couple shared was after her suicide attempts, Lili said she did not believe Paul showed her the love or tenderness she needed. She later confessed that she could love a man forever, but that "he would have to court me continuously—to constantly show he cared."[76] Whether she was particularly needy or Paul particularly unkind is unknown, but Lili felt unloved, bossed around, and "inferior."[77]

It seems Paul may have also felt inferior. Despite his own professional successes—Valentine landed a movie contract with RKO studios and starred in the Marx Brothers' film *Love Happy* during his marriage to Lili—he had, for the most part, hitched his star to his wife's garter. Paul owed much of his regular work to his wife, relying on her to include him in her act or the club's show. Perhaps he was envious that his wife made more money and received top billing.

When he landed his own roles, he often rubbed the cast the wrong way and rarely worked with people a second time. "He thought a great deal of himself. He was arrogant, very full of himself, and inflated the truth," recalled Bruce Gordon, who appeared in *Love Happy* with Valentine and was offended that he would show nude photos of Lili around on the set.[78] "It was 'see what I bagged here,' one of those things. I didn't think much of that." "He was kind of uppity," said actor Frank Aletter, who appeared in Josh Logan's Broadway hit *Wish You Were Here* with Valentine.[79] "His demeanor was that he was an enormous star. He was egotistical."

His lack of success compared with Lili's star sheen clearly rankled him even after their split. More than five years after their divorce, a gossip columnist noted that "Philadelphia is still echoing with the screams heard when Lili St. Cyr and her ex-husband Paul Valentine played the same nightclub bill. Both wanted to close the show, and the impasse could be heard for miles."[80]

After his divorce from Lili, Paul married a woman who claimed to be an Iranian princess. The couple had two sons and rented a house in Los Angeles. Paul continued to work on his career, but had little success. "Nobody wanted to hire him," said Roberta Ralph, the Valentines' land-lord.[81] "He was really frustrated about that."

It is part of the capricious nature of show business that Paul just "fell by the wayside," explained casting agent and friend Claire Shull.[82] "He was a lovely, striving artist who started what could have been a brilliant career. He had everything. He had beauty, charm, ability. He just fell through the cracks."

Eventually Paul and his family made their living holding garage sales and selling autographed photos. "The family was not in good shape," said

Marsha Schoen, their neighbor for nearly fifteen years.[83] "They were sort of like gypsies, had a lot of problems, and he went off the deep end." When Ralph decided to sell the house the Valentines were renting, the family filed for bankruptcy and tried to fight the eviction. After much legal wrangling, the Valentines were finally evicted, leaving the house a complete disaster. "It was a mess," said Ralph.[84] "I've never seen a place treated that badly." According to the new owner, Bob Canny, the house was infested with rats, overgrown with vines and weeds, and "absolutely disgusting."[85]

Long after their divorce, Paul continued to take credit for Lili's success. Fifty years later, he told Canadian filmmakers working on a documentary about Lili St. Cyr that he developed her famous bathtub act to circumvent the censorship laws of the time. Paul died in early 2006, still best known as one of Lili St. Cyr's husbands.

Lili, on the other hand, was primarily charitable and benevolent in her comments about Paul, their marriage, and his work. Whereas he complained that "everybody in the country could see more of her than I could," Lili said little to reporters during the divorce proceedings.[86] When he complained she sulked in her room and was unpleasant to guests at their home, she echoed her idol Greta Garbo and said, "When I go home, I want to be alone. At the theatre I love a big crowd, I need a big crowd. At home, no crowd."[87]

Throughout the divorce proceedings she remained in Montreal, the city to which she once again escaped. Perhaps inspired by her own attempts, Lili was performing a new routine called "Suicide." In the act, she played a woman despondent and heartbroken at being abandoned by her lover. Clutching his photo, she danced in front of a set showing the New York skyline, and slowly peeled off her clothes. When her lover failed to appear, she climbed up to the window, a body double jumped, and Lili continued to dance as an angel until the curtain fell. Of her real-life suicide attempts, Lili made the seemingly prescient admission. "When it comes to physical harm, I only have to fear myself. My destruction comes from the inside."[88]

4.

Togetherness
and Trouble

A liberated woman is one who has sex before marriage and a job after.

— GLORIA STEINEM

As the wartime forties faded into the fifties, the United States breathed a collective sigh of relief and watched as the pendulum swung to the extreme. After two decades of depression and war, the country embraced frivolity, femininity, and family: hula hoops, 3-D movies, sock hops, full petticoats, high heels, and family barbecues in suburban backyards were all the rage. The roaring economy and generous veterans' benefits spurred a mass move to the newly created suburban developments and a consumer culture that encouraged the purchase of big cars and new appliances. Of course, underlying all of this innocent, happy fun trickled a stream of paranoia and frustration.

For women, the fashions that paraded through catalogs and down runways seemed emblematic of the era's duality. Women slipped out of the sturdy, masculine, practical styles of the forties and into frills and full skirts. The new look emphasized full breasts with tight sweaters, ballet-dancer skirts over full petticoats, and spiky heels. Women looked soft and feminine with their high, pointy breasts, tiny waists, and round hips, but to achieve the look required robust, armorlike undergarments. Howard Hughes asked his aircraft engineers to create a bra that lifted and separated the breasts; actress Jane Russell donned the garment and made it a hit. Women strapped themselves into waist-cinchers, corsets, and girdles. The delicate exterior belied the well-built foundation.

When the men came marching home from war, the women ditched their jobs and coveralls and teetered in their high heels to the suburbs. The entire country seemed to yearn for marriage and domesticity, creating what *McCall's* magazine termed the era of "togetherness."[1] Almost half of American women were married before they were twenty, and after falling for much of the previous century, the rate at which married couples had children soared to the point where the country's population growth rivaled that of India's.[2] The proportion of female to male college students dropped from 47 percent in 1920 to 35 percent in 1958, with many women acknowledging they went to college in search of a Mrs. title, not a degree.[3] "Never before had so many people agreed that only one kind of family was 'normal,'" wrote *Marriage: A History* author Stephanie Coontz.[4] "The cultural consensus that everyone should marry and form a male-breadwinner family was like a steamroller that crushed every alternative view."

For women, the country's reaction to the changes that began to take hold during the first half of the century must have, at times, caused emotional whiplash. They forgot they were ever sexually experimenting flappers, independent New Women, and professional Rosie the Riveters, and instead squeezed into girdles, stiff petticoats, and impregnable, fortresslike bras just to vacuum their house in the 'burbs. "Women seemed to have been catapulted back in time to the nineteenth century, to the cult of the True Woman and the corset that went with it," wrote *America's Women* author Gail Collins.[5] "They dropped out of college, married early, and read women's magazines that urged them to hold onto their husband's love by pretending to be dumb and helpless. They were isolated in the suburbs, marooned in a world of women and children while their husbands drove off every day to careers in the city."

Perhaps released from the grip of the poverty and war of the past two decades, women felt they could do worse than aspire to a middle-class, if occasionally bland, life. As Coontz pointed out, "even people who had grown up in completely different family systems had come to believe that universal marriage at a young age into a male breadwinner family was the traditional and permanent form of marriage."[6] Lili's sisters seemed to embrace the family-centric attitude, but Lili rebelled against society's expectations.

Lili's half-sister Idella Ruth Blackadder had performed as Barbara Moffett with Lili at the Florentine Gardens, experienced a short-lived career as a starlet with RKO studios, and traveled with the USO during the war. Returning to the United States, she settled in New York and shared an apartment with Lili, who was performing in town. In her French-Canadian memoir *Ma Vie de Stripteaseuse*, Lili writes about her friend Babs Adderly, a showgirl whom she met at the Florentine Gardens. This friend also had a brief career with RKO, traveled with the USO, and after the war sublet an apartment with Lili in New York. When Lili's book was published in the eighties, she and Barbara had not spoken in years so it is likely Lili did not want to identify "Babs Adderly" as her sister, but clearly they are one and the same. The split between the two women seems more unfortunate than the usual family rifts considering that in her book Lili described Babs as her best friend.

The falling out between Lili and her half-sister was precipitated by Barbara's spring 1947 marriage to Louis Marx. Born in 1896 to German immigrants, Marx was a self-made "toy king." Marx's company made some of the era's most popular toys. That, combined with his short, rotund appearance, led journalists to compare him to a "defrocked Santa Claus."7 One reporter described Marx as a "roly-poly, melon-bald little man with the berry-bright eyes and beneficent smile of St. Nick touching down on a familiar rooftop" and his new bride as one "who looks the way sleigh bells sound."8

Marx's first wife, Renee, died of breast cancer, leaving her husband with their four children. Once married, Marx and Barbara quickly had four boys of their own. The entire gaggle rambled through a large house in the New York suburbs. In a photograph from the period, Barbara, who'd shed her showgirl name and was once again going by Idella Ruth, is shown with her husband wearing a full, crinoline-lined skirt with a cinched waist and "I like Ike" embroidered across the front; it is the picture of fifties togetherness.9

That togetherness did not extend to Marx's in-laws. "It was a different life," said Patricia Ellsberg, one of Marx's daughters from his first marriage.10 "That part of her family wasn't connected to us at all." And Louis Marx definitely did not want his wife connected to her striptease dancing sister. "[My father] was attracted to Hollywood, but also thought it was disreputable," said Curtis Marx, one of Idella Ruth and Louis' sons.11 "He had a lot of Hollywood friends, but when it came to his marriage he wanted some separation."

Marx wanted more than just some separation; he insisted that Idella completely sever her relationship with Lili. "After he married [Idella], he called Lili, and offered her one hundred thousand dollars in cash and financing for a lingerie boutique if she would stop working," recalled a friend of Lili's.[12] "Lili said, 'Go to hell. I don't need you.' She was very independent. And so this man forbade his wife from talking to Lili. Lili was very upset about it."

The Marx family's togetherness did not last, as Idella and Louis divorced in the late sixties. Lili and her half-sister had had virtually no contact during all of those years. The schism in their relationship was deep and permanent. Idella, like her aunt Rosemary Blackadder and her father, suffered from depression. After Idella committed suicide in 1986, the family scattered her ashes into the ocean from aboard a boat. Lili did not attend the ceremony.[13]

In many respects, Lili's youngest sister Dardy accepted the 1950s family values as well, but she put her own spin on them. Dardy had followed her older sisters into show business, working for Earl Carroll throughout the early forties. While there, she met and married Jimmy Greenleaf, a saloon manager, and had a son. After the couple divorced in the summer of 1948, Dardy left her son with Alice and followed Lili into the bump 'n' grind world.[14]

Casting off her California life, Dardy went to Montreal, where she joined Lili, who was in the midst of her affair with Jimmy Orlando. Lili helped her sister follow her hip-swiveling steps. Soon a much blonder Dardy, who at her sister's prompting had taken the name Dardy Orlando, was dancing throughout Montreal and the United States and advertising herself as Lili St. Cyr's sister. But despite their similar appearances and Lili's assistance, Dardy never commanded the same attention. "She was an imitation of Lili," said jazz pianist Vic Vogel, who played for Dardy.[15] "She was younger and she didn't have the charisma that her sister had. She kind of leaned on Lili."

It might also have been Lili who introduced Dardy to Harold Minsky, a burlesque producer whose revues often starred Lili. Harold, as one reporter noted, looked "like a man who could be in the furniture business . . . aside from his diamond pinky ring."[16] Short, compact, round,

and balding, Harold Minksy, the adopted son of one of the famous burlesque Minsky brothers, was carrying on the family burlesque tradition and
staging shows at various clubs. The four Minsky brothers had drifted apart.
Besides business disagreements, there were family squabbles as well.
When family leader Billy Minsky died in the thirties, Abe split from his
other brothers and opened up two competing theaters in New York. The
family quarrels continued with Morton Minsky describing Abe's productions as "a much rawer show."[17] Eventually, Abe teamed up with his son
Harold to stage productions around the country. After Abe's death in 1949,
Harold carried on producing shows in Miami, Chicago, and Newark,
New Jersey, before settling in Las Vegas in the late fifties. Joan Carter, who
performed in a Minsky revue, thought "he was a typically Jewish businessman. He was quiet, but very intelligent. He had very good manners
and he handled himself very, very well. He never used vulgarity. He was
not crude or gruff in any way."[18]

By the end of the forties, Lili enjoyed several regular engagements.
One Miami reporter described her "as a Minsky girl in the winter and a
Montreal maid in the summer."[19] She and Harold held each other in the
highest regard and seemed legitimately fond of one another. "Lili is strictly
an exotic, in the most precise sense of the word," Harold said of her in the
mid-sixties when striptease had changed drastically.[20] "She's not a stripper
as we accept the term, but she immediately excites the audience. Class sur-
rounds everything she does on stage, from the stately way she lifts a mirror,
to the lithe way her hands move over her body. Women appreciate Lili as
well as men—although, of course, not for the same reason. They comment
on her gowns and furs, on her instinctive dignity. And they're right. Lili has
lady-like appeal." And Lili thought that Harold was "the Florenz Ziegfeld of
burlesque" and that he had "an uncanny sense of visual values."[21]

In early 1950, Harold Minsky married Dardy Orlando. Marriage didn't
mean Dardy shucked her career of shucking her clothes. Rather, she
became an almost equal business partner, helping Harold stage his
Ziegfeld-esque burlesques. The Minskys were creative in their efforts to portray burlesque as an acceptable form of entertainment. And one strategy in
their endeavor to make burlesque acceptable and avoid protests was playing
up their ideal fifties family status. One dancer described Harold and Dardy
as "the happiest couple I ever met . . . and they have two of the cutest
kids."[22] Dardy may not have been the typical fifties wife, but she knew

how to play the role. In November 1955, the Minsky family appeared on Edward R. Murrow's television show *Person to Person*. Wearing the fifties uniform—a dress with a cinched waist, full skirt, and heels—Dardy proudly showed off her home and children and let Harold do much of the talking.

Throughout the fifties it seemed that Dardy managed to strike that elusive balance between family and career. Lili, on the other hand, shed men in much the same way she did clothing. It's unclear whether Lili was jealous of her sister's life and work equilibrium or whether Dardy was jealous of Lili's star status, but there was a definite sibling rivalry. A few months after Dardy and Harold married, a columnist reported that "Lili St. Cyr, the stripper, is feuding with her sister, Dardy Orlando, whom she accuses of stealing some of her best routines."[23] The two would have a rollercoaster relationship for the rest of their lives. "I think there was a little competition between them," said Joan Carter.[24] "Lili became a bigger star than Dardy, but Dardy ended up marrying very well." Dancer Betty "Ball of Fire" Rowland also heard "they were not exactly friendly. Both of them were rather quiet people, soft-spoken, so there wasn't yelling and screaming or anything like that, but they had their differences."[25]

Reflecting on her family in the eighties, Lili said that early on her mother had hoped Lili would set an example for her sisters. But the example Lili set wasn't what her mother had in mind, and her mother was afraid Lili would "pull them off the right course."[26] But while the fifties dressed up the family and domestic life in an elegant set of pearls, the right course was difficult to navigate. What bubbled under the surface rarely matched the outward veneer. Bob Hope joked that there was so much togetherness "the old folks have to go out to have sex." Betty Friedan discovered housewives downed tranquilizers at an alarming rate; by the end of the decade consumption reached 1.1 million pounds a year.[27] Even the fifties' ideal family, Ozzie and Harriet Nelson, gilded their TV image. "The low-key Ozzie Nelson of the sitcoms had little in common with the real-life Ozzie, who was a workaholic," wrote David Halberstam, author of *The Fifties*.[28] "He was not merely a man who put great pressure on his children, but in contrast to the readily available Ozzie of the show, who always seemed to be around, he was gone much of the time—albeit at home, but gone. . . . The Nelsons were, therefore, for all their professional success, very different from the family depicted on the show, they lived with an immense amount of pressure and unreconciled issues."

For the Minsky family, what bubbled under the surface was Harold's drinking problem—Dardy tolerated it for many years, perhaps sharing the attitude suggested in a *Redbook* magazine article: "Few women would want to thumb their noses at husbands, children, and community and go off on their own. Those who do may be talented individuals, but they rarely are successful women."[29] Lili, of course, was the exception. She thumbed her nose at the fifties ideal, preferring to live by her own erotic code. But she did not snub love. When she met Armando Orsini in the summer of 1950, he "chased all others from my thoughts"[30] including her recently divorced husband Paul Valentine and lover Jimmy Orlando. Armando, an incredibly handsome dark-haired, swarthy Italian, was, by chance, born in New York. His father, the captain of an Italian ship, was in port with Armando's mother when the child arrived several weeks early. It was a fortuitous accident because though the family returned to Italy, Armando could claim American citizenship and was able to come to the United States after World War II. Trained as a civil engineer, Armando found work with a construction company in Queens. While he spoke little English at the time, when Armando and Lili met at a party they began a romance. "She was a beautiful woman," said Orsini.[31] "We fell passionately in love."

Despite the language barrier, Lili found Armando charming, genteel, and caring. "With Armando, I felt safe, a sentiment that I hadn't felt in years," she wrote.[32] "He was the only man in my life who chased from my memory the dreams of my lost loves. He was the only one to present himself as he is, nothing more or less."

After a two-month romance, Lili and Armando left New York and drove across the country. En route, they stopped in Flagstaff, Arizona, to get married. It was a civil ceremony with just Lili and Armando. "The judge started to talk, but I didn't know what he was saying because I spoke little English," said Armando.[33] "I just had to mumble. The judge said, 'I understand that marriage is not as serious a thing as it used to be, but you are making a joke about this thing.' Lili explained that I didn't do it on purpose." The judge proceeded, Armando and Lili picked up their marriage certificate, and they drove on to the West Coast.

It wasn't just ideas about family that were changing, but the entire zeitgeist. Even in Montreal, a city that reveled in revelry, a more conservative atmosphere took hold. In 1949, the politicians' many bogus attempts at reform backfired when they hired Pacifique Plante, a dark, lean lawyer, as the head of the city's Morality Squad. As one reporter later put it, Plante "scared the underworld kingpins out of their red flannel underwear by taking the whole thing seriously . . . [and] proved to be thoroughly uncorruptible."[34] Plante was so effective that he was fired. But then he began reporting on the vice and corruption he had witnessed in a series of articles for Le Devoir, a conservative Montreal newspaper. Plante made 15,000 specific allegations and contended what was lacking "wasn't knowledge of the law, but respect for it."[35] The articles, later gathered into a bestselling book, outlined just how the gambling and prostitution houses worked around the law. Plante also detailed public officials' involvement in protecting and profiting from the vice industry. The public outcry resulted in an official investigation that lasted over four years, dragged in over three hundred witnesses, and collected more than one thousand exhibits.

In October 1954, the scandal climaxed with the presiding judge taking over four hours to read a 100,000-word report to a courtroom packed with reporters, politicians, and lawyers. The judge found twenty high-ranking police officers, including the director, guilty of various charges. He fired the director and barred both him and the former head of police from public office. Eighteen other officers were fined as much as seven thousand dollars each and discharged. Plante was vindicated and less than three weeks later was elected mayor with a clear mandate to clean up Montreal.[36]

During the years it took for these legal proceedings to conclude, the reform-minded and the pleasure-minded Canadians fought other battles. Emboldened by the public tumult, various religious groups began a campaign against Lili. In early June 1951, when she was out of town between performances, Jesuit priest Marie-Joseph D'Anjou kick-started a crusade to run the dancer out of town in an article in the newspaper Le Devoir. "Who's ignoring the repugnant obscenity of the shows presented in Montreal by Lili St. Cyr," he wrote.[37] "All affirm that a stench of sexual frenzy plagues the theater the whole time this dancer's exhibition lasts." Citing scripture and several articles describing her performance, D'Anjou ended by demanding that the authorities prohibit her "from appearing in Montreal on any stage whatever, from now until forever." Particularly upset by her religiously inspired routines like "Eve," in which she danced around a large apple, D'Anjou wrote, "The Feast of St. John the Baptist approaches. Will we tolerate the fact that our national feast risks being soiled by the presence . . . of a woman who's already . . . ignobly profaned, on stage at the Gayety, the image of the sacred master, our God and Master Jesus Christ?" He then called upon others "to make [their] protests heard and heeded [because] Montrealers aren't dogs."

The article ignited a firestorm of protests. Youth groups, the Federation of the Sacred Heart League of Montreal, and church parishes bombarded City Hall with letters and telegrams. In a typical letter, the Committee on Public Morality wrote that it had "decided to appeal to the municipal authorities and police department to obtain an order banning all shows in the City of Montreal, given by Lili St. Cyr . . . We insist that public morals be respected. And we believe that the shows given by this dancer . . . are immoral."38 The letter included a copy of D'Anjou's article.

When Lili arrived in town to perform at the Gayety a few days later, several police officers were in the audience. After watching her dance around a large apple in her interpretation of the story of Adam and Eve, the police told reporters their presence was "simply a routine observation job" and that "everything seemed to be in order."39

The protests grew loud enough that the brouhaha even made news in the United States. *Variety* reported that "stripper Lili St. Cyr is the center of a storm of protests which may bring about a city by-law revision intended to bar her from appearing here."40 Finally bowing to pressure, the city's officials instructed its legal department to clarify laws that dealt with performances considered likely to offend public morals. And on June 19, 1951, Lili and Gayety manager Tommy Conway received a summons which ordered them to appear in court to "answer charges under a section of the Criminal Code dealing with 'offensive, immoral, or indecent exhibitions.'"41 The summons did not prevent her from performing although dancing in front of so many policemen each day led her to quip, "I'm afraid to move my fingers and take off my gloves."42

The trial, on June 27, 1951, lasted just two hours. Wearing a boxy suit, blouse buttoned to the neck, and white hat, Lili sat in court, but understood none of the testimony presented against her as she did not know French. The head of the juvenile delinquency prevention squad offered a lengthy statement in which he said her performance would have a depraving effect on youths. But when asked if he was scandalized by the performance, he said no. Another witness said he, "condemned such spectacles, although she did it in as decent a manner as she could have."[43] While the secretary of the Committee on Public Morality said "there was a quality of evil" in her performances, a police officer who watched both the afternoon and evening shows said he saw nothing "immoral or depraved" in Lili's routine.[44] Three women selected at random from that night's audience agreed. In the end of the two-and-a-half hour proceedings Judge Edouard Archambault ruled that the evidence against Lili was insufficient and acquitted her. He declared, "It seems to me that those who made the most noise here today were persons who didn't even see the performance complained of."[45]

No one seemed more pleased than Montreal's business owners, who fully recognized Lili's bottom line appeal. The *Commerce Montreal*, a newsletter for the city's businesses, cheered her acquittal in an article titled "Bravo Lili! Bravo Lili! Bravo Lili!" The article claimed that "one must never have seen the chaste and statuesque Lili to be able to decry her thus. She is the ideal woman incarnate . . . she has us experience the entire spectrum of emotion, by a gradation of personal pleasures, by all degrees of hope, desire, and enjoyment. . . . With a sparkling light she executes the most fantastic dances of eternal theme. . . . She gives a wake-up to adolescence, a stimulant to the young man, comfort to the middle-aged man, sweet memory to the old man. . . . Lili is the goddess of love reincarnate . . . She is at the same time immortal desire, and immortal enjoyment. Bravo to all those who refuse to let themselves be moved by these false cries of conscience. . . . We'd be a city dead to love and to pleasure."[46] The article warned that if the reformers triumphed the city would not only lose its reputation as the capital of nightlife, but millions of tourist dollars as well.

Just weeks later, several audience members trying to cool off from the summer heat were standing on the fire escape of the Gayety during Lili's performance when the fire escape collapsed. One man died and three others were injured. She was in no way responsible for the accident on the fire escape, but coming so soon after her trial, it was an unpleasant end to her seven-year reign over Montreal. The summer of 1951 would be the last time she would perform in the city for nearly fifteen years. Instead she would reign over another pleasure-seeking center—Las Vegas.

Montreal wasn't the only place that experienced a shift in attitude during the early fifties. In the spring of 1951, Tennessee Senator Estes Kefauver, as chairman of the Special Committee on Organized Crime in Interstate

Commerce, led the government's charge against illegal gaming. Known as the Kefauver Committee, the group began a cross-country tour investigating political corruption and the mafia. The hearings were held in Miami, Tampa, Kansas City, Chicago, Los Angeles, New York, New Orleans, Las Vegas, Philadelphia, and Washington, D.C., among other places. In an effort to describe the committee's aims, Senator Kefauver recalled to Kitty Kelley that "the Mafia is a shadowy international organization that lurks behind much of America's organized criminal activity. It is an organization about which none of its members, on fear of death, will talk. In fact, some of the witnesses called before us, who we had good reason to believe could tell us about the Mafia, sought to dismiss it as a sort of fairy tale or legend . . . The Mafia, however, is no fairy tale. It is ominously real, and it has scarred the face of America with almost every conceivable type of criminal violence, including murder, traffic in narcotics, smuggling, extortion, white slavery, kidnapping and labor racketeering."

The investigation also exposed the connection between strip clubs and the mafia and examined the connection between pornography and juvenile delinquency. During World War II, many looked at pinups as a morale booster for the soldiers. As the dancer Margie Hart, who tried to donate 4,000 of her pinups, told *Life* magazine, "I'm helping the Allies win the war, every time I unhook my brassiere."[47] That attitude helped striptease and pornography become more visible after the war. But this sexual frankness clashed with the amplified attention on family. So in the same decade that Hugh Hefner launched *Playboy*, Senator Kefauver and the purity crusaders launched campaigns against what they considered obscene and pornographic material.

In New York, the inquiry focused on Irving Klaw, a short, balding man who is most famous for his bondage photos of pinup Bettie Page. Klaw and his sister Paula operated Movie Star News, a storefront and catalog company that sold photos of movie stars and pinups of burlesque dancers. They also made burlesque films, starring Lili St. Cyr, Tempest Storm, and other dancers. The pictures, similar in style to the ones soldiers tacked up in their barracks during the war, drew the attention of the Kefauver Committee. They called Klaw to testify, but he pleaded the Fifth. Bettie Page refused to testify at all, telling the committee privately "that Irving Klaw never did any pornography at all, not even nudes, and that I would say that if they put me on the stand."[48]

The Kefauver Committee had it all: a shadowy criminal organization, sex, drugs, and even rock and roll. The investigation was a hit: broadcast on national television, an estimated twenty to thirty million viewers watched some or all of the proceedings. In the end, the investigation resulted in the formation of more than seventy local crime commissions and the Senate Permanent Subcommittee on Investigations.[49]

The Kefauver Committee represented just one player in the country's moral clampdown. The United States was in the midst of the Cold War. The confrontation, which developed after World War II, spawned a series of crises and fostered a general sense of fear and mistrust. In the United States, the fear was fueled by rhetoric like Senator Joseph McCarthy's unsubstantiated claims about the number of communists in the country and evidenced by the boom in the sales of backyard bomb shelters. To cope with the insecurities of the world, the country focused inward on the family and religion while outwardly focusing on the buy, buy, buy of a whole new consumerism. Anyone who deviated from the accepted cultural, political, and sexual mores was considered dangerous, deviant, and subversive. In his memoir of life in a Levittown-like, mass-produced, planned community, D. J. Waldie described the result. "You and I were trained for a conflict that never came," wrote Waldie.[50] "At my grade school, the Sisters of St. Joseph made me hate Communists, then intolerance, and finally everything that could break the charmed pattern of our lives." Far removed from the charmed pattern of suburban fifties life, Lili, who columnist Walter Winchell said "outstrips" Gypsy Rose Lee, her predecessor as the nation's top stripper, became a prime target.[51]

In September 1951, Lili headlined at the El Rancho in Las Vegas for the first time. In 1941, the El Rancho had been the first of several hotels to open along what is now known as the Strip. By 1946, Associated Press reporter Bob Thomas declared, "the town has been converted to an opulent playground." Yet when Lili arrived in the early fifties, some were still trying to fight Vegas' eventual designation as Sin City.

Roger Foley, the Clark county district attorney who was described by one reporter as "a veteran of the 'battle of the red light' district . . . and a scourge of would-be Las Vegas bordello operators," interrupted Lili's performance and had her booked on charges of lewd and indecent exposure.[52] After being freed on $1,000 bail, she returned to Los Angeles before the matter could be resolved, skipping her hearing entirely.

Of the increasing legal scrutiny and moral protests to her act, Lili simply told one reporter that "everyone has a right to his opinion, but a lot of people are prejudiced who would not be if they could see my act. I don't like vulgarity—I think it is ugly—and on the burlesque circuit they think I'm high-hat."53

Objections to burlesque and striptease had long been tied to class anxiety. Florenz Ziegfeld and Earl Carroll showed off near-naked women to rave reviews. Yet when Billy Minsky moved burlesque uptown, a brouhaha erupted that eventually led to the demise of burlesque in New York. Similarly, when Lili performed in burlesque theaters, she only occasionally attracted unwanted attention from the law. As she became more of a fixture in the upscale nightclubs, trouble was guaranteed.

5.

Sin Cyr-ities

*The great artists of the world are never Puritans,
and seldom even ordinarily respectable.*

—H. L. MENCKEN

On October 18, 1951, Lili stood on the stage of Ciro's nightclub on the Sunset Strip dressed in a glimmering, softly draped cream evening gown. She gazed at her appearance in what was made to look like a bedroom mirror and shook her blonde curls in disapproval. Slowly she pulled each finger out of elbow-length gloves and deliberately peeled off each glove. She slipped the side zipper down to her narrow waist, let it skim across the contours of her hips, and gingerly stepped out of the dress, revealing a silky, creamy-skinned back and the long legs of a dancer.

Caressing her legs, Lili deliberately slid on one thigh-high, black silk stocking, then the other. With the help of a maid, she carefully stepped into a lacy, black, strapless dress. Gracefully, she glided toward the mirror, studied her reflection, and again shook her head in disapproval. Slipping out of the second gown, she wrapped a filmy, almost transparent robe around her body and cinched it tightly around her waist.

Relaxing on a chaise on the side of the stage, she stared at the photo of a dark-haired boyfriend while her maid reached up Lili's long legs so as to slide off each of her stockings and then her panties. While Lili lounged on the elongated seat, languorously tracing imaginary lines over her neck, breasts, hips, and legs, the maid began a bubble bath.

As bubbles floated above the tub, Lili leisurely rose from the chaise, untied the soft, thin robe, let it fall off her shoulders, drift down her back, and hug her body as it slipped to the ground. Still dripping with rhinestones, she sank into the tub, showing just hints of her curves through the soapy water. Reaching for a washcloth, Lili lathered and massaged each arm, then dropped back further into the tub, jackknifing a leg up through the bubbles, and pulling her knees to her chin. She gave the audience a sly coquettish smile, then lowered her eyes.

Water droplets and bubbles clung to Lili's body as she rose tantalizingly from the tub to step behind the monogrammed towel held by her maid. Drying off, she allowed glimpses of her smooth skin, then slipped into a slinky, white beaded dress. She twirled and turned in front of the mirror and then, pleased with her reflection, sashayed off stage. The nightclub crowd erupted in cheers, claps, and whistles as the curtain closed on the dance Lili called "Interlude Before Evening."

Lili had been doing variations of this routine for years before nightclub owner Herman Hover caught her show during a trip to New York. Hover, a portly man who had worked for impresario Earl Carroll, began running Ciro's, the club *Variety* hailed as "the swankiest club in glitterland," in the early forties. In his unpublished memoir, he immodestly described it as a "posh palace where money was spent with abandon; where the tables that customers occupied opening night was said to determine their social status for the entire year; . . . where a poorly aimed, alcoholic-inspired punch assumed the headline stature of a heavyweight championship . . . ; [and] where autograph addicts formed a phalanx around the entrance."[1]

Hover understood what made a nightclub sexy: "longing, envy, lust, and glamour were the staples of a club you never wanted to leave."[2] In search of a new act, he decided to add a striptease routine. "The girl I was looking for need not have been . . . pure . . . but I definitely did not want anyone looking like a doorway hooker," he explained in his memoir.[3] In one of New York's Fifty-second Street clubs Hover found what he was looking for in Lili St. Cyr. "Her main claim to fame was the voluptuous beauty of her figure," he wrote.[4] "She was, to put it politely, the personification of sex." Hover was particularly struck by her "cold dignity," which reminded him of Grace Kelly. She seemed to "dare anyone to lay a hand on her." And so Hover hired Lili to inspire longing, envy, lust, and glamour at Ciro's.

Returning to Los Angeles, Herman hired Lili's long-time friend and interior designer Tom Douglas to build her a seven-thousand-dollar set, which included a solid silver bathtub that had reportedly been used by the Empress Josephine of France. Lili first slipped into the tub at Ciro's in the spring of 1951. "I'm always nervous [on] opening nights," she told one reporter later.[5] "But I was a little more jittery at Ciro's because so much more was expected of me."

Lili's onstage splash more than met expectations. The hugely successful opening night drew celebrities like singer Dean Martin and future president Ronald Reagan. "Everyone was plenty excited by the show," Hover recalled.[6] "Chalk it up to the exquisite taste of the production, the costuming, and the extra stage I had built for Lili. The whole idea was daring, and most important, it had caught on." In fact, Lili St. Cyr was the club's second biggest draw to date after Dean Martin and Jerry Lewis.[7]

Reggie Drew, a cigarette girl at Ciro's at the time, recalled Lili's act fondly. "It was unusual at that time to take a bubble bath on stage," she said.[8] "I remember her getting out of the tub with this big towel and doing her dance to this terrific music. She was elegant and classy and she had a beautiful body."

One magazine declared that, "Lili turned the chi-chi set of movietown on its ear when full-to-capacity crowds jammed the swank Ciro's in order to get to see what the whole town was talking about."[9] The crowds included Mayor Fletcher Bowron, Sheriff Eugene Biscailuz, and "more than 100 city fathers."[10]

Actor Humphrey Bogart was one of Lili's many fans, explained Armando Orsini, who was her husband at the time. "One night at Ciro's, Humphrey Bogart came to see Lili, and when everybody left, he stayed. The headwaiter said 'We're closing,' but Bogart kept saying 'I want to see Lili, I want to see Lili.' And so, the headwaiter came to me. I went to the lobby and said, 'Mr. Bogart, she's not going out. Please leave, she's not going out.' And he kind of pushed me. So the PR guy at Ciro's said to me, 'Armando, punch him. Punch him and we'll photograph you and it'll be in the papers tomorrow.' I didn't punch him, but it was funny. He was drunk. He was very drunk."[11]

With that first engagement, Lili had apparently slithered easily from grind house to ritzy supper club. She was such a success that gossip columns batted around rumors about a TV show. She even began to sell her own line of bubble bath in the lobby of Ciro's.

Although Lili left Los Angeles for engagements in Montreal and Las Vegas, it was with the promise of future gigs at Ciro's. When she returned in October 1951, she found herself in a heapful of trouble. While movie stars and gossip columnists relaxed at small tables and lounged in deep red banquettes, police officers Captain Walker Hannon and Captain Pete Sutton quietly arrested Herman Hover. And as women in strapless gowns and mink stoles and men in black tie returned to their cocktails and gossip, Sergeant Ann Hunter seized Lili's G-string and net bra and arrested her on a charge of having given an indecent performance and "lewdly exposed her person."[12] Perhaps her legal wrangles in other cities bolstered her L.A. critics. Perhaps she outraged some by swirling into such an exclusive club. As one newspaper reported, "That's what got Lili in trouble. She went highbrow . . . and began stripping at a plus nightclub, the patrons of which wouldn't be caught dead in Lili's old Main street haunt."[13] Perhaps the authorities did receive complaints from anonymous sources and church groups. Perhaps recognizing the era's growing conservatism they saw a way to further their own careers.

Jim Byron, the club's publicist, insisted the arrest was a media stunt. "Everybody on the Strip knew everybody in the sheriff's department," he told Hover's niece Sheila Weller in her memoir *Dancing at Ciro's*.[14] "They knew what was going on. They weren't seriously interested in giving Herman a hard time." If the arrest was a publicity gimmick, it was a roaring success. The story and Lili's suggestive photo covered the next day's *Examiner* and *Herald Express*. Unfortunately, the district attorney was not inclined to dismiss the case, so the bubble bath landed both Lili and Hover in court, but this only lathered up the press further. When the court proceedings began, papers around the country debated whether Judge Henry Draeger should allow Lili to demonstrate her act in the courtroom and deliberated on her court attire. To extricate her from this hot water, she hired famed attorney Jerry Giesler.

Before high-profile celebrity attorneys like Johnnie Cochrane, Robert Shapiro, or Mark Geragos, there was Jerry Giesler. During his career, the Hollywood criminal attorney represented Charlie Chaplin, Errol Flynn,

Lana Turner, and Marilyn Monroe. Because of his reputation for representing celebrities in trouble, "Get me Giesler!" became a laugh line in Hollywood hangouts. But his performance in the courtroom was far from a joke and today the Criminal Courts Bar Association honors outstanding criminal lawyers with the Jerry Giesler Memorial Award.

Despite his association with movie stars, the stout attorney with the reedy voice knew he wasn't Hollywood glamour. "No motion picture producer or director would think of casting me as a criminal lawyer in a film," Giesler wrote in his autobiography.[15] He was, however, a strong advocate for some of the biggest stars in the business, and many of his cases revolved around sex. As Giesler explained it, "It's because sex is not only one of the facts of life, it's also—at least in my experience—one of the most prevalent bases of legal strife."[16]

Now Jerry Giesler was to represent the sensuous Lili St. Cyr. "When I heard that Lili St. Cyr had been arrested in Ciro's . . . while she was doing a strip bathtub act, I wondered why," wrote Giesler.[17] "She had done much the same kind of act for years, and I couldn't imagine why anyone had suddenly decided to take her to task."

On Monday, October 22, 1951, Lili St. Cyr faced charges of putting on an indecent performance. Before going into Beverly Hills Justice Court to answer the citation, Lili, clad in a gray suit and stone marten fur piece, declared "I didn't do anything naughty up there . . . I'm going to plead innocent—I am innocent. My net bra and my panties covered up all the vital spots."[18]

Surrounded by fans and reporters, Lili breezed into court on the arm of attorney Jerry Giesler, who won a three-day continuance in order to study the complaint. Then, with his usual flair, Giesler stated that the stripteaser would be willing to perform her act for the jury.

As Lili and Hover, who was charged with procuring and assisting the alleged lewd performance, plotted their defense, the arresting officers recommended to Sheriff Eugene Biscailuz that Ciro's entertainment license be revoked because Hover had broken his promise not to rebook the dancer at his nightclub. During a press conference after the arraignment, Biscailuz decreed: "Let Miss St. Cyr dance if she wants to. If her act is indecent, arrest her again. If it isn't, she can dance until kingdom come and it's all right with us."[19] That broke up the conference and ended Lili's three-week engagement of public bathing at Ciro's. Three days later, she and Hover pleaded innocent and Judge Henry Draeger set the jury trial for December 4, 1951.

On the first day of the trial, necks craned as Lili walked into the Beverly Hills courtroom between her husband, Armando Orsini, and her chief counsel. On the first anniversary of Lili's fourth wedding, Giesler again proposed to bring a tub and bubble bath into court so she might reveal her onstage artistry. "I'm ready to demonstrate the decency of my act any place, any time," Lili, wearing a demure midnight blue suit, green gloves, and a full length mink coat, told the panel of thirty prospective jurors—many of whom were women.[20]

Giesler's next stunt came during jury selection, when he demanded a jury of her peers. "Your honor, my client is accused of indecent exposure. It is our contention that, far from being indecent, the performance for which she was arrested is artistic. We therefore demand a jury made up of people capable of judging such things on their artistic merit."[21]

Giesler didn't get such a jury—he got a jury of ten women and two men, none of whom worked as painters, writers, or dancers—but he made his point. "Everybody began to look at Miss St. Cyr and wonder if he could possibly have made a mistake in thinking of her merely as a stripper who made her living peeling, when all the time what she was doing might have some vague artistic meaning," wrote Giesler.[22]

The first witness to take the stand was police Captain C. H. Conner, who described Lili's act and testified that all of the dancer's body, except for the briefest net bra and G-string, was uncovered during the undressed moments of her performance. But under Giesler's cross-examination Conner also admitted he had applauded at the end of the act.

When Sergeant Ann Hunter took the stand, Giesler held up Lili's panties and bra to show she was lawfully clad during her act. Then he asked Hunter if she had seen Lili drying herself as the performance ended. "Yes, she made a sort of hip motion like a bump," the sergeant testified. "Well, what was it, a full bump, a half, quarter, one-eighth, one-sixteenth or one-thirty-second bump?" Giesler asked.[23] "Almost a full bump," she replied. "Please tell me, Mrs. Hunter, was it a baby bump, or a bumpity-bump-bump," Giesler followed. Asked for a definition, she explained she had once before seen a dancer perform such convolutions in Ensenada, a town in Mexico where more scandalous behavior was tolerated.

Captain Walker Hannon was less bashful when he defined the bumps as "Mae West wiggles." When he testified Lili wore "black lace panties over People's Exhibit A (a G-string)," six elderly women walked out of the courtroom. Lili, demurely garbed in a black suit, pillbox hat, and veil, sat and watched the ensuing circus.[24]

Lili's jury trial bumped along with Herman Hover's testimony. Under questioning by Giesler, Hover stated it was impossible for the audience, and therefore the sheriff's vice raiders, to see through the scanty costume that she wore in the barer moments of her scene. Lights reflecting off the rhinestones on the costume, he said, rendered this out of the question.

Hover bristled at the notion that anything so vulgar as a "bump" had marred the "interpretive dancing" of the act. Giesler reminded him that the deputies had sworn during the past two days that they saw her do bumps and grinds. "What is a bump?" he asked. Hover, his brows furrowed, replied: "A bump is a sort of pelvic propulsion, and, ah that's it! Now a grind is a circular movement of the hips where the feet don't move and the body shouldn't." Asked to demonstrate a bump, Hover looked shyly at the ten women among the jury and pleaded: "Shall I do it in front of these ladies?" Told he must, the short, plump manager rose from the witness chair, placed his hands above his head, reared back and thrust forward in a bump. The courtroom laughed. Then Hover was asked the big question: "Did you observe any bumps or grinds in Miss St. Cyr's act?" "There were none, sir," said Hover.[25]

Persistent cross-examination by Deputy Attorney Bernard Gross brought Hover to his feet, declaring, "You're deliberately trying to confuse me." Hover insisted Lili's movements about the stage between dressing and disrobing were ballet steps to the rhythms of classical music. Even the dancer's actions when going through the routine of drying herself in a bath scene, he said, were extraordinary, but not as extraordinarily nude as the sheriff's vice detail insisted. In fact, he added, he had attempted to have the act previewed by the sheriff's deputies but that never happened. "I always lean over backward," Hover said.[26] In answer to the query as to why he asked the sheriff's men to view the show, he responded it was "to do right in the operation of my place."

Red-haired columnist Florabel Muir followed Hover to the stand and corroborated his testimony that at no time had she seen the dancer "improperly nude" on the night in question.[27]

But Lili's testimony really grabbed the court's attention and became the highlight of the battle over the distinction between an artistic and an indecent performance. As she took the stand, all eyes focused on the shapely blonde who, as one reporter said, "[had] more curves than a pretzel."[28]

Under questioning from Giesler, Lili, dressed in a gray wool suit that partially concealed a strapless white blouse, testified that the art of stripteasing was an expensive business. She had $11,750 invested in props, she said, including $6,000 for the lavish set of mirrors and walls, $4,200 in costumes, $1,000 in the script, and $550 worth of music. In addition, she paid her maid $60 a week, her agent $125 a week, and she wore out $50 worth of hosiery and brassieres and garter belts weekly. Her salary, she noted, was $1,250 a week and "I'm lucky, after taxes, to keep $1,000 of it."[29]

Lili carefully described each scene of her act, pointing out she was covered at all times, either by some flimsy under-things, a semitransparent black negligee, or her designer gowns. Afterward Giesler introduced into evidence the bath towel she used in her performance, measuring it to show it was sixty-two inches wide. He asked Lili to show him how she stepped out of the bubble bath and wrapped the towel around her, and as she pretended to step from the tub, Giesler, playing the part of her maid, handed her the towel and she wrapped it around her shoulders. The dancer then demonstrated how she dried her legs with the towel and climbed into a dress. Her modesty, she insisted, was always protected by her maid, who stood between her and the audience during the undressing and dressing. "Did you have any intent to expose your person lewdly at Ciro's in your performance?" Giesler asked. "No," she replied quietly.

"At no time in my performance did I ever take off People's Exhibit A and B," Lili testified, referring to the flesh-colored brassiere and G-string that had been introduced into evidence. The garments she discarded, Lili added, consisted only of her mink coat, dress, slip, stockings, black lace bra and garter belt, hat, gloves, shoes, and pearl earrings. "But the flesh-colored bra and panties always stayed on, and anyway, when I got down to that much, either the maid, or a negligee, or a bath towel was between the audience and me." she said. The negligee, she admitted, may have been transparent.[30]

Lili explained she knew before she went on stage that the law was present. "Yes, I was told by a waiter," she said. In later cross-examination by Gross she noted, "I did not change the performance because they were there." In further cross-examination she admitted she had been introduced onstage as "the best dressed, undressed lady in the theater." But, when the prosecution made a big point of asking her where People's Exhibits A and B were during the various phases of the act, she indicated they were just where they should be, on her body. The dancer denied the maid was a device to "shield" her, but in the bath scene, at least, she "was there to support me while getting into the bathtub."[31]

When Lili stepped down from the witness stand, Gross attempted to introduce the testimony of the Reverend Bertil Van Norman, who witnessed her performance at Ciro's, in rebuttal. Giesler objected on the grounds that the witness could not testify to any new evidence and therefore could say nothing material. The judge agreed. Still, outside the courtroom, Van Norman explained he had gone with another minister to see the act because of anonymous telephone complaints he had received.[32]

The curtain closed on Lili's testimony and opened again for closing arguments. Gross, in his argument to the jury, charged the defense with having "tried to make a Roman holiday, a burlesque, out of this action."[33]

Gross continued, "Actually, this issue is very simple. It's a question of whether this defendant willfully and lewdly exposed her person in a public place. And the real problem is who are you going to believe, the deputies or the defendant? The deputies have nothing to gain. They get no bonuses for arrests."

Gross also attacked defense testimony concerning the expense of the production staged at Ciro's. "A rose by any other name would smell as sweet," he told the jury, "so all this conversation about the expense of the act doesn't affect what was done that night."[34]

Giesler took sharp exception to Gross' statements that the defense had attempted to make a burlesque act of the trial. "I have tried this case with every ounce of respect for his honor, the jury, and the integrity of the court," he declared.[35] "There is no intended buffoonery here."

After this attack on the prosecution's arguments, Giesler told the jury the burden of establishing what occurred, as well as proving whether the defendant intended to commit a lewd performance, rested on the prosecution. He said the evidence produced by the prosecution proved neither point. "Let me start with the . . . deputies who have testified on behalf of the People. Captain Sutton said that he saw neither bumps nor grinds. Officer Conner continued to eat throughout Miss St. Cyr's performance, but, as he testified, he applauded when she finished. Deputy Ann Hunter was different from them all—she said she saw this defendant with a towel two by three feet." Dramatically, he waved the towel before the jury. "The towel is larger than two by three feet. You can wrap yourself in it. I'm not two by three! I wish I were!"[36]

Giesler further emphasized the testimony given by Captain Sutton, particularly his statement that there were no fixed rules of what was considered proper as far as striptease is concerned. "Just think," Giesler cried, "one individual can tell an entire community what is right and what is wrong."

In rebuttal, Gross continued to press the theme that the jury had only to consider whether the testimony of the raiding vice officers had been true. The prosecution closed its arguments by labeling Lili's act as "shameless, defiant, and aggressive." But Judge Draeger in his instructions cautioned the jury that "even if she did indecently display herself, you must find her not guilty if it was done without specific intent to do so."[37]

After seventy-eight minutes of deliberation, the jury of ten women and two men returned to the courtroom. Lili perched on the edge of her chair, twisted a white lace hankie in her hand, and waited for the verdict. As the words "not guilty" rang out in the crowded courtroom, she smiled and threw her arms around Giesler. The jurors crowded around her like a gaggle of autograph seekers. She shook hands with them, a group who had given her performance the official stamp of decency, and declared "This is a real victory for the profession."[38]

The six-day trial climaxed with a happy ending, and Lili St. Cyr became a celebrity outside of burlesque circles. Just days after her acquittal, a group of Marines listed her as one of the stars with the most "orality," a word they coined to mean "a desire to be kissed frequently and thoroughly." In the "pucker-up poll," published in Virginia MacPherson's *Hollywood Report* gossip column, Lili came in after Lana Turner, Jane Russell, Faye Emerson, and Ava Gardner.[39] MacPherson's readers also wanted to know about the men Lili liked and the writer devoted an entire column to Lili's list of the ten most "nondivorceable" men in America. Among those on her nondivorceable men list were President Eisenhower, Pittsburgh Pirates outfielder Ralph Kiner, Gene Kelly, Irving Berlin, Henry Ford Jr., and her attorney Jerry Giesler. "It's time the family men got a little recognition," Lili told the reporter.[40] "Just because a girl's a stripper, you know, doesn't mean she hasn't got homespun values."

College officials didn't always seem to think Lili instilled the best values. In the spring of 1952, a panty raid craze took hold of college campuses. One night in May, more than a dozen schools across the country held raids. "About seven hundred students at the University of Maryland swept past the school's four-man police force and invaded ten sorority houses," reported the United Press in a story that detailed raids at Stanford, University of Southern California, Cornell, Michigan State, and the University of Georgia. Unhappy with the thought of having their underwear stolen, the female students challenged their fellow classmates. "The three hundred Stanford raiders were met at one point by five hundred screeching freshmen women who tried to fight them off. Only about fifty men succeeded in gaining entrance to the women's quarters, but they emerged holding the loot aloft." Women at some universities were more successful: "Some four hundred raiders at Cornell University were greeted by a bucket brigade of co-eds. After a thorough drenching, the boys were convinced they should go home."[41]

Lili disagreed with the female college students and got in on the craze by promising a pair of her panties to one male representative at each of the colleges where raids were attempted. "I think they should get a sort of reward," she suggested.[42] "It's such a nice sign when men show an aggressive interest in a girl." Comparing the craze to a man giving a woman flowers, Lili said, "It's really not the panties, you know. The boys just want to show how strong and brave they are. It's a way of getting attention from the girls, too. And you really shouldn't discourage a young boy about things like that."

Bill Middlesworth, a college senior at Capital University in Ohio, publicly asked Lili for a pair of her undies in a letter in the *Columbus Citizen*. In a letter signed by several of his other classmates, Middlesworth wrote, "We, the men of Capital, understand that you have offered to give to any group of college men a pair of your panties and a bra if they had pulled a panty raid on one of the girls' dorms. If you would send us a pair of your panties and bra, we feel it would satisfy all the men on our campus and we wouldn't have to have a panty raid. It would alleviate our raiding a dorm and the bad publicity it would bring, along with the wrath of the administration."[43]

The request only further frustrated college officials, however. Nearby Wittenberg College issued a statement that "participation in such activities would result in immediate dismissal from the college and notification to selective service boards." Middlesworth's letter caused such an uproar at Capital that he was threatened with expulsion. To keep from being kicked out he made a public apology and burned his letter in front of three hundred fellow students.[44]

Meanwhile, Lili took her new notoriety to the bank. Ads for her shows enticed potential audience members with the Ciro's scandal. One ad teased, "See What Hollywood Saw—Was the Jury Right?"[45] Gossip columnists whispered that her salary had increased to more than three thousand five hundred dollars a week. She endorsed a gadget called the Relaz-A-Cizor, a weight-loss device that promised to reduce hips and stomach without dieting or drugs. And she began to appear in movies.

The first movie Lili performed in was a burlesque short called *Love Moods*, which recreated her bubble bath routine. The film was shot at the Follies in Los Angeles shortly after her trial. "We had a little orchestra there, and they already knew what to do," Lili told author Eric Schaeffer, author of *Bold! Daring! Shocking! True!: A History of Exploitation Films*.[46] "We were all acquainted with the stage, which made it easier."

"We had a hard schedule there," Lili explained.[47] "We'd start at twelve noon and go until midnight, two a.m. on Fridays and Saturdays. So we had to squeeze [these movies] in between the shows somehow."

Short films of burlesque acts grew increasingly popular after World War II. The shorts would be pieced together and packaged as a burlesque feature or shown between live acts at burlesque houses across the country. The shorts that were shown between live acts meant that audiences outside of big cities could catch headliners like Lili. Beyond spreading striptease to less cosmopolitan areas, the films offered an alternative image of female sexuality in the fifties. Whereas Hollywood portrayed women as passive, the women of burlesque were anything but. "The burlesque film was directly confronting viewers with the sight of women who were uninhibited in their sexual expression," wrote Schaeffer.[48] "In burlesque films, women strutted, pranced, swung their arms, bumped their hips, poured out of and stripped off their costumes in what appeared to be a flood of uncontained sexual display. The women onscreen met the gaze of the spectator, acknowledged that gaze, and defiantly invited him to look further."

Censors, religious groups, and certain civic organizations targeted the burlesque films. The Ciro's trial and acquittal hardly granted Lili free rein to perform the same act on film, and *Love Moods* met some resistance. The Knights of Columbus and Young Ladies Institute attacked a California theater for showing the "morally degrading" film. The theater's manager eventually caved, saying, "If there's anything objectionable, we're sorry. We will refrain from booking any more questionable pictures."[49] Since burlesque films were made and distributed independently, Hollywood's oversight groups had no control over them. Some theaters did bow to local pressure, but in general little could be done to prevent the film's exhibition.

Of course, Hollywood's studio system worked quite a bit differently. The Production Code Administration, Hollywood's self-censoring group, also known as the Hays Office, maintained much tighter control over what the studios put out. And even before Lili St. Cyr signed on in May 1953, RKO's *Son of Sinbad* was having trouble getting approved.

Son of Sinbad told the tale of a Middle Eastern adventurer who romances Nerissa, one of the Khalif's harem girls, by reciting his friend's poetry to her. Knowing more of the story is unnecessary, for the film, as the *New York Times* reviewer declared, "is merely a routine action adventure with a more than normal complement of diaphanously clad young women doing some cool dances."[50] As co-star Vincent Price explained, the film was a way for producer Howard Hughes to fulfill his commitment to various starlets and beauties. Apparently, Hughes had awarded contracts promising film roles to women all across the country. With *Son of Sinbad*, Hughes could satisfy his obligations at once. The script, wrote Price, would call for "girls, girls, girls! Instead of the forty thieves, we had the daughters of the forty thieves in a cave. Every marketplace was wriggling with girls, selling their wares, among other things. Twenty girls who had won a Midwest Hughes-inspired beauty contest at least ten years before were rooted out of their happy homes. The price had been a part in a movie — now they were to have their unwonted chance. They were exported from the Midwest to Hollywood . . . and flung onto the set embarrassed to death in the flimsiest costumes."[51]

It is no surprise that the Hays Office took an interest in such a cavalcade of half-dressed women. When RKO first submitted the script, the office responded by reminding the studio that it was "mandatory that the intimate parts of the body — specifically, the breasts of women — be fully covered at all times." The letter went on to detail particular concerns, including that there be no suggestion of nudity in the bath scenes, the kissing be close-mouthed, and that "the frenzied dance described . . . be handled with great care. Specifically, the dancers should employ no bumps, grinds, or other suggestive movements."[52]

When RKO hired Lili St. Cyr as Nerissa, she thought her former beau and Hughes' assistant Walter Kane wanted to alleviate any possible guilt he might have played in her earlier suicide attempt. But she was "profoundly grateful to him" and thought she "was the only person responsible" for the suicide attempt and acknowledged her "own fears, confusions, and fatigue" were the catalyst.[53] Regardless of Kane's role in Lili's hire, the Production Code was clearly troubled when RKO hired a woman who made her living performing bumps, grinds, and other suggestive movements. In fact, when the office received stills featuring Lili as Nerissa, the head of the harem, they wrote they were "gravely concerned."[54]

The Hays Office was less than thrilled with the hiring of Lili, but the columnists were in heaven. *Los Angeles Times* columnist Hedda Hopper said Lili "holds the position Gypsy Rose Lee once held as America's foremost stripteaser."[55] Hollywood columnist Sidney Skolsky spent a day on the set watching her co-stars do a scene, but admitted he was "more interested" in Lili. Skolsky was surprised to learn her voice was "kind of shrill and untrained, didn't . . . go with her face—sexy and sophisticated—and her figure—worldly, and just about the best in town."[56] Other columnists dished the fact that another actress dubbed Lili's lines, wondered if she'd been signed to a long-term contract, and speculated on her costume—"a smile and not much else" hoped one.[57]

Reporters were enamored with Lili's appearance in a mainstream Hollywood movie but she did not like filmmaking. "I don't like the hours," she told one reporter.[58] "Up at six and work for twelve hours. It's hard work." She admitted she had a terrible time remembering lines. And, she told Sidney Skolsky, "I'm not going out of my way [to become a movie star]. I don't care that much. If it happens, it happens."[59]

Moviemaking clearly took a toll on Lili, who was still performing at a local club in the evening. One day during filming, she was rushed to the hospital with abdominal pain. Doctors thought she might have appendicitis, but she would let them do little because she was afraid of affecting her looks. "People said that I was destroying myself," she wrote later.[60] "They were probably right. . . . If Lili St. Cyr had a certain worth in the eyes of others, she got it from the beauty of her face and her body. If I lost these advantages, I would lose them. . . . I'd rather have died. . . . My force came from my beauty. Thanks to these advantages, I obtained all I wanted by my own means, in my own way. I wouldn't risk them."

Lili's newfound success took its greatest toll on her marriage to Armando Orsini. Early in their relationship, Lili and Armando agreed that she would work for two more years and then quit. After that point, Armando and his friend would open a retirement village, a novel idea for the time. "She told me she hated the kind of jobs she was doing," recalled Armando, who said Lili seemed excited about the change.[61] "She told me she really did it because of the money and to survive. If she liked it, she would have said, 'Listen, I love what I'm doing, and . . .' She knew that what she was doing wasn't worth anything more than showing her body."

Lili also expressed some discontent about her job to others. She told columnist Earl Wilson she was tired of taking her clothes off, but quickly added, "My husband doesn't care for it. He's going to be very happy if I go into something else. I may be making more pictures. It's a little more impersonal."[62] It is unclear whether Lili wanted to stop working, whether she just wanted to make Armando happy, or whether she was saying what she thought others wanted to hear. She wasn't always honest or forthcoming with Armando. She led him to believe that her mother and grandmother had died, when they were in fact still living. And he believed she couldn't have children despite a string of abortions both before and after she married Armando.

Lili was also dishonest with Armando about her work. She told him she kept getting offers for jobs and asked him if they could delay their plans because it would be "very stupid to refuse so much money."[63] Several months went by, as Lili again postponed her retirement. Finally, her agent called when she was out, spoke with Armando, and said how lucky Lili was because while everyone had been complaining about business, she was booked for the next year. "It really hit me that she would never quit," said Armando.[64] "And why should she? She was at the top of her career then, making big money. Why should she leave all that glamour for this Italian guy who wanted to build houses in Connecticut?" Armando left and the two eventually divorced. But Armando did not build houses or a retirement village; rather, he opened up the first of many successful restaurants and cafes in New York.

Of Armando, Lili wrote later that he was the best of her husbands and "the one I regretted losing the most." At the time, Lili told one reporter, "I don't know exactly what happened to our marriage. Armand and I get on well enough . . . I guess we just drifted apart."[65] With time, Lili seemed to admit that she felt trapped. "The longer I stayed with Armando, the more I felt responsible to him. I was afraid and I wanted to flee."[66] She also admitted she was not willing to give up her career. "I had sacrificed too many years to struggle to arrive where I was . . . I wanted it too much. I was too young to bust myself."[67]

In 1953, Armando divorced Lili. But more than ten years later, she thought "it was a foolish, stupid mistake. I sometimes think back on those days and can't figure out what made me tick. Armando was a prince among men. . . . If I could be lucky enough again to attract someone like him, I'd handle it better. It took many years to see things in proper perspective."[68]

In his unpublished memoir, Herman Hover described the Sunset Strip as a "boulevard littered with deception, frustrations, foiled ambitions, and hopes cruelly shattered. It was a magnet for dreamers, idlers, and easy money, but it was also a place where only the shrewd, the able, and the practical survive." Lili was a dreamer who was also able and practical. Her time on the Strip thrust her on an upward swing in the pendulum of the intoxicating frenzy that is Hollywood life, but the upturn was temporary. As Hover's niece Sheila Weller wrote in *Dancing At Ciro's*, "when you live in a Hollywood nightclub, whether you're prepared or not, your life is destined to follow the curve of melodrama."[69] Lili's success in the glamorous, wild, seductive nightclub life would not shield her from the misery Hover described. Rather, it would give her a higher stage from which to stumble. But in the meantime, she would head to another glitzy, neon-lit boulevard, the Las Vegas Strip.

6.

The Anatomic Bomb

The night before I left Las Vegas I walked out in the desert to look at the moon. There was a jeweled city on the horizon, spires rising in the night, but the jewels were diadems of electric and the spires were the neon of signs ten stories high.

— NORMAN MAILER

Throughout the 1950s, Americans waved at each other from their suburban lawns and tucked themselves into twin beds—at least publicly. So in the midst of this *Father Knows Best* era, Las Vegas became an oasis. In Las Vegas, the undercurrent that coursed beneath the white-picketed facade around the country seeped closer to the surface and tinged the air with a neon glow.

Las Vegas underwent several false starts after a Spanish trader en route to Los Angeles first discovered the water-rich valley in the early 1700s and named the city for the Spanish phrase "The Meadows." Mormon settlers from Utah tried to develop an outpost in the 1850s only to give up after the Indians rejected their teachings and continued to raid the fort. Early in the twentieth century, the Union Pacific Railroad established a train stop, but it served mainly as a resting point on the way to the coast. In the thirties, the state of Nevada legalized gambling and made divorce easier to obtain. At the same time, the building of the Hoover Dam helped the desert town flower. "Writers who came to Las Vegas during the boom years of the 1930s to tell the story of the dam and the nearby community generally wrote about a wild frontier town where alcohol, prostitution, quick marriage and divorce, and gambling were readily available," wrote Robert D. McCracken, author of *Las Vegas: The Great American Playground*.[365] "These stories promoted Las Vegas' image as a place where fun and flirtation with immorality were possible without causing real harm to anyone." So while Las Vegas would remain a small town for almost twenty more years, the "image persisted and engendered the spirit by which the city and its reputation would grow."

In 1940, legend has it, hotelier Thomas Hull's car broke down along U.S. Highway 91 right outside of Las Vegas. As he watched the traffic whoosh by, he noted the many out-of-state license plates of the tourists returning from the Hoover Dam or a weekend of gambling in the city's small downtown. In April 1941, Hull opened El Rancho Vegas, the first hotel on what would become the Vegas Strip. While some argue that Hull's decision to build the hotel was less whimsical, the transformation of a dusty roadway into a neon-lit Strip had begun.

El Rancho Vegas glamorized the Wild West, cashing in with an upscale rustic ideal. The main building housed the casino, restaurant, gift shops, and boutiques. The décor throughout featured wood paneling, exposed log beams, and western paintings. Bungalows dotted the grounds. And as visitors zoomed toward downtown, the El Rancho's windmill, outlined in orange neon, served as a welcoming beacon. The hotel was the first to use big-name entertainers to attract crowds. Chico Marx, Betty Grable, Dorothy Dandridge, Lena Horne, Sophie Tucker, Tony Bennett, Abbott and Costello, and Nat King Cole all performed in El Rancho's Opera House. "My folks could get a room with two double beds for six dollars or seven dollars a night at El Rancho Vegas," wrote *Las Vegas Sun* reporter Dick Odessky in his memoir *A Fly On the Wall*.[2] "All-you-could-eat 'chuckwagon' dinners, the forerunner of the buffet, were a buck. Seeing a top-flight entertainer in a fancy showroom was free. If you wanted to eat during the show, you could pay two-fifty or three dollars for a complete steak dinner. Gambling subsidized all costs incurred to attract the players and Las Vegas was the least expensive holiday spot in the land."

Less than two years later, the Last Frontier, another western-themed resort, opened. The Desert Inn and Mafioso Bugsy Siegel's Flamingo soon joined the Strip. Still a small city, most of the entertainment happened downtown near Fremont Street. But the Strip began to glow a little brighter.

In the mid-forties Hull sold El Rancho, and the hotel changed hands several times before Beldon Katleman took over in the late forties. The Katleman family made their money in real estate deals around the country, and rumors circulated that they purchased El Rancho to keep Beldon away from the rest of the family business. Katleman, an average-built man with dark hair slicked back in a way that accented his receding hairline, had the Nixonian look of a used-car salesman. He "was a maverick in every way, shape, and form," wrote Odessky.[3] "A true contrarian, he did everything backward from what seemed reasonable or obvious. . . . As sole owner of one of the town's major properties, Beldon Katleman believed he was entitled to his own set of rules." Odessky reported one incident of his go-it-alone style: Later in the fifties, the major property owners wanted to keep the entertainers' salaries down and agreed to stop raiding each other's talent. Despite the agreement, Beldon approached comedian Joe E. Lewis just days later and offered to double his salary if he came to El Rancho. Betsy Hammes, a Vegas lounge singer, was more damning and described Beldon as "shifty." Hammes refused to go back after bad experiences with Beldon during her two appearances at El Rancho. "He would charge his performers for their rooms and if they wouldn't pay he'd have them beat up," said Hammes.[4] "I don't think he was connected to the mafia. I think he was mean all on his own."

The Strip still wasn't much of one when Beldon Katleman hired Lili to perform at El Rancho in the fall of 1951. Vegas had not yet turned into the "sun-baked, neon-swathed, water-fraught desert pleasuredom"[5] with the moniker Sin City. Some, like district attorney Roger Foley, tried to keep it that way. Foley ordered Lili arrested on charges of lewd and indecent exposure, but the dancer left town before the hearings. By the time she returned to Las Vegas over a year later, she had been acquitted of similar charges at Ciro's in Los Angeles and had become a household name. Foley dropped the more serious charges after she promised her act would be "acceptable to public taste." She pleaded guilty to creating a public nuisance, and paid a $250 fine before she returned to work at El Rancho.[6] She put on what was initially billed as a fashion show—one in which the model changed outfits onstage—before all pretense was lost.

A huge success, Lili regularly headlined El Rancho. She often teamed up with comedian Joe E. Lewis, who once shook his head at a young man sitting at a ringside table and joked, "I saw you eating while Lili St. Cyr was working. I hope I never get that hungry in my life."[7] The pairing, as *Cult Vegas* author Mike Weatherford described it, was a "popular co-bill of booze and broads; her choreographed musical routines provided the perfect classical prelude to his roadhouse jokes and songs."[8]

It wasn't just Lili St. Cyr who was taking off; Las Vegas was shedding its frontier town feel for a more gilded image. Six months after her return in late 1952, the *Washington Post* reported "the joint is jumping. The casino is noisy with the clink of silver dollars, the shouts of the lucky players, and the moans of the losers. . . . Each weekend an estimated 25,000 to 30,000 citizens, the majority from booming Southern California, crowd into this glittering town, doubling its population. The pleasure-seekers or suckers—according to which view you take—sleep in hotels, motels, or their own cars. Some don't sleep at all. They stand at the tables all night transfixed by the frolicking dice."[9] Over the next six years, several more resorts lit up the Strip, including the Sands, Sahara, Riviera, Tropicana, and Stardust.

In the beginning, Las Vegas appealed to Lili the same way Montreal and the ocean liners had before. In those early days, explained El Rancho publicist Tricia Hurst in a 1986 article for *Nevada* magazine, the city "was more posh, glamorous and laid back than it is now. [It was a] more romantic era, men dressed black-tie and women wore evening gowns and cocktail dresses once the sun had set." She wrote that "this never-never land of around-the-clock-living" was a "tight-knit community," but Hurst sensed a darker element that Lili's life in Montreal and aboard the cruise ships lacked. A "great deal of in-fighting and competition" went on in this "place where good judgment often went out the window."[10]

The in-fighting and competition, at least in the world of burlesque, also subsisted outside of Las Vegas. In her autobiography *The Lady Is A Vamp*, dancer Tempest Storm detailed an argument she had with Lili at the Follies in Los Angeles. Apparently, another dancer left straight pins on the stage after her performance. When Lili took the stage, she stepped on one as she danced and was embarrassed and angry that she had to stop dancing and remove the pin. She accused Tempest of dropping the pins and the two argued before Follies owner Lillian Hunt stopped the fight. "If [Lili] hadn't been such a snob, perhaps I wouldn't have reacted as I did," wrote Tempest.[11] "But she didn't deserve much consideration because she didn't give much."

Lili herself later acknowledged that most other dancers didn't consider her one of their own and, as a result, she kept to herself. "Lili was shy and quiet and when you consider what she did for a living, she was unlike anything you could imagine," said Mildred Katleman, Beldon's wife during the fifties.[12] "She was a darling, warm, lovely person, and had a good sense of humor. She used to make me laugh a lot. She could make fun of things. She was a decent person and not at all what you would expect from a stripper. Of course, she teased a lot, but didn't really strip."[13]

Perhaps more in-fighting occurred in Las Vegas. Perhaps something else about the city bothered Lili, but she recognized something in Vegas' vibe that made her uncomfortable. "It's an artificial city, which seems to have surged out of the earth overnight," she wrote.[14] "It never stops growing, becoming more illuminated and burning, and, in my opinion, getting worse." But she also acknowledged that Las Vegas treated her well. In many ways, it was good to women in general—at least financially. The tourism economy provided plenty of job opportunities in what was considered "women's work," explained Joanne Goodwin in *The Grit Beneath the Glitter*.[15] "They could serve drinks, type letters, clean rooms, or wait tables in a small city that offered better tips and more diverse forms of entertainment than they had back home. Slightly over 40 percent of women workers found jobs in the sectors most likely to be related to tourism: entertainment and recreation, hotel and lodging, eating and drinking establishments, and retail."

In fact, in Las Vegas, a pretty girl was the ching-ching of the silver dollar that kept the city humming along. "They are the storm troopers of the Vegas entertainment industry, and in the large production shows are the principal selling point," wrote *Las Vegas: City Without Clocks* author Ed Reid.[16] "Everybody likes pretty girls, and within the two-mile limit of the Las Vegas Strip there are more pretty girls than in any area of similar size in the world. All kinds of pretty girls."

Lili's nearly decade-long reign at El Rancho Vegas coincided with the rise of the showgirl. Quickly Vegas Vic, a forty-foot high neon cowboy that towered over Fremont Street and represented the city's early frontier feel and western-themed attractions, was bumped for the bejeweled showgirl. In much of the country, burlesque and vaudeville were slowly dying. But a mutant, more schmaltzy, far more naked form took hold in Vegas. In 1954, *Newsweek* estimated "2,000 of these bright-plumaged creatures are now shedding their fine feathers in plush nightclubs as well as drafty burlesque houses across the country."[17]

In Las Vegas, the showgirl and exotic dancer were firmly knit into the silver and gold lamé fabric of the city. And as one of the city's best draws, women became a bigger part of the Vegas workforce. In the mid-fifties, dancers at the Sahara worked two shows a night, seven nights a week and made ninety-five dollars a week, compared to the average secretary who made about forty-five dollars a week. Perhaps this is one of the reasons "the prototypical white, All-American 'feminine beauty' aroused admiration and respect from female as well as male viewers," wrote Joanne Goodwin.[18] Regardless, she found that few "perceived the showgirl or dancer as either a pawn or a victim. . . . As consumers of American culture, they saw a kind of power in the showgirl image; one available only to women, that could lead to wealth and social influence. They admired the image uncritically and wanted what it symbolized. . . . The sex-gender system that promoted sexualized portrayals of women and prevented gender equality for all women offered individual women great economic advantages."

However, the financial rewards Las Vegas offered women remained immediate and temporary. Rarely did showgirls or burlesque dancers earn pensions, sick leave, vacation pay, or other benefits. Some spun their earnings into other ventures. Some married and left the business. And some ended up destitute, having missed their opportunity to better themselves. Lili's husband Armando Orsini, with whom she remained friendly until her death, believed this would eventually cause Lili problems. "The success of her was only monetary," said Armando.[19] "She was more requested, making more money than anyone else. It wasn't a question of money. It didn't change her life, her social life. She didn't better herself. That was the biggest mistake she made in her life."

In the short term, Las Vegas did indeed provide Lili great economic advantages. During one six-week engagement in Las Vegas she reportedly earned five thousand dollars a week for seven hours' work. A three-week engagement at El Rey in Oakland, California, purportedly earned her over ten thousand dollars. Salaries ranged drastically, but few dancers made more than a couple hundred dollars a week. Lili's scandal- and trial-induced fame and experimental routines blasted her into an astronomical salary range. She was often inspired by classic femme fatale stories and regularly developed new routines with titles like "Carmen" or "A

Geisha Fantasy." "Carmen" was Lili's takeoff on the opera about a Spanish gypsy who through her beauty and dancing leads men astray.

Of course, most came to see her now famous bubble bath routine. But Lili even offered variations on this performance. In one deviation she called "Wedding Night" she danced and bathed as a new bride preparing for bed instead of her usual routine of getting ready for a date. But as *Newsweek's* description made clear, "Wedding Night" remained quite similar to her Ciro's number. "[The curtains] opened on a young bride," wrote the *Newsweek* reporter.[20] "Tall, shapely, with feathery blonde hair and almond-shaped eyes, she stood demurely for a moment center stage, then began moving dreamily about an elegantly appointed gilt and crystal bedroom, laying out a filmy black nightgown and a pair of electric blue pajamas to the muted accompaniment of 'Tenderly' and a lavender spotlight. As the music modulated into a rhythmic passage from 'Rhapsody in Blue,' the blonde slipped behind a translucent screen, removed her wedding dress, and emerged in veil and blue underthings. At the footlights she flung a garter, bra, and panties to a frantically grasping audience, slipped in and out of a diaphanous negligee; took a bath in a glass-walled tub, and rubbed herself with a jumbo-size towel. While the orchestra thumped out 'Temptation,' she donned the black lace nightgown and threw herself tempestuously on the antique double bed."

With such routines, Lili pulled down not just her thigh-high stockings, but as much as one hundred thousand dollars a year. Financial security is likely the only reason she performed in Las Vegas, because each time she returned, she "noticed changes that always seemed to be for the worse. Vegas is a city where the inhabitants are either on the road to success or on the path to failure. People are either trying to arrive or find an exit. . . . It was very good to me, but it's a place that corrupts its inhabitants."[21]

Besides Las Vegas, Lili continued to spend much of her time in Los Angeles and New York. In fact, her Ciro's-inspired notoriety and Las Vegas-provided financial security enabled her to open her own New York nightclub, The Boudoir. At the very small nitery located above another club on Fifty-third Street, she performed on a tiny stage which was surrounded by mirrors to make it seem larger and to multiply her near-naked dance moves. She did not tease at The Boudoir for very long; after another run-in with the law she abandoned the club entirely. But she glided around The Boudoir long enough to meet the aspiring actor Ted Jordan.

Born Eddie Friedman, Jordan moved with his family in the early forties from Ohio to Los Angeles. Soon he pursued an acting career and changed his name to Ted Jordan. The new name was, in part, a homage to his uncle Ted Lewis, a musician most known for the songs "Is Everybody Happy" and "Me and My Shadow." Jordan certainly shadowed his uncle, using his fame to gain entrée into Hollywood circles. Later, he even billed himself as Ted Lewis Jr.

In early 1954, Jordan, a tanned twenty-nine-year-old with thick, course brown hair that he kept cropped short, had a small part in the Broadway play *The Caine Mutiny*. He was not Hollywood handsome, but he had an amiable quality that endeared him to some. One night after the show, Jordan and *Caine* stars John Hodiak and Lloyd Nolan visited The Boudoir. Jordan was completely taken with Lili when he saw her onstage.

"Ted happened to catch my act one night and immediately made up his mind to meet me," explained Lili, who was now thirty-seven years old.[22] "But my defense against stage-door Johnnies proved to be too effective. . . . One night he parked himself outside the club and told my maid that he would wait for me to come out—all night, if necessary. So our meeting was unavoidable."

Lili never swooned over Ted the way she did over many of the other men in her life. But she thought he had "a very frank approach" and a "charming innocence."[23] Jordan was clearly more besotted by her. "The eyes that looked at me were among the most beautiful I had ever seen . . . an astonishing shade of green in color; they were practically hypnotic," he wrote of their first encounter.[24] "The parallels with [Marilyn Monroe] were striking: the same rampant sexuality that oozed from every pore, the same stunning physical beauty, the same striking figure. The difference was sophistication: Lili was entirely self-controlled, aware every moment of exactly what she was doing. . . . I found myself almost in a sweat as I sat beside her. . . . This is a woman I must have, I told myself."

Lili and Ted began dating. When she abandoned The Boudoir and returned to Las Vegas, he quit *The Caine Mutiny* and followed her. Jordan claimed that she proposed to him, though she maintained he was the one who wanted to marry. Regardless, she was hesitant. "The more I tried to dissuade Ted, the more discouragement possessed him until the day when he almost foundered in depression," she wrote.[25] "His state worried me so much that I succumbed to the pressure." Although Lili was linked to actor Victor Mature, cowboy star Monte Hale, and singer Vic Damone around the same time, she announced her engagement to Jordan in the fall of 1954.

Even so, Lili remained indecisive, clearly torn between husband and career. One day she joked with reporters that "Ted is planning to change his last name to St. Cyr after we're married [because] we think that will help him get ahead in pictures."[26] Just days later, she said she was "tired of working" and would retire in the spring when she finished her contracts. "Ever since I was a little girl I liked designing and sewing and things of that nature," she told one reporter when discussing her plans to open a Beverly Hills lingerie shop.[27] But a few days later she flip-flopped again and postponed the wedding. She had scheduled the wedding for 2 a.m. at El Rancho so that the marriage wouldn't interfere with her performance. This frustrated Jordan, who told reporters Lili placed too much importance on her career before he left for Hollywood.[28] Lili denied the reports that the two canceled the wedding because she wouldn't give up her own career. Instead, she said she delayed it to help Jordan's career. "There would be a certain antagonism toward an up-and-coming actor if he were married to a stripteaser," she told reporters.[29] "But once he's established as a star it won't make any difference."

Despite Jordan's insecurities and Lili's vacillations, they finally married in February 1955. For the small ceremony at El Rancho, she wore a gown made of twenty-two yards of imported white chiffon—the first time she wore a white wedding dress. But the cake, shaped to resemble the mushroom cloud of an atomic bomb, was far more predictive of the couple's future life together.

In the early fifties, the Atomic Energy Commission chose Nellis Air Force Base, just over sixty miles northwest of Las Vegas, as an atomic test site. The entire city became fascinated with the explosions. "It was the most awesome thing I have ever seen," recounted John F. Cahlan, an editor for the Las Vegas Review-Journal.[30] "The device is exploded, and you see this terrific flash of white light, and then there is a rolling purple ball. The smoke just seems to roll around the ball, and as the ball grows bigger, it turns into all colors of the rainbow, and then, all of a sudden, the sound of the shock wave'd hit you, and it's just as if somebody took a bat and hit you in the stomach. . . . And all the time, this roiling, boiling cloud—or fireball—is rising in the air and picking up the dirt off the ground. It seems to suck the dirt from the ground into the stem of the mushroom. The most awesome thing is the red fire, because it looks like the fires that Dante describes in the *Inferno*."

While the desert exploded with tremendous nuclear power, Las Vegas cashed in. Tours tromped into the desert to watch the blasts. Hairdressers designed mushroom-cloud hairdos. Restaurants served atomburgers. The Sands staged a beauty contest to choose Miss Atomic Bomb. The Las Vegas Chamber of Commerce distributed calendars with the dates of the tests so visitors could properly plan their visit. And Beldon Katleman got Lili, his star attraction, mentioned in countless papers across the country by celebrating her wedding with that mushroom-cloud shaped cake and the inscription, "Happy wedded days to El Rancho's own anatomic bomb, Lili St. Cyr."[31] While most papers included a snapshot of the happy couple in front of the cake, gossip columnist Dorothy Kilgallen chided the bride. "Lili St. Cyr didn't even give her newest bridegroom billing on the wedding cake," Kilgallen wrote.[32] "The icing wished her a happy marriage, never mind him."

But Lili did attend to Ted Jordan, or at least to his career. As with Paul Valentine, she found Ted a place in her act. He alternately served as an impresario or singer. The couple spent weeks at a time in Los Angeles so she could introduce him to people she thought might be able to help him. They also planned a stage comedy entitled "Kiss Me Goodbye" that was set to open at El Rancho, but it never came off.

The notion of the male breadwinner and the stay-at-home wife remained an entrenched cultural ideal at the time, even if it wasn't always the reality. In one way or another, Ted relied first on his uncle, then on Lili, and finally on the memory of Marilyn Monroe by writing the book *Norma Jean*, among other things. "I don't think he worked a day in his life," said Mildred Katleman.[33]. He didn't seem to want to work, despite society's expectations. And Lili was not willing to give up her career. Mildred didn't think she liked stripping, but that she did it for the money and independence. Whether or not Lili enjoyed stripping, she recoiled at the idea of being a stay-at-home wife and mother. So perhaps she included her husband as a nod to social norms and to give Ted some pretense of providing. Clearly, however, she was frustrated by her dependent husbands and she once lamented, "I always seem to be married to somebody I have to support."[34]

Lili was very much the provider. As a wedding gift, Beldon Katleman gave his favorite torso tosser a five-year contract, guaranteeing her twelve weeks of work each year at four thousand dollars a week. Katleman recognized Lili was one of El Rancho's top draws and well worth the quarter-million dollar deal. She also continued to pack in standing-room-only crowds at Ciro's and Larry Potter's Supper Club in Los Angeles, Minsky's Adams Theatre in Newark, the Old Howard in Boston, the Casino Royal in Washington, D.C., and various clubs in New York, Chicago, and Philadelphia. Lili made news everywhere she performed. Sometimes, her routines captured headlines. In Washington, D.C., her interpretation of Sadie Thompson—a routine that again required her to splash around in an onstage tub—was a hit. One reporter wrote, "When blonde Lil begins her sensuous cavorting around a stage-prop version of Sadie's South Sea Island thatched hut—even author Somerset Maugham would be proud of her."[35] Sometimes Lili's personal life landed her in the gossip columns; within months of her marriage to Ted Jordan there were reports of a rift. Sometimes, a gimmick, such as providing the voice for the telephone company's new automatic answering device, a machine that let callers listen to a pre-recorded message, secured her a few newspaper inches. And sometimes, her movie career garnered some action in the news.

Son of Sinbad was released nearly two years after the filmmakers captured Lili's bathing moves for the project. RKO Studios had been battling the Motion Picture Association of America (MPAA) over whether the film would be granted a Production Code seal of approval. Much of the Production Code's complaints involved Lili. In the board's notes to RKO they criticized her bath scene because there was "apparently nothing covering [her] breasts" and "St. Cyr's dance before the girls contains bumps and grinds, ends in simulated strip tease." Overall, the Production Code staff listed a litany of complaints, including "indecent solo dances; scanty costumes of women; nakedness and breast exposures throughout."[36] The film won approval only after most of Lili's disrobing scenes were cut.

Still, Son of Sinbad was really just a big tease—colorful, pulpy, and silly eye candy. "It does have girls," wrote one reviewer.[37] "Leggy girls, girls with half-bared bosoms, girls with . . . pretty faces—all in Technicolor and all inflated to positively blurry proportions. . . . When these concubines, coryphées, and cooch dancers are not draped around [the male stars], they are simply draped—or undraped." The local censors were unhappy and many theaters refused to book the girl-laden movie. Memphis' City Censor Board, in a typical reaction, banned the film. The eighty-eight-year-old chairman explained, "It was a pretty good picture, but it had one of the vilest dances I ever saw."[38] The Legion of Decency, a Catholic group that evaluated movies for its congregations, gave the film a C grade, explaining that it was "a serious affront to Christian and traditional standards of morality and decency because of its blatant and continuing violation of the virtue of purity." The group complained that "throughout, it contains grossly salacious dances and indecent costuming. This picture is a challenge to decent standards of the theatrical entertainment and as an incitement to juvenile delinquency, it is especially dangerous to the moral welfare of youth."[39] RKO exploited the film's notoriety, keeping *Son of Sinbad* and its leggy leading stripteaser in the news for months. In fact, Lili attempted to use the *Son of Sinbad*'s renown in her onstage productions. She approached RKO about buying her costumes for her nightclub act, but the studio preferred to keep them in a warehouse.

Lili also continued to appear in burlesque films and did a series of them with Irving Klaw, the photographer famous for his Bettie Page pinups and bondage photos. "Irving Klaw had this loft [in New York] and he was acquainted with an awful lot of strippers," she told author Eric Schaeffer years later.[40] "He'd take them one at a time and shoot their various acts . . . [then] he would take these separate segments—one with me, and one with Bettie Page, and all these other girls—[and] he would splice these together until he had enough time . . . to make what he would call a full picture. But actually it was nothing but a bunch of segments of ten or twelve different girls doing their various acts."

Klaw's film *Varietease* was typical of such a picture. In that film, the camera first found Lili arriving backstage in her dressing room and then treated audiences to a voyeuristic view of her preparations. She slipped in and out of various outfits allowing the camera a glimpse of her bra, garter belt, and sheer thigh highs. She shimmied around the stage and with each change teased viewers by sliding her hands down her long legs or twirling around in body-hugging gowns before she again undressed. Finally she changed into a red net bra, garter belt with a floor-length tulle panel down the front, a strapless red velvet and gold trimmed gown. She was ready to perform and twirled around the stage showing off her gown, letting the audience admire her long, lean lines. She turned her back to the audience, swiveled her hips, and used the curtain to play peek-a-boo. Slowly shaking her hips back and forth, she slid the zipper down her body and shimmied out of her gown. She pirouetted around stage with a sheer red scarf and slowly ground her hips while sinking down to the floor. She slipped behind the curtain, which opened to reveal her seated cross-legged on an ottoman. The lights dimmed and cast a shadow behind her, magnifying her motions. She wiggled around, flung her legs in the air, arched her back, and ended the routine splayed out in the red net bra and garter. The entire routine was interrupted several times by other performances spliced in to draw out Lili's headline performance. In between Lili's segments Bettie Page performed a belly dance, comics told jokes, a couple danced the tango, another dancer twirled around in a sparkly bikini bathing suit with feathers attached to the bottom, and yet another did the can-can.

Lili confessed she only made both Irving Klaw's films and Hollywood movies for the paycheck. "All the films in which I appeared are, for the most part, excusable," she admitted.[41] "I made them because the occasion presented itself without any effort on my part." At the same time, she clearly understood that the burlesque producers and Hollywood's heavyweights were simply interested in cashing in on her reputation. Discussing the pieced-together films that Klaw produced, Lili told Schaeffer, "They'd put my name up in front, making it look like I was the star of the show and I was going to be . . . in the movie for two hours. And I was only in the movie for, like, fifteen minutes. Now let's face it, that's what I was used for in *The Naked and the Dead* and *I, Mobster* and *Son of Sinbad*. I didn't have a legit part. I was a name they could put on the marquee and I was worked in in a way that might have looked like I was part of the story, but I really wasn't. They were doing the same thing, only in a grander manner."[42]

Lili didn't mind the exploitation, perhaps because there was some reciprocity to it. But what did bother her was Irving Klaw's practice of taking still photos after a film shoot and selling them without paying her. "Every time I see those pictures, I have a fit because they're not good pictures," she told Schaeffer.[43] "I was used to working . . . with wonderful photographers like [Bruno] Bernard. Bernard and I spent hours working on our pictures, spending all this time and making such a fuss over them. And then having these pictures from Irving Klaw show up. . . . It made me angry every time I looked at them."

And at best, Lili remained ambivalent about moviemaking. She hated memorizing lines and found the process dull. "I found moviemaking the most boring job of all," she told *Autograph Collector's Magazine* in 1988.[44] "There was so much standing around, so much doing nothing. For me, I enjoyed the action of the stage." Later she wrote, "Onstage, I had control over my interpretation. I could decide what I wanted . . . and change the game if the audience didn't go for it. In the cinema, it's impossible. Too many people intervene."[45] She told Schaeffer that making movies involved a "strange kind of pressure . . . [because] you know every move you make is going to be there forever. At least on the stage if you blunder the audience has probably forgotten about it five minutes later."[46]

Lili also stayed in the news and advanced her career by joining the new profession of "sexpert." The credit for taking sex advice from bathroom walls to public debate goes to Alfred Kinsey. In 1953, Kinsey published his second report on sexuality, *Sexual Behavior in the Human Female*. The tome caused an even greater furor than his earlier study, *Sexual Behavior in the Human Male*. Both books made sex a subject of public debate.

Kinsey, a professor of zoology at Indiana University, found himself leading the shift to greater public frankness about sex after teaching a course on marriage and family for undergraduates in the thirties. He found his students craved accurate, unbiased information about sex. Since little scientific data was available, Kinsey set out to record the sexual history of several thousand men and women. The resulting data offered a revealing look at Americans' sex lives. Among the more surprising revelations, Kinsey found that almost ninety percent of men had premarital sex and half had extramarital sex. The public was more shocked that half of the women in America engaged in premarital sex and a quarter in extramarital sex. The studies also discovered that a significant percent of both men and women masturbate, engage in homosexual activity, and experience wet dreams resulting in orgasm. Kinsey became a household name, his reports became best-sellers, and the entire country rumbled with sex talk.[47]

Kinsey and his reports peeled away the stereotypes many Americans had regarding female sexuality. The country's ecdysiasts were happy to get in on the act. "After 'K-day,' as it was called in publishing circles, St. Cyr and other strippers became informal spokespeople for Kinsey's book, as if, by virtue of stripping, they knew more about sex than civilians," wrote Rachel Shteir in *Striptease: The Untold History of the Girlie Show*.[18] Before detailing what made a man special, Lili touted her expertise. "I've had plenty of opportunity in my life to study men, to form an opinion of my own," she wrote in *Top Secret* magazine.[49] "Dr. Kinsey interviewed a 'sample' of 5,300 males to get the facts for his famous report, but as many as Kinsey's whole 'sample' come to see me in a single three-performance day. Men are my audience and, in my ten years in show business, I suppose I've been in closer contact with more men than any other woman in the world." After she detailed the characteristics that would make a man special and gave examples of men that met these ideals, Lili actually went on to scold the famous scientist. "So here we are, Dr. Kinsey! This is my own report on the males of America. I tried to do what you missed when you took love out of sex and looked at humans as if they were animals whose relations between male and female are of concern only to the zoologist."[50] When another reporter asked her about Kinsey's reports she said, "People have lived by a false set of values for years, but I don't believe in hiding anything."[51]

As a sexpert, Lili wrote articles with titles like "How to Tame a Wolf" for the booming pulp and men's magazines. When she wasn't dispensing advice or commenting on Kinsey, she publicly embraced her own sexuality. "I've heard philosophers say the three most important ingredients of life are health, sex, and money," she wrote.[52] "The order in which we regard them tells the kind of person we are. I always put sex first."

Television depicted Mom and Dad pecking good-night from separate beds, but Kinsey and his army of self-appointed sexperts brought the sexual undertones to the surface. For every virginal Doris Day or Ward Cleaver that the fifties conventionality served up, a skin-barer like Lili St. Cyr or a hip-swiveler like Elvis Presley shook things up. Each time someone like Ed Sullivan censored Elvis' swinging pelvis, someone like Hugh Hefner splashed a nude Marilyn Monroe across the pages of *Playboy*. It was the last time the entertainment industry was uncertain about selling sex. It was the last time it tried to squash such open sexuality. Others, including Lili, knew the real scene. "As far as sex is concerned, let's face it," she told a reporter, "no matter how popular baseball may be, it will never be our national game, no matter what baseball writers tell you."[53]

Ted Jordan wasn't a star player, at least not as far as Lili was concerned. "I had no feeling for him and I don't think he did for me," she wrote.[54] "It's just that I sort of fascinated him. . . . There never was any great passion between us and we were hardly man and wife."

Within months of their wedding, the gossip columnists reported about fissures in their marriage. "She was very independent," said Ben Friedman, Ted Jordan's brother.[55] "And if she liked a guy, he could be a waiter, he could be a boxer, he could just be a nice young guy like my brother Ted . . . well, she didn't know what the word faithful meant."

In August 1956, Derek Goodman, a South African millionaire and beau of Zsa Zsa Gabor, came to blows with Jordan over Lili. Goodman sat down with her at El Rancho's restaurant between her acts. Jordan arrived, started shouting, and yelled, "How dare you talk to my wife like that." Goodman reportedly replied, "If she were my wife, I wouldn't leave her sitting here alone." A fight broke out and the dueling men crashed into the chuck wagon buffet. Eventually, casino guards separated them.[56]

Lili acknowledged other dalliances, including one with singer Vic Damone and another with a steward when she was on a cruise with Jordan. "Ted told me one time [he went] to Europe and she took off with some guy," said Ben Friedman.[56] "And then she comes back, all refreshed, and ready to go to work again, and expects my brother Ted to accept that kind of a relationship. Well, he got very upset and he threatened divorce. And she said, well it's up to you, you know. It's up to you."

The heady exhilaration of having won the attraction of a goddess had worn off for Jordan. He felt detached from Hollywood and his own life. "I had cut myself off from that process and now what?" he wondered in his memoir.[58] "Mr. St. Cyr was one answer, and it was an answer I didn't like; who I was had a direct relation to my connection to Lili. . . . [I was a] kept man." The marriage limped along and it would take a few years for the two to divorce, but their relationship was all but officially over.

Lili continued to appear in movies and perform around the country, and she remained a fixture in Las Vegas. "Every time I left Las Vegas, I turned around and watched it for a long time out of the back window of my car," she wrote.[59] "It was a circus and I can't believe that I got out of there alive or that there existed another world beyond all that neon. . . . [It is a place where people] lose their illusions and their dreams. The city frightened me more and more, and I was like an animal in strange territory that I should never have ventured into." But even the world beyond the neon lights of Las Vegas began to take a toll on Lili.

7.

The Striptease Mystique

A woman is handicapped by her sex, and handicaps society, either by slavishly copying the patterns of man's advance in the professions, or by refusing to compete with men at all.

—BETTY FRIEDAN

As the fifties hurtled toward the sixties in a cloud of multi-megaton nuclear tests, the schizophrenic quality of the decade became more and more apparent. The fifties are often portrayed as a simpler, more innocent, happier time. Certainly, the television shows, movies, and magazine articles of the time often played up an American-as-apple-pie life. Later, movies like *Grease* and TV shows like *Happy Days* stoked the nostalgia for the era. But the stereotypical and sterile image of the fifties ignores Hugh Hefner, Jack Kerouac, James Dean, Nikita Khrushchev, Elvis Presley, and Rosa Parks. People flocked to the suburbs, but books like the 1955 novel *The Man in the Grey Flannel Suit* explored the empty lives behind the white picket fences. Families congregated together around the television while noshing on newly invented TV dinners, but Kinsey found a high percentage of Moms and Dads were also sneaking off to meet a lover. It was a wholesome era of coonskin hats, tailfins, and poodle skirts. It was a fearful period of red baiting, atomic testing, and Cold War. It was an unruly, sometimes violent time of race riots. It was a chaste time when *I*

Love Lucy wouldn't use the word "pregnancy" on the air. The decade was at once sexy and innocent, unruly and restrained, contented and distressing. And with the approach of the sixties and the sexual revolution, feminist movement, and the civil rights battle, the push and pull of the late fifties' irreconcilable ideas and emotions was more palpable.

The era's contradictions showed themselves in the torso-tossing world of striptease. At times it seemed Americans lost interest in burlesque and stripping. Television reigned as the entertainment of choice. While in 1948 only 2 percent of Americans owned a TV, by 1960 almost 90 percent did and on average watched roughly five hours a day.[1] Americans went to the movies, nightclubs, and theaters much less often; it was easier just to cuddle up on the couch in front of the television. Approximations of nudity also became more common. The bikini's arrival poolside and at the shore meant more of a woman could be ogled in public than ever before. And *Playboy* and the other men's magazines laid out even more tantalizing pulchritude that could be enjoyed in the privacy of one's home. Yet none of this tolled the death knell for striptease. The tassel-twirling moves of exotic dancers were still the heart of many clubs, carnival shows, and Las Vegas. Of course, to counter all the competing forces, the old bump 'n' grind was getting a cheeky makeover.

Once again a Minsky adjusted the strip. After a protracted battle with the city government, Harold Minsky closed the Adams Theater in Newark, New Jersey and moved to Las Vegas. Minsky had staged performances there before, but the desert oasis now became his permanent home. Major Riddle, the new owner of the Dunes Hotel, was redesigning the property with an Arabian Nights theme. When Riddle finished, the sprawling hotel, with more than two hundred rooms and a shopping center, was topped off with a giant neon sultan and harem girl. The centerpiece of the main building was the Arabian Room, a vast restaurant with a sixty-five-by-thirty-five-foot stage and Broadway-caliber equipment. Here Harold Minsky staged *Minsky Goes to Paris*, a show that tossed aside the twisting, shaking blur of the peel for an exhibit of topless showgirls who merely paraded across the stage. The showgirls strut across the stage in costumery that altogether comprised "three hundred pounds of rhinestones, two miles of nylon, two bushels of sequins, [and] 1,650,000 pieces of mirror glass."[2]

Of the change from dancing to sashaying across stage, Minsky said, "Well, it's a pretty good job. You don't have to really do anything. You have to be pretty and have a good figure. And you have to have good breasts—

they don't have to be big, but you know, attractive, because they're bare-breasted in the show. We never show total nudity though—I think something should be left to the imagination."3

Good looks were key and in a tone reminiscent of Florenz Ziegfeld and Earl Carroll, Minsky was inordinately particular in choosing his beauties. The ideal Minsky girl needed to have legs "like tapered rose stems and her ankles sufficiently narrow so that an ordinary man's hand can completely close around them," Harold told one reporter after fully detailing the appropriate measurements, hair color, and complexion of a Minsky girl.4 "She should have small feet, but not so small they look like clubs. . . . Her eyes must be large, her lips full and she must have a chin, so she doesn't resemble an egg. Her neck should be long and swan-like, her shoulders narrow, but never drooping, and her back cut like a figure eight vertically cut in half." With such a spectacle of the female form, the revue, the first topless show in Las Vegas, became a huge sensation and ran for four-and-a-half years. The Tropicana, New Frontier, and the Stardust all quickly mimicked the Minsky formula. Of the show's popularity, Minsky said, "We have something people can't get on television."

Several years later, a reporter reflected on what made Minsky a hit. "Two things made Minsky's a success—the decision to switch from overblown, Lillian Russell types to younger, slimmer girls; and an emphasis on what Harold Minsky refers to as a 'more modern approach.' Others, particularly *Variety* editor Sime Silverman, would call it dirty."5

The other change in striptease owed its garter belt to El Rancho's favorite peeler, Lili St. Cyr. As dancer Jessica Rogers told *Striptease: The Untold History of the Girlie Show* author Rachel Shteir, "They no longer holler 'take it off,' they want to see why you take it off."6 In Las Vegas, the striptease dancers followed Lili's lead and began developing story-telling gimmicks with scenes that more naturally led them to disrobe. Sharon Knight, a protégé of Lili's who was a virtual look-alike, performed a routine called "The Tramp." The routine began with Sharon portraying a tattered vagabond asleep on a park bench. Through her dance she showed the tramp's dreams of being a rich young lady in silk gowns, furs, and jewels.7 The transition from tramp to refined lady back to tramp allowed Knight to dress and undress several times.

"The stripper who gets ahead is the one who knows how to bring her personality across the footlights, not the one who simply removes more articles of clothing than her competitors," explained Harold Minsky.[8] "Girls become star strippers because they know how to act better, conduct themselves better on stage, and make every man watching her believe, during the time she's in the spotlight, that she's performing exclusively for him."

Minsky's Vegas showgirls may have held a "pretty good job," but during the fifties fewer and fewer earned star status. Burlesque queens in the vein of Gypsy Rose Lee, Ann Corio, and Sally Rand vanished. "The form of celebrity glamour created by Hollywood made achieving legitimacy difficult for many strippers, whose franker sexuality was antithetical to it,"[9] wrote Rachel Shteir. All of this made it increasingly difficult for burlesque dancers to star in supper clubs, movies, and Broadway shows.

With her tall, slender figure, movie-star face, high-end production numbers, and elegant spin on the dirtier business of sex, Lili ruled as one of the last real queens of burlesque. "Lili does the best production numbers I ever saw—a tremendous job," Harold Minsky told *Sir Knight* magazine.[10] Besides her bubble bath bit, she continued to play the female sirens of history—Cleopatra, Aphrodite, and Salome—and found herself drawn to these characters because they "used their charms and their talents to leave a mark on the world, to carve a niche that belonged to them."[11] She now also performed a "Geisha Fantasy," a naughtier version of Cinderella, and a matador routine. Each told a story. In her matador routine, Lili, dressed as a Spanish lady, appeared on a stage designed to look like an apartment. On the wall of her bedroom hung a poster of a matador. Through her movements, the audience understood she was in love with the handsome bullfighter, but that he did not return her affection. To win him over, she tempted him with a suggestive dance, promised to caress him, undressed, and ultimately offered him her body. At the end of her performance, she was so taken with her own attempts to win him over that she believed her matador was there making love to her.

Whether they rushed the stage in a haze of motion or presented a mini-play like Lili, striptease dancers held an ambiguous position in American life. To some, they were artists and knowledgeable sexperts; to others, they were deviants and gold diggers. They were both the quintessence and aberration of femininity. Millions who never saw Lili and her rivals held views about them due to the new and intense attention that the media paid to public figures' personal lives. The strongest force in this trend was Robert Harrison and his salacious gossip magazine *Confidential*.

Raised by her grandmother and step-grand-father, Alice and Ben Klarquist, Lili believed they were her parents until she was in her early teens. Alice, in particular, molded Lili into an independent and adventure-loving woman.

{Collection of Ellie Hiatt}

Initially, Idella Peseau seemed to embrace the fun-loving, free-wheeling attitude of the Roaring Twenties. She gave up Lili, her eldest child, to her mother and went on to have four other children with two other men. Any trace of that young Idella was long gone by the time Lili spent any significant time with her.

{Collection of Ellie Hiatt}

Lili and her mother had an incredibly tumultuous relationship. But the photos of her famous daughter that lined the walls above the piano indicate Idella was proud of Lili.

{Collection of Ellie Hiatt}

Lili was born Marie Frances Van Schaack on June 3, 1917. When she became Lili St. Cyr she told reporters her name was Willis Marie Van Schaack. Apparently the Willis was for her uncle William, but her birth certificate lists her middle name as Frances, the feminine version of her two grandfathers' names–Frank Van Schaack and Cedric Francis Peseau.

{Collection of Ellie Hiatt}

SUMMER THIRTY - SIX

Born in Minneapolis, Lili and her family moved around for several years before settling in Pasadena, California. She attended Eagle Rock High School but did not graduate.

{Collection of Eagle Rock Junior/Senior High School}

Lili left high school early to marry motorcycle racer Cordy Milne. She later admitted she used his proposal as a way to escape Pasadena, California. The two wed in England in front of a throng of racing fans on July 25, 1936. The two split within months.

{Collection of John Chaplin}

Lili began performing at the Florentine Gardens under her given name, Marie Van Schaack, in 1940. She quickly earned the attention of celebrities like Orson Welles and Anthony Quinn.

{*Collection of Genevieve Kop*}

Lili and her younger sister Idella Ruth Blackadder, who performed as Barbara Moffett, worked together at the Florentine Gardens. When Barbara married toy tycoon Louis Marx, he forbade her from having anything to do with her stripteasing sister.

{*Collection of Genevieve Kop*}

In the early Forties, Lili married Florentine Gardens head waiter Dick Hubert. The marriage did not last and Lili later admitted, "what should have been a brief, weekend affair had foolishly been spread out over a year–a year that couldn't stand up with what we had to offer."

{*Collection of Ellie Hiatt*}

Lili reigned supreme in Montreal. There she met Jimmy Orlando, a Montreal nightclub owner and retired hockey player with the Detroit Red Wings. The two carried on an affair for several years during the late Forties. They reconnected over fifteen years later.

{*Collection of Doris Quinn Godfrey*}

Lili married Italian Armando Orsini in 1950 and honeymooned in Rome. The two divorced in 1954 but remained friendly until Lili's death. She wrote later that he was the best of her husbands and "the one I regretted losing the most." *{Collection of Armando Orsini}*

Lili's routines always told a story, often with themes from history, literature, and even religion. She said she tried to create scenes where it was normal for her to undress. "I created characters of women who were torn by passion and sexual desire," she wrote.

{**Movie Star News**}

Lili routines were mini plays, and she loved playing sirens like Cleopatra and Salome. However, it was her bathtub routine in which she took a bubble bath on stage for which she was most famous.

{Bruno Bernard.
Courtesy Bernard of Hollywood Pub.}

In 1951, Lili performed her bubble bath routine at the swanky L.A. nightclub Ciro's and landed in legal hot water. Famous celebrity attorney Jerry Giesler defended Lili using her net bra and panties to prove she had remained scantily clad throughout her performance. She was cleared of all charges, and the trial gave a huge boost to her career.

{Corbis}

After her arrest and trial, Lili appeared in several short burlesque movies and feature films. The burlesque shorts, like the photos from this Irving Klaw short, were filmed recreations of her stage act. She didn't like making movies and admitted she only did it for the paycheck.

{*Movie Star News*}

Lili's 1951 arrest and trial were not her first run-ins with the law. In December 1947, she was arrested at the Follies Theater in Los Angeles over a performance about the lonely wife of a sultan who commits adultery with a slave. After a two-day hearing, she received a $350 fine. The mug shot first surfaced publicly in a Fifties tabloid called *Confidential*.

The word most often used to describe Lili was classy. This in part came from her natural talent as a dancer. This series of photos by Bruno Bernard captured the grace of her movements.

{Bruno Bernard. Courtesy Bernard of Hollywood Pub.}

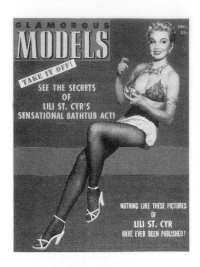

Lili was regularly featured in the men's magazines of the era. In the beginning, it was primarily photo spreads. As she became more famous, she also penned articles about life as a stripper and the kind of men she liked.   {*Collection of Bob Bethia*}

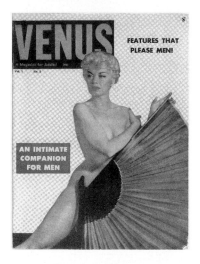

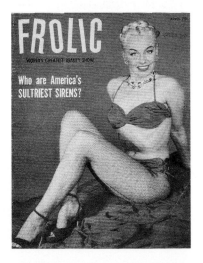

Despite a rocky engagement, Lili and Ted Jordan wed at El Rancho hotel in Las Vegas in February 1955. It was her fifth marriage and the first time she wore a wedding dress. However, the cake, designed to look like an atomic mushroom cloud, was more telling of their relationship. The two divorced in 1958. {*The Las Vegas News Bureau*}

Lili married her sixth and last husband, special effects technician Joe Zomar, in 1959. At first, Lili put her career on the back burner and planned to settle down. But the relationship did not last and the two divorced in 1964, with Lili telling the judge that Joe was often drunk and mean to her.

{Collection of Gloria Zomar}

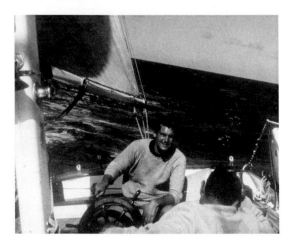

Long fascinated with Lili, when Donald Markick returned from a sailing trip to Hawaii the two met and were romantically involved until her death. Their relationship lasted over thirty years—far longer than any of her marriages—but the two never wed.

{Collection of the Markick Family}

In the years before *Confidential* appeared in 1952, Hollywood studios controlled what writers reported about its stars through its power to give journalists credentials and access. As *Hollywood at Sunset* author Charles Higham wrote, for years the "fan magazines carefully sustained the public illusion of Hollywood, since the hard-drinking, whoring reality would scarcely have interested a naïve mass audience."[12] But after watching the Kefauver hearings on TV and noting the public's fascination with sex and scandal, Harrison realized the magazines were wrong. He decided to work around the Hollywood system and served up a regular dose of tittle-tattle. Using private investigators, paid sources, and sometimes even unethical methods, *Confidential* aired out Hollywood's dirty laundry with the tag line "tells the facts and names the names." Its lurid reports of promiscuity, affairs, and drunken misadventures pushed its circulation to 4.6 million by the mid-fifties. Readers of dozens of copycat magazines with titles like *Exposed, Hush-Hush, The Lowdown, Top Secret,* and *Whisper* boosted gossip tabloid circulation overall to 15 million a month.[13]

The hip-shaking world of a striptease dancer was both a perfect and a popular topic for the innuendo-laden, pulpy prose of *Confidential* and its smudgy-ink spawn. "A popular tale was that of the powerful man brought down by the gold digger," wrote Rachel Shteir in *Striptease.*[14] "This tale appealed to a public hungry for scapegoats and exposes." The magazines also focused on what many considered to be the abnormal behaviors of a stripper's personal life. Ann Corio, a burlesque queen who reigned during the thirties and forties, made the tabloids when a wiretap a jealous wife paid a detective to place on her phone was discovered. Candy Barr, a dancer who began performing in the early fifties in Dallas, was also great fodder for the scandal rages, particularly after her arrest for marijuana possession. Another magazine detailed a "Roman orgy" that several of the lesser-known dancers indulged in.[15] And it was *Confidential* magazine that first outed to the public Lili's earlier suicide attempts and first published the mug shot from her 1948 arrest for indecent exposure.[16]

By 1957, *Confidential* had annoyed a critical mass of powerful people, leading to a concerted effort to shut the magazine down. That spring, California Attorney General Edmund Brown brought various employees of the magazine to trial on a litany of charges, including libel and conspiracy to commit libel. The six-week trial ended in a hung jury, but a settlement eventually caused the magazine's economic downfall. By 1958,

Harrison had sold *Confidential*. "The irony was that despite its scurrility and underhandedness . . . most of the pieces printed in *Confidential* were true — or at least came with full verification," wrote author Neal Gabler in his comprehensive look at the magazine's trial for *Vanity Fair*.[17] "Harrison spent more than one hundred thousand dollars a year on the prestigious New York law firm Becker, Ross, and Stone to vet each story, and contrary to [another editor's] assertion, Harrison never overruled his attorney in matters of libel, only in matters of taste."

The rag that author Tom Wolfe once called "the most scandalous scandal magazine in the history of the world,"[18] disappeared, but it left a tawdry tattoo on the culture. For striptease dancers, it amplified their insalubrious image. For celebrities and other public figures, it permanently opened the door for all to view their personal lives, peccadilloes and all. *Confidential* may have fallen by the wayside, but it changed the way magazines reported on public figures and launched an entire industry dedicated to exposing celebrity secrets.

But nowhere was the era's ambivalent attitude toward striptease more apparent than in Hollywood. Burlesque and the cinema had long pilfered from each other. In the 1929 film *The Blue Angel*, Marlene Dietrich tipped a hat to the take-off, playing a flamboyant cabaret singer who appears on screen in black stockings and garters, her groin highlighted with lace. In 1946, Rita Hayworth peeled off long, black gloves in *Gilda's* bump-and-grind dance number. In 1959, Jayne Mansfield squeezed into a sheer dress with sequins sewn over strategic places for *Too Hot to Handle*. "Indeed, by the end of the Fifties, Hollywood portrayed striptease as being both a morally corrupting force and a daily part of show business life," wrote Rachel Shteir.[19]

Burlesque just as often dipped an elbow-length gloved hand into the mine of Hollywood material. In the forties, Alice Jewell traded in on the popularity of *Gone With the Wind* and performed as the "Scarlett O'Hara of Burlesque." Throughout the fifties, Dixie Evans made a career out of mimicking Marilyn Monroe. Known as the "Marilyn Monroe" of burlesque, she portrayed Monroe on the casting couch and, using a dummy, with husband Joe DiMaggio. And inspired by Grace Kelly's wedding to Prince Rainier, Lili turned her usual bedroom scene into a "Wedding in Monaco."

The irony of the seemingly easy back-and-forth appropriation between burlesque and Hollywood is that very few stripteasers made the transition to movies or television. The men of burlesque, like Bud Abbott and Lou Costello, Phil Silvers, and Jackie Gleason, jumped to the more respectable and higher-paying realm of television and movies. But the women of burlesque rarely managed to parade off the runway into more mainstream media. Part of the reason laid in the barriers to the sexual spectacle of the striptease dancer posed by the Hays office and local censors. When Gypsy Rose Lee's book *The G-String Murders* became the movie *Lady of Burlesque*, actress Barbara Stanwyck portrayed the stripper; an actress as burlesque star was more acceptable than the real thing. Success was rare even when the dancer shed her stripteasing career and took a role that didn't involve the bump 'n' grind. Gypsy Rose Lee appeared in several films, but according to Morton Minsky, studio executives "were terrified that her frank and charming sexuality would come across so they changed her name back to her maiden name [Louise Hovick] and made her wear costumes that covered her from her ankles to her neck."[20] Partly, strippers failed to become movie stars because the Hays office and local censors forbade them to perform their specialties in the family-oriented cinema of the day. And partly, strippers stayed in their demimonde because of the public's contradictory attitudes toward them. They were alluring and yet repellent. They were at once enticing and scary, desirable and repugnant. Strippers had no one place in the public mind or the social order, so Hollywood hesitated to take a chance. It was often just easier to ignore her.

However, Hollywood did not totally ignore Lili St. Cyr. Unlike Gypsy, Lili most often portrayed a striptease dancer, mostly in short "novelty" roles. Her inclusion regularly caused problems with the censors, but her glamorous, ladylike spin on the strip put the public at ease and helped compensate for the more tawdry aspects of sex. Her star status helped reel in both news coverage and audiences. In 1958, she starred as a striptease dancer in the film version of Norman Mailer's *The Naked and the Dead* and the Roger Corman flick *I, Mobster.*

Mailer's war novel shocked America in 1948 for its rough language, blunt sexuality, graphic violence, and general pessimism. When angry, its characters said "Fug!" and Aunt Sallies everywhere ran for cover. Rights to the book changed hands several times and it took years for the movie to be made. Directed by Raoul Walsh, the movie slightly brightened the ending and added the role of Jersey Lily, a stripper played by Lili St. Cyr. "There wasn't really anything in the script at the time that had to do with a striptease," explained Paul Gregory, one of the film's producers.[21] "[Lili] was the rage of the moment and Raoul Walsh was intent on having her in the film. They seemed to want her to buck up the word naked in *The Naked and The Dead*. I didn't want a trampy stripper, so she fit the bill perfectly. She was very classy and built like a Venus."

According to Gregory, Lili caused quite a stir on the set. People from all over the studio came to get a peek at the famous peeler, and Gregory even claimed that Walsh's glass eye popped out due to the enthusiasm with which he watched her scenes. The combination of Mailer's explicit and striking book and Lili St. Cyr's scandalous undulations should have been explosive, but the unimpressed Hays office would not approve "scenes of obscene, lewd, and lascivious spectators."[22] The office believed Lili's "strip tease number [was] unacceptable"[23] and her dialog too salacious. Many of Lili's scenes were sloughed off onto the cutting room floor. Despite her limited role, the film's publicists plastered her lissome figure over most of the film's posters and marketing materials.

The film was still a critical flop, largely due to the forced whitewashing by the Hays office. One critic wrote, "Producer Paul Gregory has managed to clean up *The Naked and the Dead* for the screen so well that all that remains is the title. Norman Mailer's World War II novel emerges as a routine movie of the war . . . whose characters are close to caricatures."[24] The *New York Times* called it a "surface recounting" of Mailer's book.[25] The *Washington Post* thought "the angry vitality of the book is totally vitiated with a patly white-washed ending."[26] And *Variety* wrote, "It catches neither the spirit nor the intent of the original yarn . . . and becomes just another war picture."[27]

I, Mobster, a film in which Lili starred as herself, was equally forgettable. The crime drama was produced by Roger Corman, a filmmaker who has been called everything from the King of the Bs to the Pope of Pop Cinema. Corman mastered the low budget exploitation film by understanding that "the whole idea was to tell an interesting, visually entertaining story that would draw young people to the drive-ins and hardtop cinemas, and not take yourself too seriously along the way."[28] Seeming to take a lesson from burlesque, he made films "about something wild with a great deal of action, a little sex, and possibly some sort of strange gimmick," Corman explained in his memoir *How I Made a Hundred Movies in Hollywood and Never Lost a Dime*.[29]

Once again, Lili provided the little bit of sex. Corman filmed her scene for *I, Mobster*, taken directly from her bubble bath act, three times. "In the first version Lili had a small towel draped around her waist," reported UPI.[30] "The second time the towel covered her from shoulders to hips. On the third trip the second towel was missing." In the third take, Lili made "movieland history . . . when she appeared in a scene for a new picture in the altogether—that is, absolutely nude."[31] Lili, who confessed she'd never been entirely nude for an audience before, told one reporter, "I don't know what they'll do with the shots except show them to their friends."[32] The filmmakers knew censors would cut the sequence, but hoped it would remain in the picture for foreign audiences. And at the very least, the crew enjoyed the takes. "Electricians, grips, prop men, and carpenters crowded around the camera, hung from overhead catwalks, climbed ladders, and generally resembled the front row at Minsky's," reported UPI.[33] Lili thought the film was "second-rate" but believed it eventually became a cult classic in France because of her nude scene. "I don't know why I consented to do it," she wrote later.[34] "I didn't believe in total nudity. Roger Corman must have employed irresistible arguments."

In admitting she didn't believe in total nudity, Lili acknowledged the real power in her routines; that the imagination was more vivid, more wild, more potent than any act she performed onstage. As former showgirl and producer Helen de Cenzie told *Variety* years later, "I told Gypsy, 'Girl, be demure, be languid, do not race to the finish line. Take your gloves off slowly, make 'em scream for more. The name of this game is tease! tease! tease!'"[35] Helen and Lili knew the tease was far more compelling than the strip and this was, in part, what worried the Hays office.

Despite these roles and the short-lived crossover success they gave her, Lili still did not enjoy making movies. It was something she did only for the money. She remained realistic about her movie career, writing, "I have done many motion pictures. None of them ever made any impact though, and I'm sure Doris Day or Audrey Hepburn aren't worried about my unseating them as box office champions."[36]

The schizoid nature of the era—on the one hand bold and brassy, on the other buttoned-up and conventional—clearly confused Lili. Her doubts about her career first surfaced publicly during her engagement to Ted Jordan. But at a time when she scheduled her wedding after her last show, her promises of retirement came across as insincere. Two years into their marriage, in October 1957, Lili's misgivings received an even more public airing and the qualms she shared about her career seemed far more genuine. On *The Mike Wallace Interview*, she spoke with the yet-to-be venerable journalist about her career, marriage, and her future. She had been hesitant about appearing on the program. "I still can't figure out why Mike Wallace wants me on his show," the forty-year-old dancer told another reporter just days earlier.[37] "I'm not a crusader or anything like that. . . . I know I'm probably crazy. I'm already so nervous that it takes six sleeping pills to put me away at night. But, after all, how many chances does a girl like me get to go on TV across the nation for a half-hour? It will give me a chance to be myself."

Wallace, who previously interviewed Frank Lloyd Wright and Eleanor Roosevelt for the program, teased the interview in the show's opening saying, "Tonight we go after the story of a beautiful blonde who has made a fortune by taking off her clothes in public. . . . She's the leading strip teaser in America, Lili St. Cyr, whose uninhibited dancing is matched only by her uninhibited attitudes toward marriage, alimony, religion, and politics. . . . Let's try to find out what attitudes, what ambitions, what needs and emotions make a striptease artist."

Sporting a short, curly hairdo, Lili looked demure wearing small pearl earrings, a multistrand pearl necklace, and simple black dress. Plumes of smoke swirled around the two from the cigarettes both Wallace and Lili puffed on throughout the interview. At first, she seemed confident, telling Wallace in her high-pitched, Minnie Mouse–like voice, "I don't believe that I'm arousing any lust in the audience. I never do anything that I believe is wrong." Wallace pressed her to elaborate, saying, "Yesterday you told our reporter, 'If I do demoralize an audience, as some people might say, then I'm glad I do it.' You said, 'People need some loosening up. Most of the people in this country are too hypocritical. Underneath we're all the same,' you said. 'Only too many put on a front of being shocked by certain kinds of behavior.' What did you mean by that, Lili?" Defending herself and her profession, she responded, "Well, it's a joke to think I could demoralize anyone with this little act. If one has morals, then they can't be taken away by me or anyone else." She argued that those who made such claims did so for commercial reasons, to financially support the vice groups they ran or belonged to. "Otherwise, they would go after things that are of more importance, but more difficult . . . [like] crime," she told Wallace.

Lili even teased Wallace a little bit. When he asked if she'd ever done anything she was ashamed of, she joked, "Yes. He was so handsome I couldn't resist." But as Wallace pushed, she admitted she did not think burlesque was art and that she was not proud of what she did for a living. "I would rather be doing something else," she explained. "I must make money and it's the only thing I'm trained for. I don't know how to do anything else."

Wallace turned to Lili's marriage to Ted Jordan, which was falling apart. Gossip columnists had linked both to other lovers and they had repeatedly separated and reunited. Wallace asked about the effect her career had on her marriage. "Last night, I went to see you at the Crescendo, where you're dancing here in Hollywood, and I must say that it's a very effective, really kind of a beautiful act," he said. "And I thought to myself, I wonder how I would feel if my wife were up there, performing in that fashion, taking off her clothes in front of a bunch of people who are vaguely intoxicated. . . . How does your husband feel about this?" Lili admitted Jordan was anxious for her to stop performing, but that until recently she hadn't been in the financial position to retire. Now that she was financially able, she laughingly told Wallace, "I'll be the housewife and forget the bright lights gladly." She also admitted she didn't believe in the institution of marriage or see any need to legalize her relationships. "If you love someone and want to live with them, the moment you decide that, you're married without any law to say so," commented Lili, who then explained the reason she kept getting married was because of the culture and American laws. She also told Wallace she believed alimony was unfair and "if there were no marriage there would be no alimony and no divorce."

When Wallace asked if she would have children when she quit, Lili said she had no intentions of raising a family. "I think the world is overpopulated as it is," she said. Wallace pressed saying, "Every psychologist since Freud has said that childbearing is as important to a normal woman as love and marriage. You don't feel the least bit unfulfilled or incomplete without a child of your own?" The blonde dancer said no, but if she did she would adopt and that she believed "quite often women who have no other interest certainly need children."

Her smile faded, though, as Wallace continued to pursue her attitudes on the entertainment world. "I gather from what you say that you don't like show business really at all," remarked Wallace. "Well, it's a false sort of business," Lili admitted. "You're not being yourself. You're not contributing anything really . . . to anything. . . . I think doctors and nurses and people who build houses and people who work constructively contribute much more and I'd be much more proud of myself if I could do that." Looking very serious for the first time, she confessed she didn't like herself very much because of her job and that she worried about growing old and losing her beauty. She was so concerned that a year earlier, afraid of the scar, she refused surgery and had her appendix "frozen" for a fifth time. It was not until doctors promised she wouldn't have a scar that Lili let them operate.[38] Now, Wallace asked, "Do you have anything in your emotional bank or your spiritual bank, so to speak, to keep you when you have lost your beauty?" Looking down, Lili paused before saying quietly, "I don't know."[39]

After watching the program, one television critic thought Wallace "left that rather naïve . . . and simple girl dangling before the nation with her life as naked as an open wound."[40] It was a drastically different image of Lili St. Cyr, one that revealed the effects of the era's push and pull. Reflecting on the fifties, Betty Friedan wrote in *The Feminine Mystique*, "over and over women heard in voices of tradition and of Freudian sophistication they could desire no greater destiny than to glory in their own femininity." Women were encouraged to be dependent and to conform to the wishes of the men in their lives. Performing onstage, Lili found a way to glory in her femininity and conform to men's fantasy. Doing so onstage enabled her to maintain her independence and freedom offstage. As her namesake, the fictitious Diamond Lil, said, "Men is all alike. Married or single, it's the same game. *Their game.* I happen to be wise enough to play it their own way."

Most of Friedan's work explored the stifling boredom that came with the idea that "fulfillment as a woman had only one definition for American women after 1949—the housewife-mother." But she briefly acknowledged that women who rejected that notion had their own struggles. Talking to the few female editors at women's magazines, a group of women who helped put the housewife-mother on that pedestal, Friedan found they were embarrassed about being career women and wondered if they had missed out on something. One *Mademoiselle* editor told Friedan,

"The girls we bring in now as college guest editors seem almost to pity us. Because we are career women, I suppose. . . . When I remember how I worked to learn this job and loved it—were we all crazy then?"[41]

Pockets of opposition existed, but given the postwar emphasis on children and family, those who rejected motherhood clearly struggled. One study in the late fifties found most Americans believed parenthood was key to happiness. Movie stars and pinups whose sexual appeal was celebrated during the war were now pictured as happy mothers; magazines showed actress Dorothy Lamour at her son's birthday party and Joan Crawford mopping her kitchen floor. Whereas during the war, a women's sexuality was considered a powerful weapon, a bombshell, and defense against the terrors of battle, now children were viewed as such. "Parenthood was much more than a duty to posterity," wrote Elaine Tyler May in *Homeward Bound.*[42] "The joys of raising children would compensate for the thwarted expectations in other areas of their lives. For men who were frustrated at work, or women who were bored at home, and for both who were dissatisfied with the unfulfilled promise of sexual excitement, children might fill the void. . . . [In having children] they also demonstrated their loyalty to national goals. . . . Rather than representing a retreat into private life, procreation was one way to express civic values."

As parenthood reached mythological heights, those who remained childless were considered deviant and selfish. One could not escape the notion that motherhood was the ultimate fulfillment of femininity and the source of a woman's identity. The women's magazine editors Friedan interviewed, Lili, and other women of the fifties who found a way to use their femininity to cobble together something outside of the "image of those pretty pictures of the American suburban housewife, kissing their husbands good-bye in front of the picture window"—all were often left ensnared in the same contradictions as their stay-at-home counterparts. The tension between the image and the reality corroded both.

Sex and striptease opened up a world of possibilities for Lili, a world that might not otherwise have been possible because of her background and the era in which she came of age. As Helen de Cenzie pointed out when defending burlesque, "Burlesque was not the evil, sinful influence on morality, so commonly believed. It was a door, sometimes the only door, open to aspiring comedians, dancers, musicians, acrobats—yes, and even choreographers, set designers and costumers."[43]

Moreover, watching Lili's performances from the time, one sees a woman who is powerful, graceful, and even triumphant in how she expressed her sexuality. She does not appear to be a woman ashamed of her work or conflicted by her job. But if she truly was herself during her interview with Mike Wallace, he revealed the clash between her onstage and offstage life and the cracks in her rhinestone-covered armor.

Despite regular separations, Lili and Ted Jordan kept getting back together, but within a few months of her television interview, she and Ted broke up for good. He was clearly jealous of her success. And according to Lili, he was incredibly upset when Paul Gregory, the producer Jordan worked with on *The Caine Mutiny*, cast her, but not him, in *The Naked and the Dead*. "At our best, Ted and I tolerated each other," she wrote later.[44] "We weren't really linked to each other . . . Ted used me . . . as a sort of anchor, a life buoy."

Having left yet another man in her wake, Lili distracted herself by "playing seductresses"[45] and plunged herself into her work. Fred Carson, a stunt man who doubled for one of Lili's favorite movie stars, Victor Mature, was one of the men with whom she busied herself. But she could not find peace and once again she attempted suicide. Perhaps she was upset by a fifth failed marriage. Perhaps loneliness overcame her. Perhaps she spent too much time in Las Vegas, a city that left her feeling like a caged animal. Perhaps, as she told Mike Wallace, she was tired of stripping, afraid of losing her looks and her source of income. Perhaps, as she later claimed, it was simply an accident. Whatever the reason, on October 31, 1958, Fred Carson found her stretched out on the floor of her El Rancho bungalow in a blue nightgown and pink robe, unconscious after taking an overdose of sleeping pills. The police rushed her to the hospital, where doctors pumped her stomach.[46] The incident made headlines in newspapers around the country, and later she said she was more embarrassed by it than anything else.

Hush-Hush, a magazine similar to *Confidential*, wrote, "The fact is that under the glitter and glamour, this $5,000-a-week star, who brought the exotic art of stripping to an astronomical level, is a frustrated and unhappy woman whose life is far more serious than her bumps and grinds would indicate." And in the popular psychological lingo of the day, the magazine speculated that Lili suffered a "mother complex. Perhaps because she still recollects her own unhappy childhood, she wants to 'mother' and 'baby' every man she meets. She tries too hard to please—and in the end they get tired of it and walk out. . . . Under the veneer is a nice girl who is lonely, frightened, and very unsure of herself."[47]

But it wasn't Ted Jordan who walked out. Two and a half weeks after her suicide attempt, Lili filed for divorce from Jordan on the grounds of mental cruelty. She asked the judge in Reno for sealed court orders and a private hearing. Years later, she perfectly summed up the effect the tensions of the fifties had on her marriages when she said she "was never destined to be a 'respectable' married woman. You have the choice between being a respectable woman and a career woman. I needed to have a career and that came first in my life. But the world seemed to demand of me that I also have a spouse."[48]

Lili and Ted's marriage had begun under the cloud of conflict between career and family. In the end, her career won out. She spent the first half of 1959 performing around the country in clubs like Chicago's Black Orchid and Reno's Mapes Skyroom, waiting for her divorce to go through. The papers regularly linked her with men like singer Vic Damone, special-effects technician Joe Zomar, and even Ted Jordan once again. But in July 1959, her divorce from Jordan was finalized. At decade's end, the tension between the romanticized American life and the reality was about to collide in American culture, the world of burlesque, and Lili's own life.

8.

The Lust Frontier

Striptease will become irrelevant when naked entertainment becomes ubiquitous.

— Marshall McLuhan

The dance toward the cultural upheaval of the sixties started slowly. Bit by bit, Americans discarded the remnants of the fifties ideal and gave in to the frenzy of change that fully took hold after the middle of the decade. But the harbingers of the changes that melded into the national mind-set were clear even earlier.

An innocuous little white pill suggested the most powerful indication of the changes at hand. In her 1920 book *Woman and the New Race*, birth control crusader Margaret Sanger wrote that, "No woman can call herself free who does not own and control her own body. No woman can call herself free until she can choose consciously whether she will or will not be a mother."[1] Throughout her life Sanger worked to make that choice a reality. She passed out pamphlets on birth control, smuggled diaphragms into the United States, and, in the fifties, sponsored the development of an oral contraceptive. Sanger convinced a wealthy female friend committed to the cause to bankroll a team of doctors to develop such a contraceptive. By 1954, the doctors who referred to the drug as "the Pill" began human trials. In 1957, the Food and Drug Administration (FDA) authorized its use for specific medical ailments such as menstrual disorders. Sanctioned as a contraceptive device in May 1960, 2.3 million women took the Pill by the end of 1963 and more than 12 million used it by 1967. By 1970, 60 percent of married and unmarried women used birth control—the Pill, an intrauterine device, or sterilization—and birthrates fell lower than their Depression rates.[2]

"It's easy to forget how truly liberating the Pill seemed to be in 1960," reflected *Ladies Home Journal* in 1990. "Nothing else in this century—perhaps not even winning the right to vote—made such an immediate difference in women's lives."[3] The Pill completely altered the focus from sex for procreation to sex for pleasure. As *Mademoiselle* argued a few years later, "surely, nowadays, it is both aesthetically and psychologically preferable for a girl who engages in sex to do so wholeheartedly, joyously, responsibly, and responsively."[4] And with that shift, with control over childbearing, women took a giant leap forward in becoming sexually equal with men. As country music star Loretta Lynn sang in 1973:

> For several years I've stayed at home,
> While you had all the fun,
> And every year that came by, another baby come
> There's gonna be some changes made right here on nursery
>   hill
> You've set this chicken your last time, 'cause now I've got
>   the Pill.[5]

The Pill spurred sexual frankness and experimentation. Women could think seriously about careers now that they had the option of postponing childbirth. Once women felt like they were in charge of their own bodies, they started to question authority and it sparked the feminist and pro-choice movements.

The Pill changed things both in the workplace and at home, where it altered the relationship between husbands and wives. "Without a constant round of small children competing for their attention, many couples were forced to reexamine their own relationships more carefully," wrote *Marriage, a History* author Stephanie Coontz.[6] "In addition, the growing number of childless marriages weakened the connection between marriage and parenthood, eroding some of the traditional justifications for elevating marriage over all other relationships."

At the same time, a chorus of protests sang out in response to all of this change. As *Where the Girls Are* author Susan Douglas explained, "In the early 1960s, the voices of the schoolmarm, the priest, the advice columnist, and Mom insisted, 'Nice girls don't.' But another voice began to whisper, 'Oh yes they do—and they like it, too.'" Douglas argued that the "double standard exerted a powerful hold . . . [but] the seeds of doubt and eventual rebellion were planted, and they grew rather quickly."[7]

The nation's entertainment machine led the revolt. Foreign films like 1960's *La Dolce Vita*, in which the stunningly beautiful Anita Ekberg splashes around in Rome's Trevi fountain, embraced sexuality and were incredibly popular with Stateside audiences. That same year, *The Immoral Mr. Teas*, an exploitation film about a man who sees women undressing everywhere, produced by burlesque impresario Pete de Cenzie, became a cult classic hit. The Hays Office all but lost its sway over Hollywood, which led to American movies featuring more adult themes. Billy Wilder's *The Apartment*, the story of a man (Jack Lemmon) who climbs the corporate ladder by lending his apartment to his boss for trysts with his mistress (Shirley MacLaine), won the Oscar for Best Picture in 1961. The same year, the awards for best supporting actress—Shirley Jones in *Elmer Gantry*—and best actress—Elizabeth Taylor in *Butterfield 8*—went to women who portrayed prostitutes. In the next few years, *Lolita*, the film version of Vladimir Nabokov's novel about an older man and his adolescent love interest; *Tom Jones*, a bawdy British comedy; and a spate of other movies fraught with naughtier themes all made a splash on the big screen. American movies also included a new genre Douglas called pregnancy melodramas. In films like *A Summer Place* (1959), *Susan Slade* (1961), and *Splendor in the Grass* (1961), girls who enjoyed premarital sex and ended up pregnant got the boy, instead of the usual comeuppance. According to these movies, it wasn't sex that was bad, but rather the older generation's hypocrisy about it.

On the radio, the girl group music of the era doo-wopped, belted out, and sang sweet serenades that highlighted the era's burgeoning changes and reflected the tension between the old and new attitudes. In syrupy ballads and upbeat pop hits, groups like The Shirelles and The Supremes sang about the pull between self-control and indulgence, between "nice girls don't" and "yes they do." Through their songs, the girl groups gave voice to these conflicting desires and allowed women to try on the different roles. Did women want to be devoted girlfriends, as in "My Guy" or "I Will Follow Him," or sexually liberated, as in "It's in His Kiss" — or something else altogether?[8]

Shelves groaned under the weight of sexually explicit books like the novel *Lady Chatterley's Lover* and Helen Gurley Brown's nonfiction tome, *Sex and the Single Girl*, topping best-seller lists. And both men and women flipped excitedly through *Esquire* to read Gloria Steinem's "The Moral Disarmament of Betty Coed," an article which indicated college girls weren't just hitting the books, and they weren't ashamed of premarital sex. More important, they didn't believe that their sexual predilections were anyone else's business. One graduate student, seeming to repeat an attitude of Lili's, told Steinem, "Lovemaking can be good outside marriage and bad in marriage just as easily as the other way around. Sex is neutral like money. It's the way you use it that counts."[9] Whether by pen, radio, or big screen, the doyennes and titans of the mass media embraced and furthered the cultural revolution.

As the entertainment world canoodled with more open sexuality, the hootchie-cootchie world of striptease was bound to change. Burlesque was shedding its last net bra, as theaters around the country went out of business. In 1958, the Denver Victory Theater closed. In 1959, the Gayety Columbus shut its doors. And in 1960, Harold Minsky remarked that "there are only twelve cities in the country that have burlesque theaters: Boston, Philadelphia, Baltimore, Cleveland, Toledo, Buffalo, St. Louis, Chicago, Indianapolis, Seattle, and Los Angeles. Other cities advertise burlesque, but when you get to the theater, you find out they're running girlie movies . . . When Minsky's was in its heyday, there must have been fifty or sixty theaters scattered around the country."[10]

The year after Minsky mourned the fading burlesque scene, Seattle's Rivoli closed and a fire destroyed the legendary Old Howard in Boston. As the sixties ground on, it seemed burlesque was a dying entertainment. "When the theatres started to close, shows were being cut, and badly," singer and acrobatic dancer Peter "Sonny" Thomas told *Burlesque: Legendary Stars of the Stage* author Jane Briggeman.[11] "First went the lines of girls and the choreographer, naturally. Then the bands began to shrink in size. Finally, there were no bands, just taped music. Footlights that burned out were not replaced. Then the new theatre operators wanted girls working totally nude more and more. Comics and straight men disappeared, as did vaudeville acts and specialty numbers. Little by little, better feature women refused to work the remaining burlesque circuit and concentrated more on nightclubs."

But while theaters closed, some elements of burlesque found new homes. Many of television's top comedians from the day cut their teeth on the burlesque stage; Phil Silvers, the Marx Brothers, and Laurel and Hardy all learned their trade working the circuit. Variety shows like *Hee Haw*, *Rowan & Martin's Laugh-In*, and *The Carol Burnett Show* owed their riotous slapstick, rapid-fire spoofs, and bawdy one-liners, in part, to burlesque. A few lines in many sketches came from old burlesque skits and, occasionally, audiences first heard entire routines on a burly stage; Abbott and Costello polished their famous "Who's on First" routine there.

Unwelcome in the family-friendly world of television, many of burlesque's strippers retired from dancing and moved on to other careers. Betty "the Ball of Fire" Rowland opened a bar in Santa Monica. Val de Val, who performed in the Ziegfeld Follies and several burlesque shows in the forties and fifties, taught painting at a Michigan community college. Zorita, known for her dance with a live snake, opened a nightclub in Miami Beach.

Other striptease stars flicked a hip in a nostalgic homage to burlesque's version of the tease. In the spring of 1959, the musical *Gypsy*, based on the life of Gypsy Rose Lee, opened on Broadway. With music by Jule Styne and Stephen Sondheim, choreography by Jerome Robbins, and a star-studded cast that included Ethel Merman, *Gypsy* took off and earned millions. Bolstered by the show's success, stripper Ann Corio opened up an off-Broadway revue called *This Was Burlesque* in the spring of 1962. Corio's show ran for over one thousand performances, eventually moved to Broadway, and then toured the country. A year later, *Burlesque on Parade*, starring Blaze Starr, a dancer known for her relationship with Louisiana governor Earl Long, followed.

The nostalgic nod to burlesque wasn't a smash hit with everyone. "The show is a literal museum piece and just about as musty," declared the *New York Times* critic after taking in *Burlesque on Parade*.[12] "It makes pertinent a view that if burlesque had not been cut short by [Mayor LaGuardia] . . . it would have long since died of old age. Sex, under the influence of foreign films and uptown theater, has outstripped the strippers."

Striptease dancers also faced competition from Hugh Hefner, whose Playboy Clubs started heating up the nightlife scene. In February 1960, Hefner opened the first club, which *Variety* called "Disneyland for adults," in Chicago. The clubs served up food, alcohol, music, and Bunnies— women dressed in bright-colored, satin costumes that showed off their legs, exaggerated their hips and breasts, and cinched in their waists. The ensemble, topped off by bunny ears and finished with a puffy white tail, created an erotic atmosphere without the women ever removing a stitch of clothing. The clubs borrowed the "look but don't touch" appeal of striptease while shedding the tawdry reputation of the burlesque clubs. The combination succeeded and, by the end of the decade, almost a million clubs had sprung up around the world.

Of course, striptease dancers were hardly going to release their satin-gloved hold on sex. And proving audiences still wanted to watch them drop that glove, several reports indicated a shortage of trained dancers. The American Guild of Variety Artists (AGVA) in Chicago told *Variety* they received eight to ten calls a day from club operators looking for good strippers. And East Coast agents Lou Miller and Dave Cohn entertained so many requests they promised to turn every woman into a blonde bombshell.

The demand continued, but to compete with the increased availability of nudity elsewhere, a new breed of stripper slowly ground her way onstage. Topless dancing, complete nudity, and pole dancing had yet to arrive, but now stripping had much less tease. Minsky lamented the changes in the girls, saying, "The ones who work around the theaters that are left today have funny names—Candy Barr, Penny Cillin, and . . . Norma Vincent Peel are only three—but they're much less serious about their sexiness. . . . The girls aren't the kind we used to get at Minsky's. With few exceptions, we had girls who were serious about getting ahead in show business. . . . And they had to have some real talent. . . . Today, if a manager of a burlesque show sees a waitress or a cashier in a store with a whistle-drawing figure, he'll sign her up as a stripper. It doesn't matter if she's got a walk like a hippopotamus. If things shake when she walks, she'll do."[13]

Jennie Lee, a dancer who retired at the end of the decade to open Exotic World, a strippers' hall of fame and museum, agreed. "Stripping is . . . more than boobs and bottoms," she said.[14] "A good stripper has to master the art of the tease. She has to have a well-planned act that leaves the audience calling for 'more' without becoming crude or vulgar."

San Francisco Chronicle columnist John L. Wasserman held a similar opinion and thought Lili remained a success because she had "personal dignity . . . quite absent in the younger generation of ecdysiasts and their less ceremonious counterparts, the topless dancers. The reason for this . . . is that when . . . [she] began working . . . both ends of the word 'strip-tease' meant something. Today, only the former is operative. And the key component, the tease, required some class, some thought, some original-ity. Artful disrobing involves style; taking off your clothes does not."[15]

Burlesque faded and the style of striptease changed, but the demand for, and interest, in the strip held strong. In fact, as a reporter for *The Gent* magazine pointed out, "the elements that made burlesque so appeal-ing of old are more widely available to the public today than they ever were in its heyday."[16] The Pink Pussycat College of Striptease in Los Angeles gave a boost to aspiring dancers, housewives looking to spice things up at home, and everyone in between. Sally Marr, comedian Lenny Bruce's mother, taught the school's ten-session curriculum, which included courses like "The History and Theory of the Striptease," "The Psychology of Inhibition," and "Dynamic Mammary, Navel, and Pelvis Rotation." Dallas nightclub proprietor Barney Weinstein also ran a school for strippers, referred to locally as Strip-Tease University.[17] Stanley Borden's LP *Music to Strip By*, which came with a G-string attached to each album, helped striptease become even more ubiquitous. And lingerie couturiers claimed to be filling more and more orders of net panties and bras for the general public.[18]

Lili thought striptease's ever-expanding reach changed things for the worse. "Show business is a bore," she told columnist John L. Wasserman.[19] "And the reason burlesque is dying is because it's dull and, like vaudeville, out of style. It used to be 'forbidden,' and therefore attractive, but now nudity is so common that nobody thinks much of it."

Even though she grumbled about the monotony of show business, Lili continued performing her bubble bath routine, the same act she'd been doing for over ten years. In the fifties, when her onstage bathing really took off, the top ecdysiasts twirled their tassels in both burlesque the-aters and nightclubs. By the early sixties top performers like Lili worked primarily in clubs. She held regular and lengthy gigs at hot spots like the

Moulin Rouge in Los Angeles, the Chi-Chi in Palm Springs, and the Black Orchid in Chicago.

But even in the nightclubs things had changed. Men in black tie and women in cocktail dresses no longer crowded into banquettes and clinked martini glasses while watching a show. The legendary glamour of forties and fifties nightlife faded out—even in Hollywood. In the mid-fifties, the Florentine Gardens closed. The owner of the Mocambo died in the late fifties and the Los Angeles hot spot lost its earlier sheen. In 1958, Lili's former haunt, Ciro's, shuttered its doors because of bankruptcy.

"The inquisitive tourist can do as well . . . by curling up with an old Hollywood movie on TV—or by going to Las Vegas," reported the *New York Times* in an article bemoaning Hollywood's lost glamour.[20] All that was left of the glitzy, mink-coated nightlife in Los Angeles was the Cocoanut Grove in the Ambassador Hotel and the Moulin Rouge, a club that had taken over Earl Carroll's old space. "The entertainment [in Los Angeles] can be classified by the yardstick of nearby Las Vegas, Nev., which has become the live-entertainment center of the country," declared the *New York Times*.[21] "In the Las Vegas pattern there are three brackets of entertainers—the top-ranking big names who star in the main casino shows; the second-rank supporting acts; and the cocktail-lounge entertainers, who serve as a come-on for the casinos' more elaborate attraction. The Ambassador and the Moulin Rouge are the only regular Los Angeles showcases for performers in the top bracket."

Nightlife shifted in other cities as well. Without direct competition from nearby Las Vegas, big clubs clung to the nightlife image a little longer. Many New York hot spots, such as El Morocco and the Latin Quarter, managed through the end of the decade. The Casino Royal in Washington, D.C., kept on swinging until the early Seventies, but the go-go joints and porn shops gave the once-hopping Fourteenth Street area a more tawdry image by the mid-sixties. Philadelphia's Troc even made it to 1978, but the days when café society played after dark were slipping away, bumped by Playboy Clubs, go-go joints, discotheques with recorded music, and, of course, Las Vegas.

In the fifties, Las Vegas was a neon beacon heralding many of the changes that would follow in the rest of the country. Even then visitors left their everyday morality back home—a forecast for the city's tagline, "What happens in Vegas, stays in Vegas." In the sixties, as the rest of the country's principles caught up, Las Vegas relished its role as the bastion of the glamorous nightlife era. It would still be a few years before legitimate corporations wrenched control from the mob. It would be even a few more years before Elvis rock and rolled the swinging swagger out of the typical lounge scene. But change was on the way in Las Vegas as well.

Perhaps portending the changes, the city's welcoming light and first Strip hotel was destroyed. In June 1960, a pre-dawn fire ruined the El Rancho hotel, demolishing the main building, which housed the casino, theater, cocktail lounge, and restaurant. No one was hurt and the few staff and guests still in the building at that late hour escaped to the parking lot and watched the flames devastate the hotel. As a climax, the neon-lit tower that had greeted revelers to the city crumbled. "There was a cracking, like lightning before the main thunder of the bold, and the windmill fell down," reported the *Las Vegas Sun*.[22] "Down, down it came, its flailing arms winding crazily, a pinwheel of smoke and fire. It crashed with a roar, pointed to the north, and tumbled into the ruins of the casino."

The El Rancho windmill pointed north, but it was south on the Strip where pleasure seekers found the whirling dervish of Las Vegas' nightlife in the early sixties. South on the Strip at the Dunes, Vegas tried to stay ahead of the va-va-voom curve with Minsky's topless revue. And Lili headed south on the Strip to the Dunes after the El Rancho was destroyed, headlining for Minsky's Follies at the close of 1960. It was a gig to which she returned for a few week stint annually for several more years.

But with the number of supper clubs decreasing and the remaining clubs paring down their acts, things changed for Lili as well. Orchestrated music for her act was now infrequent. And in a June 1961 performance at the Mapes Hotel she was also called on to serve as comedian Ken Murray's "talking woman." When burlesque first began, female performers used their bodies and their voices to challenge society's ideas about women and to poke fun at the upper class. By the turn of the century women were silenced. "The power of burlesque language to call attention to society's categories and hierarchies was based on the fact that it came out of the mouths of women," wrote Robert C. Allen in *Horrible Prettiness*.[23] "As the burlesque performer's mouth became the only part of her body that did not move in the cooch dance, the shimmy, and the striptease, she literally and figuratively lost her voice. . . . Without a voice it was all the more difficult for that body to reclaim its subjectivity."

Certainly, as Allen pointed out, a woman's voice onstage commanded attention and held power. But a voiceless woman was not a powerless woman. "A woman taking off her clothes is a magic act. It really does activate some primal, elemental, universal principle," feminist commentator Camille Paglia told A&E for the cable channel's documentary *It's Burlesque*. "We look. We don't really listen. We listen to the music, but that puts us in a trance state. I really do think there's a mystique of women taking off their clothes that feminist discourse has never really caught up to. It isn't about woman degrading herself, exposing herself, becoming a piece of meat. It's something quite different. It's woman actually being elevated to goddess, which is why she must stop talking. It's beyond words. It's beyond the reach of language or logic."

By the time Lili stepped on a burlesque stage, a woman with a speaking role often appeared dim and obtuse. She was such a rare creature that the role was denoted simply as "talking woman" and her entire purpose was to bolster the comedian's performance, usually as a foil or as the butt of the joke. Before her appearance with Ken Murray, Lili never played the "talking woman" and rarely even acknowledged the audience. She preferred to maintain her distance, as either a way to increase the mysterious femme fatale image or to cope with her own incredible shyness. Now, however, if the added responsibility irked Lili, she didn't let on. She told reporters, "I think that the show will be a great challenge and a great deal of fun. I can't think of another performer that I would venture to start into this phase of show business with."[24]

In 1962, she landed another speaking role—the first movie part that actually tested her acting skills. In *Runaway Girl*, she still played a striptease dancer, but this time her character was the lead and Lili had a legitimate acting role. In the film, originally titled *Bend to the Wind*, Lili played a dancer named Edella who escapes her demanding agent by hiding out as a grape picker in a California vineyard. Edella falls in love with the vineyard owner's adopted son, played by future Tarzan actor Jock Mahoney. When Edella finally explains to him who she is and why she ran away, the character echoed a sentiment Lili herself felt: "I need[ed] a change . . . I felt a need to get away from everything connected to the life I had been living."[25]

She expanded on the attitude in the publicity materials for the movie, saying she believed most strippers are neurotic and unhappy people offstage. She declared most were from broken homes or bad marriages, were quick to develop an inferiority complex, and often felt like prostitutes, destined to live on the other side of the tracks. "They are an unhappy lot," said Lili.[26] "They feel trapped in a sordid world of their own making and can't seem to develop the imagination or energy to escape from it."

Shortly after *Runaway Girl* was released, Lili St. Cyr took the first real break in her career, working only sporadically until 1964. While Lili didn't perform in the sleazy world she described, her own frustration with the changing nightlife scene pushed her toward taking time off. She was frivolous with money and flippant in romance, but she was always serious about and dedicated to her career—even sacrificing relationships for it. As burlesque theaters closed and nightclubs economized, Lili found that not everyone else was as committed to the performance. "Back in the old days we worked in large theaters, had plenty of time to work things out, and a group of real pros to put the show together," she told columnist John L. Wasserman.[27] "But now, club owners care less for quality, everything is done more carelessly, and it is virtually impossible to be really creative. You're supposed to come into the club in the afternoon, take a look around, and then have opening night in a few hours." The experience, one she encountered repeatedly at clubs around the country, sucked the joy out of her work and left her discouraged.

Joe Zomar was born in Canada in July 1920, and at three years old came to Los Angeles with his family. After serving in the Coast Guard during World War II, he used the skills he learned in the military to begin a career as a special-effects technician. He worked on the Lana Turner film *The Postman Always Rings Twice* and helped create the rain for Gene Kelly's dance sequence in *Singin' in the Rain*. By the time he met Lili in the late fifties, the broad-shouldered and dark, curly-haired Zomar had switched to television work because of the changing studio system.[29]

It's unclear where the two met, though Joe was to tell his fourth wife Gloria that it was at one of the studios. What is clear is that Lili was smitten, thought Joe looked like actor Victor Mature, and actively pursued him. "She was the one that was most forward," said Gloria Zomar, who saw Lili perform her bubble bath routine years earlier.[30] "She told Joe, 'I'm gonna marry you.'" Lili admitted that she followed him to one of the locations he was working on for the Western TV show *Have Gun, Will Travel*.

Have Gun, Will Travel star Richard Boone encouraged his co-stars and cast to bring their families on location. Reminiscing about one trip, his wife Claire recalled that "the Squaw Valley location was especially fun. One of the special-effects guys said, 'I have a girlfriend. Can I bring her?' Dick said, 'That's all right. Bring your girlfriend; we're a big family here.' So who should show up as his girlfriend but Lili St. Cyr, the stripper. But she turned out to be adorable; we had a wonderful time with her."[31]

Clearly Joe enjoyed himself as well, and in September 1959, Lili, who was forty-two but claimed she was thirty-seven, and Joe married in Tijuana. A month later, while she worked at Bimbo's 365 in San Francisco, the two repeated the ceremony.

In the beginning of their marriage, Lili continued to perform at clubs like Bimbo's, which despite the name, was an upscale, hip nitery. The club was named for its owner, the bowler-hat-wearing Agostino Giuntoli, an Italian immigrant whose nickname was Bimbo, a take on the Italian word for boy. Bimbo's featured performers like Rosemary Clooney, Bette Midler, Mel Tormé, and Marvin Gaye. During the late fifties and early sixties, Lili regularly danced and bathed on Bimbo's stage.

When he could, Joe would go with Lili to the clubs where she performed and help her set up. Joe's sister, Helen Frazee, first met Lili during Christmas dinner. When Joe called to ask if she could come to dinner he warned his sister that Lili was a stripper, "but not that kind." When Helen did meet Lili she "acted just gorgeous. She was in a beige cashmere skirt and top and she looked absolutely gorgeous, anything but a stripper. She was a perfect lady."[32]

Helen and Lili hit it off well enough that for some time Helen worked as Lili's errand girl and seamstress. But eventually Lili decided to take a break. Previously, she remained staunch in her unwillingness to relinquish her independence and her ability to provide for herself. Perhaps she felt that since neither her real mother nor father wanted her, both of whom instead surrendered her to her grandmother, that she had only herself to depend on. Perhaps the independent example that her grandmother set or the fear of becoming trapped in an unhappy marriage like her mother left her reluctant to rely on anyone else. Whatever the reason, Lili had never counted on anyone else for support. And, except for Armando Orsini, none of her husbands had possessed the ability to take care of her. They were content to rely on her for financial and career support. In Joe Zomar, however, she had someone with a steady job. Later, she claimed she put her career on the back burner because she wanted to settle down and be at home. "I went into this romance determined that no matter what happened it would last," she wrote.[33] "I was sick of divorces and I had visions of spending some pretty lonely years unless I settled down."

But Joe and Lili maintained very different ideas of what settling down together meant. After years of working in nightclubs, Lili wanted to be a homebody. She played up her homemaking skills in several interviews. In an article for the *San Francisco Chronicle* headlined "I'm Really a Housewife at Heart," she dished up her recipe for chicken in cream.[34] She also served a baked ham with all the fixings to *Los Angeles Herald Examiner* columnist Bill Kennedy.[35] Nightlife columnist Wasserman wrote that offstage, she underwent a transformation "which puts Jekyll and Hyde to sniveling shame. For Lili St. Cyr is a retiring and unobtrusive homebody whose idea of a wild, impetuous evening is to cook dinner for her husband . . . keep an eye on her seven resident alley cats, and go to bed at nine p.m."[36]

"She never wanted to do anything or go anywhere," said Gloria Zomar.[37] "She was no party girl. Joe said all she liked to do was stay in bed all day and read. That wasn't much of a life for Joe." Moreover, according to Helen, Lili didn't want Joe to go out either. "He wanted to go fishing and she didn't want him to go," said Helen Frazee.[38] "Or she'd have us over for dinner, but only at certain times 'cause she liked it to be just Joe and her. She was very possessive of him." She was so unwilling to share Joe's time and attention, she discouraged his two children from his previous two marriages from visiting the house. "She told him it reminded her that he had been with another woman," said Gloria.[39]

Lili admitted they wanted different things. She claimed she would make dinner, that they wouldn't talk, and that Joe would pick an argument, and then go out to bars. "I know this sounds awfully middle class and that thousands of American marriages stagger on this way for life, but . . . I just couldn't accept it," she wrote.[40] Lili chose to return to work while their marriage sputtered to an end.

Joe's gambling and drinking was more divisive than their different outlooks on life. During the couple's July 1964 divorce proceedings, Lili told the judge that "he was intoxicated nightly and was often angry with her."[41] She also testified that Joe would start arguments when he'd been drinking. "He'd call me nasty names and accuse me of things that weren't true," she said.[42] She didn't elaborate on either. During one argument, she claimed he pushed her, injuring her back, and causing her to be hospitalized. Granted the divorce, she refused alimony and told reporters that "I'm not through with marriage, but I would have to be sure of the man."[43]

Joe's sister Helen denied he was ever abusive and contends he and Lili split because of other differences. But Joe's next wife, Gloria, faced similar problems. "He was a big drinker," said Gloria Zomar, who married Joe after his divorce from Lili and stayed with him until his death in 1997.[44] "He would drink and he would get kind of mean. He never hit me or anything, but the words that would come out of his mouth . . . you couldn't believe it. He would just ridicule me. He never did that when he was sober. He would never be sorry. How can you say all those things, and not say sorry or that he didn't mean it, or something? But I feel he loved me. And I loved him."

Lili did not tolerate Joe's drinking and felt she "had lost five years in vain efforts."[45] But despite the unpleasant end to their marriage, Lili and Joe remained friendly. Several years later she called and asked him to help her new boyfriend get a job at the studio where Joe worked. And when Gloria and Joe began dating she visited his nephew's house during Christmas one year to find a huge painting of Lili on the wall. "I don't know if they liked me too much at that time because they were all still pretty crazy about Lili," recalled Gloria with a small smile.[46]

Lili's marriage to Joe would be her last. This was the first time she tried to find fulfillment and satisfaction solely through marriage; the short experiment failed for her. Cracks started to show outside of just Lili's life as well. "The more people hoped to achieve personal happiness within marriage, the more critical they became of 'empty' or unsatisfying relationships," wrote Stephanie Coontz, author of *Marriage, a History*.[47] "Looking back on their lives a few decades later, men and women who had been in male breadwinner marriages in the 1950s and 1960s told interviewers that the division of labor in which they'd hoped to find fulfillment had so divided their lives that intimacy had become difficult, if not impossible. Wives were especially likely to regret their choices."

Lili echoed the sentiment and acknowledged that she had "learned one important thing: don't try to be what you're not. And never could I be, even after years of trying, the perfect woman of the house."[48] The experience reminded her of her earlier position that "if most women had the guts and the ability to earn a living, they'd divorce, too."[49]

Lili returned to work, not just to escape the remnants of an unhappy marriage, but because she craved the adoration of an audience. Decades later, author Elizabeth Eaves wrote in *Bare*, a memoir of her own days as a stripper, that she "wanted the devotion of one man and the admiration of many. At that time, if forced to choose, I would have taken the latter. Admiration from many meant no single one could make a claim on me."[50]

A year after her divorce from Joe, Lili appeared to share this attitude when she wrote, "I'm a girl who must have a husband—a man to love and to love me. I don't quite know where I go wrong, but obviously I do. Perhaps years of adulation have spoiled me. . . . Maybe applause and kind words have led me to expect too much from one man."[51] Even after six failed marriages, she was not ready to give up on love. But for Lili, an audience's applause was perhaps the most satisfying kiss. And so at the age of forty-seven, she returned to stripping full-time.

9.

Striptease a Go-Go

The sentimentalist ages far more quickly than the person who loves his work and enjoys new challenges.

— LILLIE LANGTRY

When Lili returned to dancing, the steady, percussive beats and slow, undulating rhythms of burlesque had wholly given way to the unpredictable, frantic tempo of go-go and topless dancing. And the changes that began to materialize at the start of the sixties emerged at a precipitous pace.

By the middle of the decade, the entertainment industry shook off any remaining hesitancy about using sex as currency and revealed the extent of the changes. In 1965, a Supreme Court decision essentially eliminated most state and local censorship boards. Convicted of showing a racy film without prior approval from the Maryland State Board of Censors, theater owner Ronald Freedman challenged the decision. In *Freedman v. Maryland*, the Court found the Maryland law violated the First Amendment's guarantee of freedom of expression and established guidelines, which shifted the burden of proof from the business or individual to the government, essentially rendering censorship boards inoperable.

That same year, a shot of a woman's breasts in the film *The Pawnbroker* won the industry's Production Code approval, a first for the business. The following year, the Code was revised altogether. The opening sentence of the new Code read in part that it was "designed to keep in close harmony with the mores, the culture, the moral sense and the expectation of our society."[1] This version reflected the practices of the present rather than the past code, which worked to protect society from breaches of the moral standard. By 1968, movies weren't censored or approved at all, but rated—G, PG, R, or X. And by the end of the decade, movies like the lascivious James Bond series and *Midnight Cowboy*, the first X-rated film to win an Oscar, confirmed the movie industry's emphasis on sex.[2]

The changes revealed themselves off the big screen as well. Television, which had brought families together over newly invented TV dinners for the likes of *Ozzie and Harriet*, now beamed riots, protests, and the Vietnam War into the living room. In mid-decade, Beatlemania reached its zenith. Not since bobby-soxers swooned over Frank Sinatra had teenage sexuality been on such open display, though in this new era girls pursued the Fab Four far more assertively. In 1966, *Human Sexual Response*, a book based on scientific studies that involved the authors observing couples having sex and men and women masturbating, became a best-seller. It spawned a plethora of sexual how-tos including *Everything You Always Wanted to Know About Sex*, which answered questions about how big a normal penis is and what dildos are, and *The Sensuous Woman*, a guide to becoming a better lover. *Sports Illustrated* made a splash with its first swimsuit issue in 1964. And by 1969, *Penthouse* and *Screw* magazines gave Hefner's *Playboy* a run with far more risqué coverage.[3] American society was happy to take the advice of Harvard professor Timothy Leary who, after downing psychedelic mushrooms, advised the world to "turn on, tune in, and drop out."[4]

Fashion, as is so often the case, also reflected the era's spirit. The leather-encased Emma Peels of *The Avengers* and bikini-clad Annette Funicellos shoved aside poodle-skirt wearing June Cleavers. Clothing became tighter, smaller, and more revealing. British designer Mary Quant began raising hemlines in the late fifties and by the mid-sixties had made the miniskirt popular. Quant summed up the sexually liberated attitude apparent in her apparel when she said: "Am I the only woman who has ever wanted to go to bed with a man in the afternoon? Any law-abiding female, it used to be thought, waits until dark. Well, there are lots of girls who don't want to wait. Miniclothes are symbolic of them."[5] Another fashion designer pushed bareness even further with a topless bathing suit— Rudi Gernreich's monokini, a bathing suit bottom held up by thin suspenderlike straps that ran between the breasts.

In June 1964, exotic dancer Carol Doda donned the monokini for her performance at San Francisco's Condor Club and transformed striptease into topless dancing. Doda, who started and ended her routine in the bathing suit, never undressed. In ditching her pasties, she removed any last remnants of the tease from the strip. The new method of simply presenting nakedness without any pretense or story and without any concealment or peek-a-boo beforehand was a huge hit; lines for Doda's show stretched down the block, and topless bars popped up around the country. Doda's brand of dancing began the move from striptease to stripping, from show business to pornography. More and more strippers began including "floor work," or shimmying and grinding while lying on the runway. Eventually, the changes gave rise to gentleman's clubs, lap dancing, pole dancing, and strip joints as we know them today. "In one evening, the formula that had defined the striptease for half a century became irrelevant," wrote Rachel Shteir in *Striptease: The Untold History of the Girlie Show*.[6]

Most of Lili's peers shunned the transformation. "The girls from my era don't want to be compared to the dancers and club people of today," dancer Joni Taylor told *Burlesque: Legendary Stars of the Stage* author Jane Briggeman.[7] "We always felt some things should always be left to the imagination, and one always looked better with something left on. Pasties and G-Strings were better than nothing, and that way we never became associated with pure smut."

Lili agreed and, despite the changes, continued to swivel her hips with the brand of burlesque striptease that had served her well for over twenty years. However, the headlines and reviews made it clear that the draw was in part nostalgic. In June 1964, she performed in a revue titled "Naughty-Naughty" at the Moulin Rouge in Hollywood, where audiences were promised "the opportunity to patronize a big Vegas-type show, like we used to have."[8] A few months later, in January 1965, she danced at a club in New Orleans. One reporter declared that the city used to be "bad and bawdy" and a "jungle of vice." It used to be a place where "the peroxide blondes in the sleazy strip joints carried their acts to astonishing limits, and the tourists who walked into any of those traps was lucky to walk out again with his wallet." But now, the city was "more mild than wild" and the "dancers conclude their performances more fully clothed than many waitresses in Los Angeles' saloons."[9]

Dave Cohn, a booking agent who called himself "the King of the Exotics," summed up the state of burlesque when he told the *Washington Post*, "What you see in a burlesque theater today you could probably see on television."[10]

Lili once again looked for respite in Montreal. Earlier, she had seen Montreal as her home, the one place she could truly be herself. "Montreal and I, we were made for each other in the 1940s," she wrote.[11] "I almost demanded the sensational, the bustle . . . [and the city] brought me a sense of security, as if I were a part of it in a way that I never felt in Los Angeles or in any other city where I worked and lived."

So in March 1965, she returned. She told one reporter that her fourteen-year absence was "much, much too long. . . . Montreal was one of the most charming cities in North America. I actually considered it my second home."[12] But as with so many other things, time altered Montreal. "There are so many changes," she said, lamenting the city's building boom.[13] "I hardly recognize it."

Indeed, as Montreal prepared for Expo '67, a World's Fair meant to bring attention and tourists to the city, officials worked to clean up the areas deemed less desirable. Old buildings were knocked down, parking lots constructed, and a stadium built for the exposition. Neighborhoods, including Goose Village, where Lili's former lover Jimmy Orlando grew up, were razed. The changes wiped out entire sections of the city and forced thousands of residents to relocate.[14] The result, Lili thought, stripped the city of much of its charm.

But Lili still charmed Montreal, and journalists and fans heralded her return. "The public [has] welcomed me in a sensational way," she told one reporter.[15] "I know that among the spectators, there are many who comprised my regular audience when I lived here. I recognize many. Some of them came to say hello personally, and were surprised to know that I remembered them."

Several new fans also sat in the audience. In fact, Lili later claimed that famed ballet dancer Jacques d'Amboise, of whom she was a huge fan, watched her perform when they were both in Montreal. According to Lili, they had met once before in New York. One night after his own performance with the New York City Ballet, d'Amboise went to watch her show. Afterward, she asked him why he had come and he reportedly responded, "To learn something."[16]

Lili's old haunt, the Gayety, was no longer a burlesque theater. Instead, she performed at Jimmy Orlando's nightclub Champ's, shattering attendance records. Jimmy was still a popular man about town. "He was very well known in Montreal even though he was out of hockey and had been out of the public eye for years," said Doris Quinn Godfrey, his third wife.[17] "People on the streets would still call out to him. He was asked for autographs all the time."

Lili enjoyed reconnecting with Jimmy, but claimed nothing of their passionate love affair still existed. "We were different now and our life was different than it had been in the past," she wrote, maintaining they spent hours discussing the good old days, but that was it.[18] "We got along much better as friends than as lovers."

Whether a warm, platonic friendship was all that persisted is unclear. Jimmy, still with the showgirl he'd married in the early fifties, later admitted infidelities to his next wife, Doris Quinn Godfrey. "I asked him one time how long he had been faithful to her," said Doris, who believed he did have a romantic liaison with Lili when she returned to Montreal in the sixties.[19] "He said, 'Ten years,' which I think was remarkable given the opportunity that he had [working in the nightclub business]."

More than forty years later, Jimmy's wife still wondered about the nature of his relationship with Lili. "Sure she was after him and, who knows, he probably wound up in bed with her," she said.[20] "How would I know? He kept saying that he never did. Of course I was accusing him, because he was working there, and he was with her. So whether he did or not, I guess I will never know. I'm sure she was trying to get him back."

Regardless of the nature of her relationship with Jimmy, Lili's return definitely placed a strain on his marriage. "When she came back to town in the sixties, my mother was very threatened by her presence," said Jamee Carangello, Jimmy's daughter.[21] "In our household it was kind of heated at that time. I remember it being very tense when Lili was back in town. Who really knows if anything was re-kindled? But I would remember them fighting and arguing and talking about her. Also, [my mother] used to be in the limelight, but now she was a housewife and this other woman was in the limelight. I guess that also must have really bothered her. I understood why my mother was so threatened and upset."

Lili returned to Montreal several times over the next two years. In an attempt to follow the times, she even donned a miniskirt and put together a show set to go-go music. "It's something new in the way of routines," she told columnist Al Palmer.[22] "Swinging music and fast dancing. Sort of a change of pace."

A forty-seven-year-old dancer following the trends of the youth culture by peeling off a miniskirt may have seemed ridiculous to some, but Montreal raved about Lili and her new look. "The 'Return of Happiness' has returned," wrote one *Montreal Star* reporter.[23] "Lili is back in town looking as chic as ever." And columnist Al Palmer thought, "When anyone else is on stage, it's a strip act. But when Lili is up there, it's art."[24] Despite the effort at modernization, it was the bubble bath routine, which had caused her trouble at Ciro's more than fifteen years earlier, that once again landed her in hot water.

In February 1967, after a two a.m. show that included her famous routine, Lili was arrested at Champ's and charged with giving an indecent performance. Wearing a heavy olive duffle coat over a white blouse, knee-length checked skirt, and calf-high brown suede boots, she pleaded not guilty and posted $100 bail. The case, which was widely thought to indicate the standards that would be enforced during Expo '67, was postponed until March 21.[25] Lili returned to work the next night, stripping off a turtleneck sweater and miniskirt. "She's back doing pretty much the same act she has been doing for the last twenty years," said one patron.[26]

In March, when her case came to trial, Lili was in New York performing at the Latin Quarter. Her absence from the proceedings led the judge to order her arrested on her return. But Lili never returned to Montreal.[27]

A few months later, Jimmy Orlando and his wife separated. "This whole thing with Lili, it just wasn't good," said Jamee Carangello.[28] "I don't know all the circumstances. I'm just assuming that [Lili] played a big role in their divorce."

"Their romance went on and off for a long time," said Doris Quinn Godfrey.[29] "I think his marriage broke up over it. Lili would come back to work at a club and his wife thought he was seeing her. I think there were times he was seeing her and she'd get angry."

Lili wasn't the cause of their separation, protested Jimmy's ex-wife, who claimed after nearly twenty years she was fed up with the nightlife world. "I just decided he was building the club business and he was gone all the time," she said.[30] "I didn't want to waste any more of my life being home alone. And he didn't want to sell the clubs."

Lili kept performing in the United States—possibly to avoid spending time at home or because she was unable to afford retirement. As most burlesque theaters and supper clubs shuttered their doors, she turned to carnival striptease. Girl shows became popular in carnivals during the Depression and boomed after World War II. Carnivals' association with grifters and their use of strippers to draw in the conmen's marks had always given tent shows a seedy tinge. While never able to completely shake off their seamy image, such shows gained a little more respectability in the fifties when the high-end operations hired marquee names like Gypsy Rose Lee, Faith Bacon, and Georgia Sothern. In the sixties, as other venues upped the sexual ante, so did carnival shows. And in some cases, they bordered on the pornographic.

The shows grew increasingly raw. Conditions were often rough and the hours long. Many girlie shows started as early as 10 a.m., and the dancers ground on in shifts until after midnight. Describing one common scenario, *Carnival Strippers* author Susan Meiselas wrote: "They work out of a traveling box, a truck that unfolds to form two stages, one opening to the public carnival grounds, another concealed under a tent for a private audience. Again and again, throughout the day and night, the women performers move from the front stage . . . to the back stage, where they each perform for the duration of a forty-five pop record. . . . The degree of suggestion on the front stage and participation on the back stage varies greatly from town to town, depending on legislation and local leniency."[31]

Talkers, men who convinced passersby to buy tickets to the show, drew audiences in with fast-talk and innuendo. "This show is strictly for the gentlemen," called one talker.[32] "You must be over eighteen and under eighty to go in this tent. There is a good reason for this rule. If you are under eighteen you won't understand it and if you are over eighty you couldn't stand it. This is red-hot burlesque, carnival hootchie-cootchie. We guarantee you'll leave our show with your hands in your pockets with a new grip on life!"

Sometimes the grip wasn't on life, but on the performers. The degree of coarseness in a show varied, but overall, as Meiselas described in her book, it was a seedy world where audience members touched the strippers and even, at times, performed oral sex on the girls while they were on stage. "I have been pulled off the stage and beaten and I've been stepped on and I've had people cut me," one of the dancers told Meiselas.[33] "I know that the guys that come in there have to be a little bit off—a lot of them are really sickies. . . . They say come on down here and they bite your clit, the blood's running down your leg. With a few exceptions, the ones that do touch you have to hurt you in some way. They think of carnival people as low anyway, and a carnival stripper they think is lower." The whole thing, another dancer told Meiselas, "fucks your head up because you don't really know who you are and you find yourself acting the same way with the man that you really like that you do with a trick, 'cause it's hard to distinguish."34

The women Meiselas spoke with believed that "the stripping profession has really evolved and its evolution has been downhill all the way." Patty, a manager and former stripper, thought that in burlesque "you were selling female glamour." By the time Meiselas interviewed the dancers in the early seventies, Patty thought girl shows had long since become about "bartering sex." Overall, "the girls think of the men the same way as the men think of the girls—as objects. They both seem to have little respect and a large amount of contempt for each other."35

Girl Show author A. W. Stencil argued that there was a difference between carnival shows and cooch shows, claiming the former tended to have a hands-off rule and remained much more clean. When Lili joined the carnival circuit it was highly unlikely she would have been subjected to or tolerated the cooch-show aspect of the carnival. In the summer of 1966, at the age of forty-nine, she performed in a nostalgic show called "The Best of Burlesque." As part of such a show and as a headliner she would have been somewhat protected from the seamier side of the carnival strip. But she spent several summers working local fairgrounds from North Tonawanda, New York, to Cleveland to Anaheim and certainly knew what other girls endured.

Even far-removed from the truly pornographic, rough side of carnival shows, the reviews made it clear that Lili's routines were a rare, bright spot. Of a nostalgic show called "Bravo Burlesque," the *Los Angeles Times* critic wrote: "Not really burlesque nor revue, nor much of anything but hodge-podge, this seedy show with its wonderfully unsubtle double-entendres and liberally exposed ladies nonetheless has a number of good people . . . that make its excessive length of two and a half hours and general mediocrity worth the trouble. [There is] the legendary, eternally lissome Lili St. Cyr, whose dance of the seven veils is a classic act of its kind and breathtakingly belies a reported fifty years."36

Another reviewer wrote that the show was "a tedious, heavy-handed, and tasteless revue which clearly demonstrates the reason for the demise of this particular theatrical format. . . . A sniggering vulgarity seethes beneath the surface of the revue, which makes no attempt to satirize the golden days of burlesque. Instead, a half-baked, juvenile re-creation of the bawdy, tinselly grind shows of the past is the show's only achievement. . . . The show's only hint of elegance and polish is the glittering presence of Miss St. Cyr whose lithe, lean lines and sensuous grace provide a brief, nostalgic glimpse of the stylish elements of old burlesque. But even her performance, as she writhes in self-caressing narcissism, frighteningly evokes the pathetic ghost of the lonely, frustrated men for whom this kind of theater was designed."[37]

It was unlikely Lili, who spent much of her career in upscale nightclubs and theaters, knew what the carnival scene entailed when she first started performing on the circuit. In fact, in the beginning she seemed excited about the tour. "They call it the Straw-Hat circuit and it's always a lot of fun," she told one reporter.[38] "Sometimes they put a stage in the middle of a circus tent and line up seats all around. It draws an incredible crowd, wherever it plays." But as she realized what she was involved with she maintained a distance. Her attempt to dissociate caused one reviewer to grumble that she "did two dance numbers under subdued lighting in the . . . tent, but failed to make an appearance in the bright lights of the finales."[39]

For Lili, who believed Las Vegas was too coarse and vulgar, the cheap, seedy carnival world must have chafed against her glamorous aspirations and so she remained as detached as possible. Her disconnect was also a result of the show's decreased production quality. Early in the sixties, she bemoaned the declining importance of settings, lighting, and music, and the problem only worsened. Eventually she cannibalized her routines down to those that required as little scenery as possible like, "Salome and the Seven Veils," which became one of her staples. For a woman who took such pride in her work, it is not surprising that she began to suffer from serious and severe ulcers.

It is likely that two other trends contributed to Lili's increasing angst: the women's liberation movement and the academic study of striptease. The sexual revolution helped launch the women's rights movement, as once women had control over their bodies and were no longer tethered to childbearing, they demanded opportunities far beyond motherhood.

Those demands began with renewed debate over the Equal Rights Amendment. Suffragist Alice Paul wrote the amendment, which guaranteed that "equality of rights under the law shall not be denied or abridged by the United States or any state on account of sex," in the twenties. Forty years later, as the women's rights movement picked up steam, the ratification of the amendment became a powerful symbol and call to action. In 1966, the call grew louder with the founding of the National Organization of Women (NOW), a group that would coordinate the growing movement and lobby for changes that would secure women's equal rights. But a small protest at the Miss America pageant in 1968 really set the women's liberation movement ablaze.

Outside the pageant in Atlantic City, a group of women protested the competition and its basic assumption: that the ideal woman needed a pretty face and shapely body and little more. They set up a "freedom trash-can," and to the delight of the TV cameras and journalists with nothing else to cover before the pageant, the protesters tossed bras, high-heels, hair curlers, and other womanly detritus into the garbage can. They crowned a sheep Miss America to play up the idea that the contestants were "judged like animals at a country fair."[40] At the end of the pageant, a few of the protesters who had snuck into the show stood in the balcony and unfurled a banner reading "Women's Liberation." As *America's Women* author Gail Collins pointed out, "It was the first time most of the viewing public had ever heard the term."[41] The small demonstration both launched the term "bra burner" and brought the women's rights movement into the forefront of the American public's mind-set.

As the movement grew and women focused on the commoditization and objectification of the female body, striptease became a target. A few years later, Harold Minsky, still staging revues in Las Vegas, weighed in saying, "Yeah, I thought once the women's lib people attacked Hugh Hefner I'd be the next to go. But here's how I feel—my wife agrees with me and she's a very women's lib person, she subscribes to *Ms.* and everything—I feel that if a girl thinks there's anything immoral or wrong in my shows, she doesn't have to take the job. I don't hit anyone over the head to work for me."[42]

Minsky lacked a full understanding about what feminists balked at when it came to striptease; men had appropriated female sexuality for profit and a thrill. "Feminists object to the image on the grounds that it reinforces the prevailing ideologically based male fantasy about women," wrote *Behind the G-String* author David A. Scott.[43] Years later, dancer Elisabeth Eaves wrote in her memoir *Bare* that, "stripping reinforces the stereotype of women that came to bother me the most: that they can be bought. For a price, a stripper will pretend to be a kind of woman that doesn't exist outside the imagination—the naked, adoring, one-dimensional sex object. She creates the idea that a woman's appearance, behavior, and sexuality are for sale."[44]

Long after Lili retired, however, others advanced the argument that burlesque actually strips away female stereotypes and empowers women. "By aggressively subverting the societal convention, the stripper takes on masculine attributes and defies feminine passivity," wrote author Dahlia Schweitzer in the *Journal of Popular Culture*.[45] "Strippers further reverse the rules of the game by exalting the role of the woman in the rite of seduction, forbidding the role of the man. On one hand, the woman is the object and the man is the possessor. . . . However, the viewer is not free to pursue his desire for the stripper. She is literally and figuratively out of his reach. . . . Strip joints provide one of the few outlets in which women exercise unchallenged command over their bodies."

For Lili, the tension between the two ideas existed as more than an interesting debate—it was an incredibly personal conflict. As early as 1965, she called herself a feminist. Striptease provided her unimaginable opportunities and financial success, and the idea that others viewed it as part of the male tyranny over women must have felt like a personal attack. At the same time, she clearly held some misgivings about her career and the choices she had made. She continued to express the conflict she had begun to publicly air in her interview with Mike Wallace—even when she was being flippant. "I'm mad about fashion—in fact I wanted to be a designer," Lili, bedecked in a $2,500 knee-length mink coat and matching shoes, told a *New York Times* reporter in May 1967.[46] "I wouldn't be caught dead wearing net hose, sequined dresses or false eyelashes. Women who wear them in public remind me of strippers." As she spoke, a woman in a silver vinyl raincoat walked by and Lili remarked, "Now, there's something that should be seen only on stage."

By the late sixties, public debate about striptease spilled into academia. Several studies examined who the estimated seven thousand exotic dancers in the United States were and what made them choose stripping for a living. Studies like the one by professors James K. Skipper Jr. from the University of

Western Ontario and Charles H. McCaghy from Bowling Green State University were common. They found that almost ninety percent of the women were firstborn children who "received little affection from their parents, especially from the father who had usually left the home by the time the women were in their teens." The study established that many of the women engaged in sex at an early age and usually left home by eighteen, often through marriages that ended in divorce. Most of the women had first held jobs where their bodies were on display—dancers, models, bar maids—before they began stripping and that they moved to stripping because it offered them more money.[47] It was a vivid snapshot of Lili's own life.

For the most part, the women the researchers interviewed and studied were nearly thirty years younger than Lili. As Harold Minsky told one reporter in 1966, "The average professional life of a Minsky girl is six years, from age eighteen to twenty-four. There are exceptions, but normally the maximum they can stretch it is age twenty-six."[48] A woman might dance as a feature until her late twenties, at which point she would be bumped to the chorus or work backstage in wardrobe or as a seamstress. Sol Goodman, the manager of Baltimore's Gayety Theater, once said, "They used up their youth. . . . Some of them went home. Some got married. And some just seemed to fade away."[49] Exceptionally Lili celebrated her fiftieth birthday in 1967 and continued to perform into the early seventies. A few other dancers like Tempest Storm and Sally Rand continued to perform far longer than the average dancer, though reporters often used their age to dismiss the women. And despite the age gap between Lili and the dancers Skipper and McCaghy interviewed, overall she fit the researchers' profile.

The researchers' findings regarding men were most striking in their similarities with Lili's own life. In general, the study discovered that most dancers had used their sexuality at an early age to attract men and gain attention. "Throughout the course of the interviews we noted the strippers' disillusionment with males," wrote Skipper and McCaghy.[50] "Many of them had bitter memories of fathers from whom they received little attention and affection. . . . When strippers do establish relationships with males, they often end in disappointment. Frequently the girls become involved with rough, unemployed males who are only interested in a financial or sexual advantage. . . . However, one should not get the impression that most strippers are anti-male or that they have severed all contacts with males. In fact, most hope to get married again."

Lili's relationships with men comprised a complicated history. The father that had left her as a child supposedly tried to contact her as an adult. And when he died in 1962, his obituary acknowledged his only child by her given name, Marie Van Schaack. Regardless, she never knew her father. Perhaps he never really reached out. Perhaps she rebuffed his attempts. She once told *Top Secret* magazine that band leader Artie Shaw, who she called "an addict of Dr. Freud," regularly analyzed her. "Whenever we are together, he promptly probes my soul and then explains everything, especially what he thinks worries me," she said.[51] "He thinks that the reason I have needed so many husbands is that I never knew my own father and that men are the pawns in my search for my own missing forebear."

Whatever the reason, Lili certainly kept men at arm's length. It was not just onstage that she presented imagined romance, imagined intimacy. Rita Hayworth said men went to bed with a movie star only to wake up with an ordinary woman. Similarly, few men ever knew the actual woman that woke up each morning and transformed herself into Lili St. Cyr. Most men never got that close. She chose husbands and lovers who were not wholly available—either because they drank, felt insecure about their own careers, knew little English, or for other reasons altogether. She picked men who could serve as backstage help or who could nurture her dance skills, not men who could serve or care for her. A profile on Lili from the era seemed to sum up her attitude. The *San Francisco Examiner & Chronicle* reported that, "she has said that there are only two things in life . . . work and sex."[52]

Unfortunately for Lili, by the end of the decade work lost most of its appeal. "Girls literally threw away their bras and the miniskirt exposed an incredible amount of flesh," Camille Paglia told A&E for their documentary *It's Burlesque*. "It made the burlesque houses seem kind of seedy and old, a kind of style of sexual display that was now in bad taste. It was aging."

Burlesque striptease could not compete with X-rated movies, topless dancing, men's magazines, or Broadway shows like *Hair* and *Oh! Calcutta*, where both men and women appeared naked onstage. As Tempest Storm, a titties-era burlesque dancer legendary for her DD-sized breasts, told NPR years later, "That's what killed burlesque . . . when they started taking off everything. I mean a woman's greatest weapon is a man's imagination, anyway."[53]

Headline dancers like Storm no longer filled the theaters. In a late sixties performance at the T and T Follies in California, only sixteen people watched her dance.[54] The tease had been stripped from striptease. As *Striptease* author Rachel Shteir pointed out, the general public learned to "prize instant gratification over anticipation."[55]

For those who had been involved in burlesque's heyday, the change was for the worse. In December 1969, one of the few remaining burlesque houses, the Folly Theater in Kansas City, closed. Manager Mark Stuber complained: "These girls they have around here all the time are vulgar, they're cheap. They have cheapened the name of burlesque."[56]

By now, the transformation from classic burlesque striptease to naked dancing was complete. The topless trend was in full swing with clubs offering everything from topless lunches to topless shoe shines. Soon, bottomless dancers joined the party. Full nudity quickly followed suit and as the 1970s progressed, some clubs featured live sex acts. "Stripping became only an adjunct to a massive sex industry of which hardcore pornographic films were the centerpiece," wrote Jessica Glasscock in her book *Striptease: From Gaslight to Spotlight.*[57] "The lines between stripping, prostitution, and other kinds of sex work were briefly blurred."

Nudity was also no longer simply erotic. It could be political as well. A group of Cornell women took off their tops and covered their breasts in jam to protest women's role as sex objects. *Hair*, the antiwar musical chock full of nudity, came to Broadway. And the slogan, "Make love, not war" popped up everywhere. Critics remained skeptical about the political power of the naked body. "What does taking off your clothes have to do with the Vietnam War?" asked *Esquire* magazine.

Lili stayed out of the debate. For her, burlesque and striptease no longer represented the world of glamour, intrigue, and excitement she had first glimpsed when she watched her idol Greta Garbo shimmering on the big screen. Striptease no longer offered her passport to the first-class life she had aspired to when she climbed aboard the grand ocean liners. And it was no longer the sensational, bustling party that she danced through, as she had when she reigned in Montreal or American supper clubs like Ciro's.

In September 1970, Lili performed her last show in Harold Minsky's revue at the Aladdin in Las Vegas. When *San Francisco Examiner & Chronicle* columnist Lew Wasserman asked her if she would miss show business, "she looked as if she had just gotten a whiff of tear gas. 'I hate it . . . I haven't been enthusiastic for ten years. And I just can't face any more openings . . . never again!'"[58] And with that, Lili St. Cyr hung up her rhinestone-bedecked pasties and G-string at fifty-three years of age.

Nils T. Granlund, the impresario for whom Lili first worked at the Florentine Gardens, wrote in his memoir *Blondes Brunettes and Bullets* that "girls in show business are subjected to more temptation in a day than most other women encounter in a lifetime. It takes a great mental and moral stamina for a girl to come through, not necessarily to stardom, but merely to retain her decency. No amount of care or guarding prepares her for this bewildering business. She picks her own way, and what she picks depends on her stamina. The dazzle easily blinds."[59]

Lili loved the dazzle and resisted most of the temptations available in the nightclub world. She found stardom and relished it. However, away from the stage lights, she would be bewildered by the shadows of anonymity. In her personal world, she would struggle with great temptations. She would need great mental and moral stamina to face her own demons. And as she herself once pointed out, she would have to face the fact that she was often the cause of her own destruction.

10.

The Garbo-esque Philosophy

The hell of women is old age.

—FRANÇOIS DE LA ROCHEFOUCAULD

At the height of her popularity in the fifties, Lili glibly told a reporter: "People say I should save my money. That doesn't interest me; I'd rather spend it. I suppose there will always be someone to buy me a hamburger and a cup of coffee when I'm broke."[1] More than a decade later, as she prepared to step out from under the spotlight, she began to consider the issue of her future more seriously. As her youthful beauty faded and she stopped dancing, Lili found other ways to take care of herself.

In the mid-sixties, Lili, now in her late forties, sold a pulpy, provocative autobiography titled *And Men My Fuel*, which was ghost-written by Leo Guild, who also ghosted books for Bob Hope, Jayne Mansfield, Barbara Payton, and Liberace. In the slim, scandalous, and photo-laden paperback, which sold for seventy-five cents, she revealed just a little about her career and instead focused on her personal life. She offered a brief glimpse into her childhood, detailed her six marriages and the reasons for their collapse, and shared her ahead-of-her-time and shocking attitudes about men, children, and abortion. She ended the book still hopeful about love writing, "Somewhere there's a man who will make me happy and who I can make happy and I'm going to find him!!"[2]

It's unlikely the book gave her the publicity boost or financial gain she hoped for. Similar in style to the gossip and men's magazines that helped make her popular, it was not covered by the day's major newspapers or magazines. Nearly twenty years later, in 1982, she sold a thicker, more serious French-Canadian autobiography, *Ma Vie de Stripteaseuse*, for which she was paid an advance of two thousand dollars—far less than she made for a week's performance at the height of her career. It's unlikely she earned more than that for her earlier book.

Always interested in fashion, Lili also opened up a mail-order lingerie business and a Hollywood boutique known as the Undie World of Lili St. Cyr. The catalog, which used both exaggerated illustrations of Lili and her glamour shots, promised that women would "be well dressed for that most delightful sport of all . . . [in styles] created to meet an unprecedented demand for the bold . . . the delicious . . . the naughty!" The sexy creations included bikini briefs, filmy negligees, lacy G-strings, and sparkly pasties, with names like Scantie Panties, Folies Bergere, Coy Miss, Lili's Love, Lolita, and Fanny Hill. Descriptions played up Lili's connection to the lingerie. The ads divulged that in her personal appearances she wore the Illusion, a robe made of "yards and yards of sheerest Nylon—draped to reveal and conceal." And they trumpeted the notion that "only Lili St. Cyr could design such a fabulous Nylon Lace dance set" as Lili's Love, a halter bra and bikini.[3] The lingerie boutique, which sold the same items as Lili's mail order business, boomed and remained a Hollywood hot spot for over twenty years, attracting many designers and celebrities, including pop icon Madonna.

Despite the claims of Lili's intimate involvement, she served primarily as the face and name of both aspects of the lingerie business. For some time, she would visit the boutique and sign autographs for fans. Jazz musician Kid Ory had been friends with Lili throughout much of their careers and after his death his daughter Babette would visit with Lili in the shop. "She would hold court and tell me stories about her different adventures," said Babette Ory, who thought it was funny that Lili spiked the lemonade she sipped on.[4] "She told me about different encounters with people and reminisced with me about my dad. One time, she saw this woman trying to come onto my dad while he was still on stage. This woman was starting to cause a scene in the club. Lili stood up and started dancing to take the attention off of the woman trying to climb up on stage."

In the late seventies, Lili's business partners in the mail-order portion of the business bought out her share. At the same time, Lana Henderson, a former ballroom dancer who started working at the boutique in the early part of the decade, bought the Undie World of Lili St. Cyr. The two women spoke occasionally, because Lili earned royalties for the use of her name. Lana, who described Lili as a "very sweet, quiet lady," recalled that her royalties amounted to roughly one hundred dollars a month.

Lili also made money selling autographed copies of her glamour shots to fans. She charged ten dollars for three autographed eight-by-ten glossy photos and regularly included letters to her fans. On stationery decorated with the heading "The Fabulous Lili St. Cyr" above a grayed-out glamour shot, she answered fans' questions, provided a brief glimpse into her life, and often began a mail-based relationship with her admirers.

When one fan asked what was the best piece of advice she was given, Lili replied, "It was, 'to save my money,' of course—I guess every one gets that one and very few people take it seriously—at least, I didn't." She wrote that she looked at striptease "as sort of an adventure, but it certainly was the last thing I had in mind as a career." Instead, she wrote that she wanted to be a "designer of fashions, and even now I design and create costume jewelry necklaces. The part of show business I found most interesting was designing my own sets and costumes."

She wrote to another admirer about her formula for success: "Most of the successful people I've known have certain traits in common . . . a definite goal, ability to sacrifice to reach that goal, patience, courage of your own convictions, [and] rich parents. Personally, I did not have at least two of these traits—but I made a living anyway!"[5]

Sometimes Lili's correspondence even led to a phone-based friendship. Bob Bethia, a movie aficionado, stumbled across one of Lili's ads for her autographed photos in *Movie Star News*, Irving Klaw's catalog of pinups and movie pictures. Struck by her stunning beauty, Bethia sent away for a few photos. "I wasn't familiar with strippers or burlesque at the time, but I was fascinated," said Bethia, who after receiving his first batch of photos began an affable back-and-forth with Lili through the mail.[6] In one of her first letters, she told him, "I now lead a very quiet life and it is a relief after so many years of show biz." When he asked if she had a fan club, she told him no and said she didn't want one because she didn't have the strength to participate.

Bethia continued to order photos. "I had to have more because they were just beautiful," said Bethia.[7] "She wrote me back and said 'oh you must be a big fan.' I wanted them because I didn't know who she was. I still couldn't find anything out about her; there were no books. I kept ordering photos and asking her questions. She finally wrote that if I wanted to find out more about her or her career, I should call and she gave me her number.

"It took me weeks to work up the courage to even attempt to call her because I didn't know what to say to her," said Bethia.[8] "I didn't know much about her, but the more I would find out, the more intrigued I got. So one day I got the nerve to call her and she answered and she was very, very nice."

After that, the two talked regularly. Over the course of a few of years, Bethia learned more about the former dancer. "I asked her if she ever dated mobsters because I know they frequented Vegas and clubs like that," Bethia remembered.[9] "She said, no, she never dated any but she was aware of their presence. She met them but she stood her distance. She would not discuss her marriages and she would just get very angry if I asked."

Much more willing to talk about her work, Lili told him about her performances and the costumes. "She was very proud of her costumes," said Bethia.[10] "She was proud of her work. I think that meant everything to her. I did ask her if she missed it. She said she didn't miss the work, but she missed feeling important." Overall, Lili was incredibly guarded, and her conversations with Bethia were mostly about him, which he thought was "strange."

"She would give me ideas about things to do with my career," said Bethia, who worked as a hair stylist in Southern California.[11] "She gave me a lot of career advice. She would always say 'I hate to start mothering you, but I think you should do this.' I think a lot of it came out of the fact that she needed to self-promote, so she was giving me advice that I needed to self-promote to get ahead. She just felt I was creative and I think she took an interest in that. She'd always try to give me pep talks on how to get out there and sell myself. It was neat."

"It's my mail that I find most enjoyable," Lili told *The Autograph Collector's Magazine* in 1988.[12] "I particularly enjoy it when people tell me a little about themselves—who they are, what they do, and what their interests are. Many of these individuals have corresponded with me over the years and we have become friends."

For the most part, these letters and phone calls became Lili's only connection to the outside world. Taking a cue from her long-time idol Greta Garbo, Lili became increasingly reclusive. By 1975, she so wholly removed herself from the spotlight that she was included in *Whatever Became Of . . .* , a book that dished on where former stars were at the time. Author Richard Lamparski reported that Lili "sees almost no one from show business and her home in the Hollywood Hills is secluded behind tall trees. . . . [She] now describes herself as a housewife. She takes in stray cats and at times has had as many as ten of them. She is a gourmet cook and reads about a book a day curled up in front of one of her five fireplaces."[13]

The same year Lili told Richard Lamparski she spent her days cooking and reading, the cult classic *The Rocky Horror Picture Show* gave a sexy nod to the former dancer. The musical, a wild mix of sexual fantasy and science fiction, regaled audiences with the story of a young couple who stumble into the castle of a transvestite after their car breaks down. In the film's "Dream It" scene, an ode to "absolute pleasure" and "sins of the flesh," Janet, played by Susan Sarandon, splashes around in the pool and ends the song with "God bless Lili St. Cyr." The reference acknowledged that the campy, kitschy, bawdy burlesque aspects of the film owed its fishnets, in part, to Lili and her peers. And that was how she wanted to be remembered—as a striking and sexy woman who evoked glamour and inspired lust.

When Bob Bethia asked Lili why she vanished from the public eye, she told him "I feel as a beautiful woman gets older, you should be remembered for how you looked and not the way you look now."[14]

Throughout her life, Lili's beauty had an intoxicating effect on men. A showgirl pal of Lili's once told *Uncensored* magazine, "There's something about Lili that brings out either the best, or the beast, in a man. But this much is sure, when they've loved her, they know they've lived. And with someone unusual."[15]

Lili used that effect to empty wallets and make a living onstage. She never relied on the woman within. When she lost her youthful beauty, she felt she lost her only asset. Years earlier, she performed a routine based on Oscar Wilde's novel *The Picture of Dorian Gray*. The book tells the story of a remarkably handsome man whose friend paints his portrait. Believing beauty and enjoyment are the only things worth pursuing in life and frightened by the realization that one day his physical appearance will fade, Dorian Gray calls out with the desire that his picture ages instead of him. When his wish is fulfilled, he embarks on a whirlwind journey of debauchery. As the painting ages, it reveals his sins and serves as a painful reminder of what he has done. It was prescient that Lili chose to do an homage to *The Picture of Dorian Gray*, as she shared the same fears of Wilde's protagonist. Yet, without the magical painting to age for her, she suffered a reverse fate. She allowed the public image she created based on her beauty to completely engulf her private identity. To her, preserving her image was worth isolation and loneliness.

"She called it her Garbo-esque philosophy," said Bob Bethia.[16] "[She thought that] the public doesn't accept when a beautiful woman gets old. To be beautiful is to be doomed, because you're going to lose it sooner or later. You just fade away and are remembered for what you were. That was very interesting."

Many speculated about the reasons behind Greta Garbo's demand for privacy but they have never been completely clear. Perhaps, as her character in the 1933 film *Queen Christina* indicated, she grew tired of being a symbol. Perhaps she was shy and depressed. Perhaps Garbo believed letting people in would belittle her emotions; she once said, ". . . your joys and sorrows. You can never tell them. You cheapen the inside of yourself if you do tell them."[17] Whatever the reason, the mystery surrounding Garbo enabled her fans to fill in the outline of her personality with the colorful brushstrokes that each needed. Lili, like much of the public, only knew Garbo through her characters, and not through self-revelation.

Women admired Garbo's characters for their "toughness and were fascinated by her willingness to acknowledge her sensuality," wrote author Marjorie Rosen in *Popcorn Venus: Women, Movies & the American Dream*.[18] "Inevitably the Garbo character's ephemeral spirit was broken and her bravado punctured. She exuded splendid élan and soul while going down, but her ship always sank. Love was inevitably the vehicle of catastrophe and ruin."

Perhaps in mimicking Garbo's hermitlike habits, Lili believed her ship would inevitably sink. But for Lili, love would be both an albatross and a buoy.

*I*n the mid-sixties, while still performing, Lili met Donald Markick, the last and perhaps greatest love of her life.

Born in February 1934, Donald was the third of four children to Yugoslavian immigrants who married when they themselves were young teenagers. In the forties, Donald, the only boy, moved to San Bernardino, California, with his family.

As a teenager, Donald hoped to become a magician. He studied under Cardini, a Welsh-born magician who specialized in manipulation tricks that involved moving cards or billiard balls with his mind, and he got so far as entertaining at private parties, but after high school Donald joined the military and served in the Korean War. The conflict in Korea began in 1950 as a civil war between North and South Korea. The United States supported the South. China and the Soviet Union backed the North. The Cold War nations entered into a proxy war that ended in a stalemate in 1953. Donald, who was only sixteen when the war began, served toward the end of the conflict.

"That's where he first fell in love with jumping," said his younger sister Andrea Hedrick, who believed he was a paratrooper.[19] Besides jumping from planes, Donald's time in Korea proved to be tumultuous and risky. He suffered from jungle rot, a fungal infection that caused him health problems for the rest of his life. According to his sister he was captured and held as a prisoner of war for some time. He also landed in trouble over drugs.

"He and some friends had purchased some marijuana," said Andrea.[20] "They got stopped and there were some repercussions. He got reprimanded for it, I guess." Unsure whether the incident led to Donald's discharge, Andrea dismissed it as "no big deal. It was just guys being guys."

When he returned home, Donald found a job in sales, but he worked just enough to fund his adventures. "He was a free spirit, a soldier of fortune," said Andrea, who heard tales about his trips diving for pearls, working on a whaling ship, and mining gold in the Sierra Mountains.[21] "He wasn't like everybody else. He was not your regular, get-up-to-go-to-work kind of guy. He wasn't a workaday Bob with a nine-to-five job. He never did that."

Like Lili, Donald ditched his childhood home, a place he called a "cowboy hick town." After a yacht trip to Hawaii he settled in Los Angeles and, long smitten with the blonde dancer, went to see her perform. "He had pictures of her all over the place way before he ever met her," said Andrea.[22] "He just knew someday he was going to be with her. It was part of his destiny."

After a mutual friend introduced them, Lili and Donald did get together. Over six feet tall with wavy, dark hair and brown eyes, he struck Lili with his handsome looks, charm, and wry sense of humor. He was completely willing to dote on her and satisfy her whims.

In many ways, he matched the ideal man Lili described years earlier in an interview with one of the men's magazine. "I like a man to be all man—rugged," she told *Sir!*[23] "Then I'd say generosity would come next. Not in its monetary sense, necessarily, but I expect a man to be generous with his affection his time and his consideration. . . . [I like] a sense of humor. He shouldn't be too serious, should be able to laugh—with me, at himself, at something funny I might say or do. Serious men, intense men, are always too wrapped up in themselves to be good lovers."

Donald's appeal also came from his interests and outlook on life. "He was artistic and well read," said Andrea.[24] "He was into classical music. He liked finer things. He liked traveling and fine dining. He liked to be well groomed. My brother liked dressing up in his suits. He was the type of person who had a cigarette holder."

But more than good looks and similar interests, what drew Lili and Donald to each other—and kept them together for over thirty years—was a willingness to play each other's games. "They were just a couple that was perfectly suited for Fantasy Land," Andrea recalled.[25] "They were a unique pair of people. They were not regular, structured people. They lived in a world of their own making."

This showed early on, when Lili decided Donald was just not a Hollywood enough name and began calling him Lorenzo. Happy to oblige, he changed his last name as well. In homage to his favorite writer, Arthur Conan Doyle, who wrote the Sherlock Holmes stories, Donald Andrew Markick became Lorenzo Holmes.

Donald's family refused to call him Lorenzo and, in general, his mother was unhappy about the relationship. Being only a few years older than Lili herself, his mother disapproved of the nearly twenty-year age gap. She "would have preferred a Susie Homemaker, which would never have been [Donald's] pick in the first place," explained Andrea.[26]

Instead, Donald chose someone who lived as eccentrically as he did. After Lili retired, the couple entertained themselves with extravagant private parties. "It could be Arabian week or whatever else they cooked up," said Andrea.[27] "They would have someone come in and set their whole backyard up as an Arabian tent. Lili would sew costumes for them both. They would dress up in these outfits and have a Scheherazade party. Actually, in a bizarre sort of way, Lili was kind of a Susie Homemaker. She was a great cook. She could sew. It's just that she put those skills to use in a unique way."

In an equally free-spirited approach, Lili and Donald shunned marriage. In 1970, after she and Donald had been together for nearly six years, Lili told *San Francisco Examiner & Chronicle* columnist Lew Wasserman that she'd been married six or seven times, and that was "usually because it made the man feel more secure."[28] Donald, apparently, felt no such insecurities.

"She just didn't feel like marriage was lucky for her," said Andrea.[29] "She thought if they didn't get married it would last longer. And it did. And it didn't matter to him, because it was just a piece of paper. He loved her absolutely with all of his heart."

Privately, the two eschewed marriage; publicly Lili called Donald her husband. In a 1967 article she told a *New York Times* reporter that her husband Lorenzo Holmes worked as a technical writer. Her short FBI file, put together after her 1967 arrest in Canada, indicated he was her husband as well. And in 1973, when her mother died from heart complications, the obituary listed her as Mrs. Lili Holmes.[30]

By the time her mother Idella died, Lili and Donald had closed themselves off from most of her family. The grandmother who had so shaped Lili's outlook on life had died at ninety-one in January 1967. Lili attended the funeral but remained in her limousine. She was so distraught over her grandmother's death that even twenty years later she had trouble talking about Alice without becoming upset.[31] She remained distant from her step-siblings.

Despite Donald's mother's initial objections, his family spent as much time with the couple as they could. "I would visit once a year," said Andrea, who chatted with Donald almost weekly on the phone.[32] "My mom would come down sometimes. But they were very private. Lili was extremely so, which is funny because onstage she had to be very outgoing. It was a bit of a paradox. As she got older, she wasn't just private. Sometimes we were supposed to visit and my brother would call and say it's not a good day to come down. She became very reclusive. She hardly left the house."

The Garbo-esque seclusion that Lili had described to Bob Bethia even affected family. "She only wanted people to see her or remember her when she was young and beautiful," said Andrea.[33] "If I saw her, it was briefly."

For the most part, Lili holed up with Donald and Tiny, her cat. Years earlier, somebody had given Tiny to her backstage, and while initially uninterested in the cat, she grew to adore it. The cat would travel with Lili in custom-made cages. "Tiny became the queen," said Andrea.[34] "Tiny was like Lili's child."

The performer who rejected having children of her own also hinted at a maternal side in a letter to one of her fans, who asked about memorable moments in her career. "There were quite a few of those, since it was a very long one, but one of the most thrilling mornings of my life was when a mother cat presented me with three baby kittens," she wrote.[35] "Watching her care for them and seeing them all grow up together really changed my life for the better."

Lili's love for her cats hardly indicated her regret at not having children. She made it clear to Andrea that she never wanted kids and told her she aborted several pregnancies. "Some people don't want to have kids, and there's nothing wrong with that," said Andrea.[36] "Some people don't think they're cut out to be a mother. Some people don't want the responsibility, or their lifestyle doesn't have time for raising children."

Lili claimed to have had several abortions during her life. But it was not until 1973 that abortion became legal. Before the 1860s, performing an abortion before the fetus first moved remained legal, and an abortion after that point was just a minor offense. During the 1860s, however, states began passing anti-abortion laws in part to protect women against the dangers and in part because the American Medical Association lobbied for such laws in an effort to drive some doctors out of business. Yet criminalizing abortion did not prevent it and experts believe that during the first half of the twentieth century, illegal abortion was the most widely practiced form of birth control.[37]

Women used a variety of abortion methods, and all were highly dangerous. One option involved scraping the fetus from the uterine wall with a sharp object. The sharp object was not always a medical instrument, but just as often could be a coat hanger or knitting needle. Often women bled to death or got infections from improperly sterilized equipment. Another method involved douching, typically with unsafe solutions that included Lysol, iodine, or turpentine. Experts estimate women received one million illegal abortions during the fifties and more than a thousand of these resulted in deaths due to infections. "In the frightening, secret world of illegal abortion in the 1950s and 1960s, most abortionists were interested in collecting their fees—usually one thousand dollars or more in cash," wrote *A Century of Women* author Deborah Felder, who explained women were sometimes forced to have sex with male abortionists before the procedure and that the use of anesthesia was rare.[38]

It is likely Lili used one of these highly dangerous methods for at least one of her abortions. In the early thirties, she sought out a doctor in downtown Los Angeles and paid him fifty dollars for her first abortion. She wrote that she had no regrets and when her mother called her a disgrace, Lili wished she'd been born a man, but vowed not to let anyone else's rules limit her. She claimed to have had as many as eleven abortions and in *And Men My Fuel* wrote, "I despise children and the thought of having any has always petrified me with shivering fear. . . . Though it is unnatural for a woman to feel that way, it is true."[39] She blamed her own childhood for her disinterest in having children and despite societal pressures to do so, Lili refused. Like so many other women, she quietly used abortion as a method of birth control. "Today, she wouldn't have even gotten pregnant," said Andrea, whose brother did not care about having kids either.[40] "She would have taken birth control."

In January 1973, when Lili was fifty-five and retired, the Supreme Court ruled in *Roe v. Wade* that an abortion was a decision between a woman and her doctor. The ruling had little impact on Lili personally, yet in concert with the changes brought on by the Pill, more and more women echoed the independent attitude to which Lili had long subscribed.

Few women spurned marriage as Lili and Donald did; nearly two-thirds of women under the age of twenty-four still hoped to become full-time homemakers. But more women reconsidered how marriage should work. Feminist Alix Kates Shulman even drew up a marriage contract with her husband. It stated that each had "an equal right to his/her own time, work, values, and choices" and that "the ability to earn more money is already a privilege which must not be compounded by enabling the larger earner to buy out of his/her duties and put the burden on the one who earns less." *Life* magazine covered the Shulman contract, *Redbook* reprinted it, and *Glamour* explained how to write one. Few husbands and wives signed such contracts, but the widespread discussion remained indicative of the changes brewing within the marital institution and women's lives.[41]

Surveys from the 1950s, when Lili was at the height of her popularity, to the end of the 1970s showed a large decline in the import placed on conformity to social roles. Instead people focused on self-fulfillment and intimacy. "More people believed that autonomy and voluntary cooperation were higher values than was obedience to authority," wrote *Marriage, a History* author Stephanie Coontz.[42] "Acceptance of singlehood, unmarried cohabitation, childlessness, divorce, and out-of-wedlock childbearing increased everywhere in North America and Western Europe."

Lili was neither solely responsible for the tectonic shifts in the zeitgeist nor even interested in effecting them. However, in living her life outside the traditional feminine sphere, she challenged marital norms, defied conventional gender roles, and became one of the many tremors that so drastically shifted the culture's attitudes between 1945 and the seventies.

Despite the turmoil around her, Lili remained reclusive, spending time with only Donald and Tiny. In fact, Andrea speculated that this cloistered behavior further irritated the problems between Lili and her half-sister Dardy. The two women had long had an up-and-down relationship, and Andrea wondered if Dardy blamed their distance on Donald, adding to the rift between the sisters. "Maybe they attributed her downfall to him," said Andrea, referring to the couple's financial difficulty.[43]

Donald never held a steady job, working odd jobs as needed. He even drove a taxi for a while. According to Gloria Zomar, Lili called her ex-husband Joe to see if he could help Donald land a job as a guard at the studio. Neither royalties from Lili's book nor her lingerie business brought in a significant amount of money and she had little left from her years onstage. Perhaps, as she wrote in a letter to one of her fans, she never saved. Perhaps, as Andrea believed, it was a matter of bad investments, poor judgment, and unethical business managers. Perhaps Donald and Lili spent the money on their drug habit, a downfall Dardy likely found more upsetting than money troubles.

Drugs were not new to Lili. Throughout her career, Lili used pills of one type or another. She regularly took sleeping pills, and when she attempted suicide twice in 1949 and once in 1958, she used them to overdose. During the latter half of her career Lili flirted with Miltown, an anti-anxiety drug, which was the precursor to Valium. At some point, Donald, who had used marijuana during his stint in Korea, switched to heroin. Eventually, he introduced Lili to the drug as well.

"Very commonly comes the point in the relationship where you let the other person know you use drugs and ask if they want some as well," said Dr. W., a former heroin addict who admitted he introduced his first wife to the drug.[44] "Addicts attract addicts."

As part of the opiate family, heroin falls into the same category of drugs as morphine, codeine, Vicodin, and Percoset. All are powerful painkillers and it is likely Donald used heroin, in part, to alleviate the pain in his legs he still suffered with from the jungle rot he contracted during his stint in Korea.

"The average non-addict person takes codeine or Vicodin or heroin and they get dizzy or uncomfortable," said Dr. W., a physician who now works in the field of addiction medicine.[45] "They may be taking it for a real medical reason. They don't want to do it again. That's almost more common than not. Most people don't want to keep using opiates. The addict has what's referred to as an idiosyncratic reaction. For them, it gives a sense of ease and comfort. They'd be less aware of any depression they may be having. It's very similar to the feeling you get when you're really, really drunk and feeling good—the good point, before you get sick. They find themselves uninhibited and able to do things they wouldn't normally do. If Lili used Miltown then, indeed that's in the opiate family, and she probably had the genetic makeup to respond to heroin or other opiates in this way."

Discussing Louis Armstrong's pot bust and Kid Ory's alcohol abuse, Babette Ory asked Lili why she thought so many entertainers used drugs or alcohol. "Her comment was that it was overwhelming to them," said Babette Ory.[46] "They just can't deal with all the adulation. They want it on one level because their ego needs it, but when they don't get a moment's peace then they need something to give them that peace."

Canadian television personality Jacques Normand believed Lili still searched for that peace. In the preface to her book *Ma Vie de Stripteaseuse*, he wrote, "Lili St. Cyr wasn't a happy woman, that was obvious in her eyes; she had such a great appetite that nothing and no one could satisfy it."[47]

After Lili retired, she found far fewer things to distract her from the emptiness Normand described and from the monotony of her new life. Heroin numbed her by drawing her into an oblivious and solitary world. As the heroin-addicted character Mark Renton explained with a thick Scottish accent in the 1999 film *Trainspotting,* "Life's boring and futile . . . We fill up our lives with shit, things like careers and relationships to delude our souls that it isn't all totally pointless. Smack's an honest drug, because it strips away these delusions. . . . It doesn't alter your consciousness. It just gives you a hit and a sense of well-being. . . . You can see the misery of the world as it is and you can anesthetize yourself against it."[48]

The psychic wounds Lili faced grew worse as she lost her financial security. It is unclear whether she and Donald lost their money through bad business managers or up their arms as they tried to anesthetize themselves in their heroin addiction. Regardless, the couple's economic problems forced Lili to slowly sell off her antique furniture and finally her home in the Hollywood Hills. By the early eighties the couple had settled into a Spanish-style apartment near Paramount Studios in Los Angeles.

"Social Security and Medicaid were enough to tide them over," said Andrea.[49] "And she still had tons of fans who wanted her autograph and memorabilia. They got by. They weren't living lavishly. The days of grandeur were gone, but they existed."

The existence was not easy. Donald's legs continued to bother him. "They would swell up," said Andrea.[50]. "They would look like they had blood blisters. It almost looked like someone with diabetes when your feet turn purple. He got blood clots in his lungs. He suffered terribly."

Lili cared for Donald, but she battled her own demons as well. "The looks were gone," said Andrea.[51] "The money was gone. Things were not the way she would have liked them to end up."

Both escaped with heroin. "Sometimes your life comes to a point when that might be the only thing that makes you happy," said Andrea. It is the only comment she will make about the situation.

11.

Gentlemen Prefer Blondes

In Hollywood a girl's virtue is much less impor-
tant than her hair-do. You're judged by how you
look, not who you are. Hollywood's a place
where they'll pay you a thousand dollars for a
kiss, and fifty cents for your soul.

— MARILYN MONROE

In the fall of 1982, syndicated gossip columnist Robin Adams Sloan responded to a reader asking what had become of Lili St. Cyr, the famous stripper long absent from the public eye. Sloan responded, "St. Cyr, at sixty-five, is eager to turn her life story into a movie. She visited California's Big Sur recently to try to convince actress Kim Novak that she'd be an ideal on-screen St. Cyr. She once thought the late Marilyn Monroe would be an ideal choice to play her."[1] Nothing came of the overture to Novak, then immersed in llama-raising, just as nothing had come of Lili's hopes of being played by Monroe.

The similarities between the former burlesque queen and silver screen sizzler Marilyn Monroe occurred to at least one other person as well—Lili's fifth husband, Ted Jordan. His version of Monroe's life firmly connected the actress with his ex-wife. He claimed Monroe was enraptured by Lili, admired her presence and sex appeal, and modeled herself after the striptease dancer. Lili, according to Jordan, gave Monroe tips about being photographed and how to move.

Monroe's erotic presence was, in part, learned from Lili. After World War II, two beauty ideals emerged: the innocent, childlike figure of a Debbie Reynolds or Sandra Dee and the voluptuous, sensual woman epitomized by Ava Gardner or Jane Russell. Marilyn Monroe earned her crown as the greatest sex symbol of the twentieth century because she combined the two. "With a slight, lisping voice, a soft curvaceous body, and a seriousness about life, Monroe projected an intense femininity and an inner vulnerability," wrote Lois Banner in *American Beauty*, a history of beauty culture in the United States.[2] "Her sensual posturings were reminiscent of Mae West, although with no hint of the parody that West intended." Similarly, Lili shed the tongue-in-cheek irreverence and satire of her burlesque predecessors and performed her routines in a humor-free, straight fashion. Her name said it all: St. Cyr was sincere, her acts were honest in their sexuality, overt in their glamour. And it was this direct and obvious sexuality and glamour that Monroe mimicked.

Lili, however, never captured the iconic status of Marilyn Monroe, not just because of her career as a stripper, but because she had long lost any childlike innocence. The early hardships in Monroe's life softened her, made her seem innocent, and inspired men to help her. The difficulties in Lili's life hardened her, made her seem cold and distant, and inspired her to shun assistance from others. Monroe's soft innocence, rather than Lili's cold hardness, combined with such blatant sensuality made her the sexual icon she became and the paragon Lili never could.

Those who knew both women, like photographer Bruno Bernard, agreed that Monroe took cues from Lili, though most also believed Ted Jordan exaggerated the extent to which that happened. Few supported Jordan's more salacious contentions of why Lili supposedly took Monroe under her wing. When Jordan asked Monroe why Lili was so helpful, the actress allegedly responded, "I think Lili's in love with me," and admitted to having a lesbian affair with the stripper. Over ten years later, during Jordan and Lili's marriage, Monroe purportedly reappeared. When Jordan asked Lili about it, he wrote that she responded, "Sex is free. If you like someone, whether it's a man or a woman, it seems to me that sex is a perfectly natural way to express your affection. I don't see any difference whether you're married or not, or whether you're in love or not."[3] This fit with Jordan's claim that Lili engaged in several liaisons with other women besides Monroe during their marriage.

Jordan maintained he knew all of this because of an alleged relationship he had with Monroe in the forties. But he did not reveal his relationship with the actress until questions about her death resurfaced in the early eighties and caused a publicity melee. Twenty years after Monroe's reported suicide in 1962, conspiracy theorists speculated that she had been murdered. During the summer of 1982, Monroe's friend Robert Slatzer claimed a red diary, which had belonged to Monroe and reportedly disappeared after her death, contained information about Kennedy, the CIA, and other government secrets, and would prove the actress was murdered. The torrent of media attention this generated prompted the Los Angeles Board of Supervisors to act. In August 1982, the board voted unanimously to ask the district attorney to reopen the investigation into her death, originally determined to be the result of a suicidal drug overdose. In response, the Los Angeles County District Attorney's office began a review of the evidence surrounding Monroe's death in order to determine whether to open up a criminal investigation into the matter.

In the midst of this brouhaha Ted Jordan decided to come forward with information regarding a relationship he claimed to have had with Monroe. During an August 5, 1982, memorial service at her grave, Jordan told reporters he had the much sought-after red diary. At first, Jordan said he found it in a trunk in a friend's garage. He also told private investigator Chris Harris that in the forties and fifties, he and Monroe lived together, but just as friends. "Their relationship was an unusual one in that it was not of sexual overtones," Harris told reporters.[4] "He was simply a good friend personally, one she trusted."

Over the next few months Jordan's story changed repeatedly. A few days after Harris described Jordan and Monroe's relationship as platonic, Jordan told reporters the two had been involved in a "long off-and-on romance."[5] Just days later, Jordan backtracked entirely and said the diary he had was not the one everyone was searching for. He maintained the book contained no information about the CIA and instead was just a book of love poems the couple had shared. "I'm not looking for money," he told the Associated Press.[6] "I'm not looking for publicity. I'm not selling her body or her memories. I do have a little bit of integrity."

The District Attorney's office disagreed. "Jordan advised that he falsely told reporters he possessed Monroe's diary," concluded a report by the office in August 1982.[7] "He did possess a small book . . . in which Monroe wrote several favorite poems. Jordan stated the book and four photo-graphs . . . were stolen from the rear seat of his automobile." A month later another report concluded, "[Jordan] lied about Monroe's book of poems. He now states that he received the book from Monroe in 1943 and . . . in 1962, he buried the book and a chain on a mountain in Ohio. . . . Jordan is planning to return to Ohio and attempt to locate the burial site."[8] Finally, a Los Angeles official who preferred anonymity told reporters, "[Jordan] is not a credible source. We don't think he ever had any diary— even if there is such a book."[9]

Jordan continued to lead reporters on for a few more months, using his alleged link with Monroe to keep himself in the news. But in December, after several months of review, L.A. District Attorney John Van de Kamp put the matter to rest and decided against opening up a criminal investigation into Monroe's death. According to the twenty-nine-page report that accompanied his statement, the "inquiries and document examination uncovered no credible evidence supporting a murder the-ory."[10] In response, Jordan told *Variety* in 1982 that, "I know she didn't take her own life."[11]

Three years later, author Anthony Summers released the most exten-sive biography on the film star since her death. In *Goddess: The Secret Lives of Marilyn Monroe*, Summers suggested that then United States Attorney General Robert F. Kennedy visited with Monroe the day she died. Summers posited that after Monroe's overdose, actor and Kennedy in-law Peter Lawford delayed the announcement of her death and quietly got Kennedy out of Southern California to avoid political embarrassment for the Attorney General and his brother, President John F. Kennedy. The new information in *Goddess*—culled from a plethora of interviews and unreleased police documents on Monroe's death—generated a glut of headlines. Jordan's name was noticeably absent from the book.

A canceled 20/20 broadcast further fueled the deluge of news regard-ing Monroe and her death. Staff at the ABC news program spent four months and several hundred thousand dollars corroborating the informa-tion in *Goddess* and put together a half-hour program on Monroe, Kennedy, and the mob. However, Roone Arledge, President of ABC News, canceled the segment and called it a "sleazy piece of journalism." Arledge, a friend of the Kennedy family, was accused of censorship, and journalists, including 20/20's own Hugh Downs and Barbara Walters, protested the decision. Downs said the story was "more carefully documented than anything any network did during Watergate."[12] The program never aired.

The fracas grew louder when the Los Angeles Board of Supervisors, prompted by the evidence in *Goddess* and a letter from Monroe's friend Robert Slatzer, again requested the District Attorney reopen the investigation. A grand jury convened to resolve the matter, but once again decided against reopening the case.

Goddess, meanwhile, climbed high on the best-seller lists. And while the 20/20 segment never aired and any further investigation into Monroe's death was quashed, the trifecta of the three events created a perfect storm of news coverage.

The 1982 uproar, the hubbub created in 1985 by the news in *Goddess*, and the glut of Monroe books landing on bookstore shelves, prompted Jordan to write his own book about the actress, *Norma Jean: My Secret Life with Marilyn Monroe*. Particularly upset by biographies asserting she was murdered, Jordan again changed his story, claimed he received a phone call from Monroe the night she died, and said he believed she killed herself. "I saw all this crap written about her, mostly from people who never knew her," Jordan told a reporter for the *Los Angeles Times*.[13] "I said, 'I'm going to sit down and write a book about the girl that my brother remembers meeting, that my mom . . . still remembers meeting, and write the true story about her.'" Yet, even his claims about how *Norma Jean* developed are not entirely true.

When discussion about reopening the investigation into Marilyn Monroe's death began, writer Ernest Volkman started working on a magazine article about it. In the course of Volkman's research Jordan's name surfaced, and he interviewed the actor for the story. The piece grew into a book, and the two collaborated on *Norma Jean*, with Volkman working as the ghost writer.

Working with Jordan was difficult. "He was a handful, a total pain in the ass," said Volkman.[14] "He had a limited attention span. He would start off professionally and then he'd start to wander off. He would have wild mood swings. Sometimes he couldn't do enough for me. He'd be falling all over himself. The next day he'd be totally different—moody, nasty, and bitter. He's like your crazy uncle. The guy you kind of dread at weddings because you never knew what you'd get." Despite the problems,

Volkman found Jordan credible. He verified what he could and never discovered any discrepancies.

Concerned about a slander suit, Volkman wanted to interview Lili himself. She refused to see him. "She was overweight, had a problem with long-time drug abuse, and wouldn't see anyone," said Volkman.[15] "Ted showed Lili either the complete manuscript or just the section of the book that involved her and Marilyn Monroe. She said it was fine. Then I called and spoke with her briefly on the phone and she also told me it was fine."

Shortly after *Norma Jean* first appeared on shelves, the William Morrow editor who worked on the manuscript defended Jordan's claims in a *Newsday* article. "We got [Lili's] approval before we decided to publish this," said Liza Dawson.[16] "Marilyn very much patterned herself on Lili St. Cyr. Her way of dressing, of talking, her whole persona. Norma Jean was a mousy, brown-haired girl with a high squeaky voice, and it was from Lili St. Cyr that she learned how to become a sex goddess."

However, when *Norma Jean* appeared in bookstores in 1989, critics and friends of Monroe called much of it into question. An edition of the book was first published in England before the release in the United States. The British media and Monroe's friends raised concerns regarding the accuracy of several incidents. In the British edition, Jordan claimed to have had a one-night fling with actress Lupe Velez in 1946 in an attempt to make Monroe jealous. Velez died in 1944. The British version also included nude photos supposedly of Monroe taken by Jordan. The pictures, though, were of another actress and were removed before the American edition of the book was published.

"He had nude photographs of Marilyn Monroe that were actually photographs of a lady named Arlene Hunter," said James Haspiel, a photographer and friend of Monroe.[17] "And he had a picture that he claimed to have taken of Norma Jean when she was young, in her teen years, that was actually a photograph that I took. [When] I took the photograph, in the bushes behind Norma Jean, I had put my initials, on three leaves: JRH. And there they were in the print of the picture that he published that he claimed was a picture he took of Norma Jean. I spoke with his publisher. The pictures were all withdrawn from the American publication of his book."

The American edition, which came out a few months later, received the same critical assessment. The television program *Entertainment Tonight* interviewed friends of Marilyn Monroe who said the actress never knew Jordan. In *Norma Jean*, Jordan claimed to be the father of Monroe's love child, but he rescinded that statement a few months after publication. During the post-publication media tour, the issue of Monroe's red diary also resurfaced. This time Jordan told reporters Monroe gave him the diary a few days before she died and that he kept it in a safe-deposit box.

In 1996, *Norma Jean and Marilyn* aired on HBO. The film, starring Ashley Judd and Mira Sorvino as the two facets of the actress, was originally to be based on Anthony Summers' *Goddess*. When Summers found out the filmmakers intended to involve Jordan in the movie, he asked that his name be removed from the credits. "Ted Jordan, initially, struck me as potentially interesting, but even on the most superficial investigation I found that he had no credibility," said Summers.[18] "Almost everything he said and did struck me as unreliable and unconvincing." The film made no reference to Lili.

When Jordan's book was released, the press did not question his claims that Lili and Marilyn Monroe enjoyed a love affair. Personal friends of each have since lambasted Jordan regarding the assertion.

"Marilyn Monroe did not have an affair with Lili St. Cyr," said photographer and Monroe friend James Haspiel.[19] "Ted Jordan is a liar. He's a very underhanded individual, who demonstrated with his photographs, if nothing else, what he's capable of."

Bruno Bernard, whose pictures of Lili were studied by Marilyn before Marilyn's own sessions with the cheesecake photographer, asked Lili about Jordan's claims. "[She told me] that she had met Marilyn casually in Las Vegas, but had never entertained homoerotic relations with her," wrote Bernard in his book *Requiem to Marilyn*.[20] "Ted Jordan's revelations came to me as a surprise in as much as I had never observed lesbian tendencies in either person. To the contrary, Marilyn once expressed to me her apprehension that her coach Natasha Lytess might be 'AC-DC,' which would put an unbearable burden on their relationship."

"Ted Jordan was careless with the truth," said former dancer Liz Renay, who dated Jordan for three or four months after he separated from Lili in the late fifties.[21] "He was very creative with the truth. He didn't tell bold lies, but there were discrepancies. He liked to embellish and exaggerate things. His version wasn't the exact unvarnished version of things. I could see if Marilyn said something along the lines of, 'If I went for girls, I'd go for Lili St. Cyr' and Ted would spin it that they had an affair. That's just my opinion. Too many people knew who Lili St. Cyr and Marilyn Monroe were. If they had an affair, there would have been rumors. When there are such big names involved, things leak out. I never heard any inkling of a rumor."

"I tell you, I think Ted Jordan's a jerk, and I don't believe it," said Armando Orsini, Lili's husband before Jordan.[22] "She was not prudish, believe me, but . . . She was a sensual woman, but she was not oversexed. She was just a healthy, sexual woman. Ted Jordan is a liar."

Even Jordan's brother questioned his story. "Well, did he confabulate, or did he imagine that he had an affair with Norma Jean?" asked Ben Friedman, though he does believe the two knew each other.[23] "Well, maybe he did and maybe he didn't." And Mildred Katleman, who was married to El Rancho owner Beldon Katleman when Lili and Ted married at the hotel, thought simply that "he'd do anything to make a penny."[24]

Jordan appeared on the television hit *Gunsmoke* for nearly ten years and lived comfortably off his earnings from the show. It's unlikely Jordan wrote *Norma Jean* just for the money. "I think he was trying to make a last grasp at fame," said Ernest Volkman.[25] "He struck me as typical California. He was a pure child of Hollywood and all that implies. He had no education, no talent, but he was good looking so he went into the movies. He used his connections with his uncle who he hated. He used his relationship with Lili where he became Mr. St. Cyr and was emasculated. And then he used his connection to Marilyn Monroe. But he never quite fulfilled what he wanted. He was bitter. He never got the brass ring."

Understanding why Lili signed off on *Norma Jean*—if she did—is not as apparent. She worked with two ghost writers on two different memoirs—the American *And Men My Fuel* and the Canadian *Ma Vie de Stripteaseuse*—and in neither instance, despite being remarkably frank about stripping, men, sex, and abortion, did she suggest she had had a sexual relationship with Monroe. Always savvy about snagging headlines, she surely would have known that to admit an affair with Marilyn Monroe would propel both books to the top of the best-seller lists. Yet neither memoir contained any confession of a relationship with the actress. Considering the lack of such an admission and the disbelief from both women's friends, it seems highly unlikely such an affair ever happened.

Perhaps Lili relished the return to the spotlight. Maybe, out of loyalty to, or her friendship with, Jordan, she refused to challenge his claims. She had managed the unusual feat of always remaining friends with her ex-husbands and she liked to joke the reason she and her ex-husbands remained friendly was because she never asked for alimony. She also maintained enough detachment during the marriage that staying convivial afterward was easier.

Jordan and Lili continued to be sociable enough that shortly after *Norma Jean* and the ensuing commotion, he and his brother, Ben Friedman, visited her. During the visit, she made no objection to his assertions—perhaps because she was reeling from the effects of her heroin addiction.

"I used to give her money," said Friedman.[26] "She'd ask me for a loan. I knew damn well I'd never get it back, but I gave her what little I could afford. Well, Ted and I went up to see her. And she was taking drugs then. I figured, I'm not going to give her money, so I bought one hundred dollars of groceries for her. And when I took the groceries up there, she looked horrible. Her voice never changed. She was just as soft-spoken. But she was old, broken-down, and had marks on her arm from using drugs."

By the time Jordan and Friedman visited Lili, she and Donald had moved again to a smaller, far more rundown apartment. "It was horrible," said Friedman. "She was living in poor conditions. She didn't have a big enough refrigerator for the groceries. She had one of these little boxes that wouldn't hold anything. The only air conditioner she had wasn't working. So I went out and bought her an air conditioner. That was the last time I saw Lili."

Telling the story of his last visit with Lili, Friedman revealed the pity he felt for her. And it is in this that Lili St. Cyr and Marilyn Monroe shared the greatest connection. It is through the prism of her death that most now view Marilyn. Her life has become simply a prologue to the tragic end, her death the real story. In this view, Marilyn Monroe is exploited and victimized, helpless, and manipulated. She is a cautionary tale about sex and objectification. Yet this view ignores the star she was before her death. During her life, reporters portrayed her transformation from Norma Jean to Marilyn Monroe as the ultimate American dream come true. Her fans saw her as sexually liberated, rather than objectified. During her life, her divorces, fights with the studios, and other problems were the typical tales of celebrity life. "If at the end of her life, Marilyn may have seemed a mess . . . there was nothing inevitable or emblematic about it," wrote Neal Gabler in a retrospective for *Playboy*.[27] "She wasn't a victim or a divided self or a commodity . . . If anything, she was an aging and disappointed actress who was trying to assert her control over a tough, misogynistic system. And to understand her popularity now, one has to see her not as a tormented, doom-laden goddess enshrouded in Freudian analysis, but as a tough-minded star who through the force of her personality and will, managed to seduce the world—and rather enjoyed doing so."

Ted Jordan bought into this view of Monroe. "I see girls who want to be Marilyn Monroes and they end up either as hookers or in the morgue," he told one reporter, noting he saw his book as a cautionary tale for actresses.[28] Jordan wrote *Norma Jean* in such a way that Monroe's actions foreshadowed the end. He felt sorry for its star. It does not fully credit the life she lived. Many fell into the same trap with Lili. Seeing her through the prism of her career as a stripper she is dismissed as a prostitute, lesbian, or deviant. Judging her through the prism of her drug addiction and death, she is disregarded as a cautionary tale of a woman who paid the price for exploiting her sexuality. Yet, viewed through the entire kaleidoscope of her life, the vision changes. One sees a determined woman who bucked the status quo and lived life on her own terms. One sees a working-class girl transformed into a glamorous, sexy star used as a model by icons like Marilyn Monroe and Madonna. One sees a woman who used what she was given to get what she wanted; a woman who used her body and sexuality for personal liberation.

Her drug addiction and impoverished death were not the comeuppance of a woman who dared to live outside the mainstream or the price she paid for exploiting her own sexuality. Rather, as she herself realized, they were the result of her own inner turmoil. "When it comes to physical harm, I only have to fear myself," she wrote presciently in *And Men My Fuel*. "My destruction comes from the inside."[29]

For people who want their world and its people neat, unruffled, and categorized, seeing a woman like Lili St. Cyr through just one prism makes sense. It retains order. For those who turn the kaleidoscope, a woman like Lili St. Cyr becomes colorful, distorted, beautiful, and messy. It is complex. As author Barbara Grizzuti Harrison once wrote, "It is hard to bear witness to the truth, and at the same time to shape messy experience in such a way as to make sense of it. The process is analogous to the art of lost wax: Something gets burned away, lost; something is refined, found." In Lili's case, as with Marilyn's, the trick is to not view the life through the prism of the end. For in this case, the end was tragic.

12.

And the Curtain Closes

"Life's but a walking shadow;
a poor player,
That struts and frets his hour
upon the stage
And then is heard no more."

— WILLIAM SHAKESPEARE

"Across the broad continent of a woman's life falls the shadow of a sword," wrote Virginia Woolf, who went on to explain that on one side lies tradition and order and on the other "all is confusion." In considering this quote, *Eat Pray Love* author Elizabeth Gilbert wrote "that the crossing of the sword may bring a far more interesting existence to a woman, but you can bet it will also be more perilous."[1]

In one of Lili's last conversations with her friend Augusto Lodi, an architect she'd met years earlier, she hinted at this sentiment. She acknowledged she'd lived a remarkable life, that she had been very rich and very happy. Now, however, she complained she didn't have many friends or very much money.[2] For Lili, the peril came as she attempted to retain her glorified image and escape the loneliness that resulted from her self-imposed isolation.

By the early nineties, Lili so fully entrenched herself in her Garbo-esque philosophy that she saw almost no one. Her former husband Armando Orsini, with whom she remained friendly until her death, went to California and called Lili to arrange a visit. "She didn't want to see me," Armando recalled.[3] "She said, 'I want you to have your memory of me from twenty years ago, not now.'"

Former burlesque dancers Betty Rowland and Margie Hart invited Lili to lunch, to no avail. "We heard she was a little down and wanted to try and cheer her up," said Rowland.[4] "She didn't want to [come to lunch] because she had to wear a muumuu [and] she couldn't get in her high heels anymore. I said, 'Well, we'll all wear muumuus, just the three of us, and talk.' Lili wouldn't come out. I don't know what her problem was. She would talk to people on the phone and write letters, but she would not go out."

At one point, Lili told her friend Bob Bethia that she'd gone through some boxes and found scrapbooks and other memorabilia. She offered them to Bob, who drove to her apartment in Los Angeles to pick the items up. "I went to this kind of nondescript apartment building," said Bethia.[5] "It was rundown-looking, with lots of cats running around, which I later found out were all hers."

When he got to Lili's apartment, Bob found a box outside and some costumes hanging on the door. One of the costumes was stuck in the door so he yelled in for Lili. "I looked in [a small window-like peephole], but I couldn't really see anything because it was kind of dark in there," said Bethia.[6] "Then all of a sudden I see this old, white-haired woman bent over with osteoporosis walk across the room very, very slowly. It looked like she was in a lot of pain. It wasn't what I expected. I didn't expect her to be twenty years old any more, but I expected her to be tall and statuesque. She was just an old woman. She went across the room as I stood there frozen, until this gentleman, who I later found out was her caretaker, came to the door. He told me she was not well. He never told me what was wrong. I think he was sworn to secrecy. I said thank you and left. It was too bad. We're all gonna get old."

The memorabilia Lili gave to Bob Bethia proved to be a treasure trove from her heyday. The box was filled with magazines with her on the cover, pictures from her scrapbook, publicity stills, a catalog from the Undie World of Lili St. Cyr, G-strings, a towel from her act, and a pair of fluorescent pink go-go boots. But shortly after he picked up the items Lili and Bethia stopped talking. "It was more on her part," said Bethia, who said the friendship ended around 1992.[7] "I think whatever her illness was, she just stopped answering the phone and the letters weren't being responded to. So that was that, and it was sad for me because it was a thrill to get to talk to her for the brief time that we did. She was very good to me. She was very generous and it was just neat."

The secret Bethia never learned before his friendship with Lili faded is that she was addicted to heroin. One of the very few people she allowed to see her was her dealer, Kash. When Kash moved to Los Angeles he fell into the city's rock-and-roll scene, going to clubs every night. A few friends from the clubs introduced him to heroin and he began snorting and smoking it casually. Soon he became addicted, began shooting it, and was traveling downtown to unsafe neighborhoods to buy it. A worried friend finally introduced him to a woman from whom he could buy heroin safely.

"I went to her house one day and there was a W magazine with the label Lili St. Cyr on it," Kash remembered.[8] "I asked her if she'd gotten it at a thrift store or antique shop and she said no, that Lili was her friend. Turned out she was also selling to Lili. So to help support my habit, I did deliveries for this woman. One of my deliveries happened to be Lili when she needed new syringes. I didn't know what to expect when I first went over there. She was an older lady, a little hunched over, with white hair."

After that, Kash saw Lili once or twice a week for several years. He would bring her heroin or clean syringes and often they would sit and chat. "We would just hang out and talk," said Kash.[9] "She was always very well made up and well dressed—usually a kimono or something. I was never there when she was doing the stuff. She'd give me the money and she'd always sign a picture for me. We'd have iced tea and we got to just kind of be chatty. It was like having tea with someone, just with this business deal involved. She was absolutely a lovely person, just wonderful, and super-friendly."

Kash and Lili talked about the news, how her business of selling the eight-by-ten pictures was going, and, of course, her days dancing. "Mostly we would just chat about trivial things," said Kash.[10] "I would ask her about when she was dancing and it was almost like she went into another world. She loved to talk about it."

Kash also met Donald, whom he knew as Lorenzo. Kash believed that Donald first introduced Lili to heroin. "Something happened to him in Korea," said Kash. "His legs were really messed up. He had a lot of trouble walking and was in a wheelchair a lot. I think Lorenzo did [heroin] to help the pain in his legs. He was very handsome, even when he was older. He was always well dressed, always in khaki pants and a polo or button-up, never a T-shirt or anything slouchy. And I think he was crazy about her. They never left each other's side. He was a good guy, a great guy."

One of the last times he saw her was during a summer in the mid-nineties. "It was boiling hot," said Kash, smiling at the memory.[11] "She said, 'Kash, I'd let you in, but it's so hot I'm not wearing a thing!' and she just started chuckling and laughing. I thought, well, I've got naked pictures of you, but you were twenty-five then."

Shortly after that, Kash disappeared deeper into his own addiction. He eventually cleaned himself up and has been sober for over ten years. Reflecting on his relationship with Lili, he admitted holding a strangely contrary and quixotic view about the entire thing. Whereas others described her apartment as slightly run-down, he thought it was a "terribly cool place. It looked like you stepped back into the forties. The living room had heavy curtains and a big, poofy couch. It was done in dark greens and reds. There were a couple of ashtrays, because she smoked. It was dynamic."[12]

Kash even felt this way about her drug use. He liked to believe she used heroin recreationally, despite the fact that he saw her once a week. "There's some weird romance thing I have about it with her," said Kash.[13] "She was one of those wild spirits. She didn't bother snorting it or smoking it, or putting it in a cigarette. She was going to do it the hard way."

Yet, the fact that Lili injected heroin revealed the deep extent of her addiction. Most people begin using heroin recreationally by smoking it— usually laced in a marijuana cigarette or in a pipe—or snorting it. As the addiction grows, most people move to injecting it. "Physiologically and medically speaking you get the biggest bang for your buck that way," said Dr. W.[14] "You get one hundred percent of the drug active in your blood. It gets people addicted to higher levels very quickly."

Kash, who acknowledged he was "a little out of it at the time," was alone in his romanticized view of Lili's life. The woman he delivered heroin for felt bad that Lili was "so old and so strung out" and "always gave her a deal."[15] Lili's former husband, Armando Orsini, was unaware of the drug use, but did know how poor and sketchy her living situation had become. When he talked about her last years, he moved between pity, anger, and regret. His voice cracked in sadness and he broke off in the middle of his thoughts.

"She always fell in love with people with no money at all," said Armando.[16] "I think what she had was a kind of mother [complex]. She took care of me. She took care of [Paul] Valentine. I'm not saying financially, but emotionally. She never had anybody to help her. Nobody. What I know now, as a businessman, I could have done so much for her in terms of investing money, all the financial things. At the time, I didn't. And she lost almost everything. Regardless of divorcing her, I could have done so much for her. She had no sense of . . . Jesus Christ, I could have saved this woman."

It is unlikely Armando Orsini could have saved Lili. As the decade progressed she became so reclusive that even take-out delivery men were pre-paid and instructed to leave her food outside the door. And the drugs so ravaged her that she often became disoriented. Just before her death, when Alan Hustak, a reporter for *The (Montreal) Gazette*, called her, she mistakenly thought it was her former pal, columnist Al Palmer. Informed of the confusion, the woman much of Montreal described as classy and elegant responded, "Too bad. Palmer was the best fuck I ever had."[17]

At some point, Lili's health failed and she was admitted into a convalescent home not far from her apartment. Unhappy, and likely going through withdrawal, she paid an employee to take her home.[18] The addiction had progressed to the point where her body needed more and more opiates to feel normal. Withdrawal for Lili, as with all heroin addicts, likely included extreme waves of dysphoria, shaking, and pain. Some have compared the pain to feeling like the muscles are being ripped from your bones. "You feel awful," said Dr. W.[19] "Every part of your body hurts. It hurts to sit, to take a shower, to wash your hair. You're shaking and miserable. You have uncontrollable diarrhea. Your nose runs. Your eyes run. All of your fluids want to leave you."

Addicts will go through whatever it takes to get the drug, including risk their life. In order to avoid withdrawal, Lili escaped the convalescent home she had been admitted to and returned to her apartment. Through it all, she succeeded with her Greta Garbo–inspired isolation. The now "old, white-haired woman bent over with osteoporosis" and addicted to heroin was remembered as a beautiful siren. In the January 1999 issue of *Playboy*, the arbiter of sexiness released their list of the one hundred beautiful women "who made this century sizzle." The magazine ranked Lili number sixty-nine, ahead of Gypsy Rose Lee at seventy-eight. Her idol Greta Garbo landed at number fifty-one. Not surprisingly, Marilyn Monroe scored the top spot.

At the end of that month, on January 29, 1999, at the age of eighty-one, Lili St. Cyr died of heart failure. Lili and Dardy remained estranged so it was up to Pat Carrol, one of the fans Lili had grown close with first through letters and then over the phone, to let Dardy know her half-sister had died. "At the end of her life, she was friends with a young man whom she considered her adopted son," a reporter for *La Presse*, a Montreal newspaper revealed.[20] "When he discovered that his idol was dead and the body [was] at the morgue, researcher Nicola Bridge, who worked on a [Canadian documentary about the dancer], gave him the telephone number of Lili St. Cyr's sister."

While newspapers across the country and around the world mourned her death and heralded the former striptease dancer, only four people attended Lili's funeral—Dardy, Pat Carrol, her caretaker, and the caretaker's wife. Obituaries in papers like the *New York Times*, the *Los Angeles Times*, *The Independent* in London, *Time*, and *Variety* recounted her routines and her run-ins with the law, and mentioned her connection to Marilyn Monroe. "They were beautiful obituaries," recalled Armando Orsini.[21] "They were not low-class. She would have been very happy, I'm sure."

"You cannot talk to anyone in Montreal over fifty, French or English, who doesn't know Lili St. Cyr," filmmaker Nicole Messier told *The (Montreal) Gazette*. "What is fantastic about her is that she really was the first woman most young men in this city saw nude, desired, and had access to."[22]

In one memorial, a reporter for *The Guardian* wrote, "They don't make entertainers like Lili St. Cyr . . . any more. The sincerity of Miss St. Cyr (say the name quickly) was what people came to see. Or at least, that was what her fans liked to believe. She was an artiste, a delightful character who practiced her art, well, sincerely; a charming lady who did everything in the very best taste."[23]

𝒫rivately, Lili's death left a more profound mark, even long after friend-ships and relationships had faded. Kash found out through the *Los Angeles Times* obituary and was "devastated." Bob Bethia learned the news through a friend who had seen the obituary in the newspaper. "I was crushed because I felt like I abandoned her for some reason," said Bob.[24] "I didn't. She's the one who stopped answering the phone and writing back. I cared for her, not as a fan—as a friend. I just felt bad, she was good to me and I was a total stranger."

After Lili died, Donald completely gave up. "He didn't want to live anymore," said his sister, Andrea Hedrick.[25] "Her family came in and took over everything. I don't think he went to the service. I don't know if he was invited or told. He called me and it was heart-wrenching. He said, 'Lili is gone. My life is over.' He was sobbing, sobbing, sobbing on the phone. She was his life. He just shut down. He loved me. He loved my kids, but his main source of happiness was gone. He had no will to live anymore."

After Lili died, Donald lived in a Veterans Administration (VA) affili-ated apartment complex. "He was pretty sick," said his landlord, Irene Terheggen.[26] "He tried to OD a couple of times. I have these big sliding glass doors in my building. He went right through 'em; he was so loaded. So, finally, I had to put him out. He was such a good man. He just got on the wrong track." Donald moved to a VA hospital, where he stayed until his death in February 2003.

In both the public tributes and private laments it was award-winning poet Dorothy Barresi's elegy for Lili that captured her spirit. In "Glass Dress," a poem included in Barresi's book *Rouge Pulp*, she wrote:

> Lili St. Cyr is dead.
> No tassel-twirling, minimum wage girl.
> No discount moon,
> no languishing feminine ruses.
> She teases the illimitable body,
> Marilyn before Marilyn,
> Jayne before Jayne.[27]

Epilogue

In the years following Lili's death, stripper chic and the neo-burlesque movement quickly gained in popularity. The lines between the interest in the raunchier strip and the classic burlesque-inspired tease sometimes blurred together, but clearly Americans had a newfound interest in striptease.

Publishing houses released several striptease memoirs like *Strip City*, in which author Lily Burana recalled her farewell tour stripping across the country, and *Ivy League Stripper*, in which author Heidi Mattson dished on how she stripped to put herself through Brown University. Former stripper Anna Nicole Smith starred in her own reality TV show. In the second installment of the film *Charlie's Angels*, Cameron Diaz performed a routine in a life-sized martini glass inspired by today's most well-known burlesque queen, Dita Von Teese. In a *New York Times Magazine* spread, Britney Spears wore a boa, a top hat, rhinestone shoes, and nothing else. The caption read, "From bubblegum princess to burlesque queen, Britney tips her hat to Gypsy Rose Lee." Even Broadway got in on the act and in 2003 named its annual fundraiser for HIV/AIDS "Burlesque is Back."

Taking it off in a striptease class became a hip way to take off a few pounds. Carmen Electra starred in a series of DVDs called *Aerobic Striptease*. Fitness clubs like Crunch offered striptease workouts. Actress Sheila Kelly started the S Factor, a class that helped women get in shape by wrapping their legs around a stripper pole. The craze sparked an interest in at-home stripper poles, with choices ranging from a basic shower-rod-like pole to one that included colored lights at the base.

Newspapers like *The New York Times, USA Today*, and the *Los Angeles Times* chronicled the trend. And *The Washington Post* noted, "The true surprise of stripper-chic is how very vanilla it has become, nestled in the bosom of family values."[1] In a CBS *Sunday Morning* segment on Exotic World, a burlesque museum and stripper hall of fame, Bill Geist admired Lili's lace thong. And in November 2003, Oprah Winfrey gave her audience makeovers, pole dancing lessons, and sexy lingerie in an hour devoted to releasing your "inner sexpot."

At the same time that raunchier stripper chic bumped and ground its way into popularity, burlesque striptease shimmied to the forefront as well. "Stripping is a man giving money to a woman in exchange for a sexual feeling," said Katherine Valentine, who performed as Miss Astrid in Manhattan's Va Va Voom Room burlesque show, when she explained the difference between striptease and the neo-burlesque movement.[2] "The burlesque thing has very little to do with that."

The neo-burlesque movement, which began percolating in the mid-nineties, wanted to put the tease back into the strip. "The revival is a reaction to the MTV, HBO, sex-is-everywhere attitude," said Michelle Baldwin, who wrote the book *Burlesque and the New Bump-n-Grind* and performs as Vivienne VaVoom in the Denver-based troupe Burlesque As It Was.[3] "Burlesque takes that step back, where it's not just about flesh and parts. It's about foreplay and sensuality and costumes and glitter. It's not so harsh."

The neo-burlesque movement glances over its bare shoulder to Lili's era of striptease. Dita Von Teese, largely credited with making the neo-burlesque movement popular with the general public, even pays homage to Lili by recreating her bubble bath routine. Yet significant differences remain. Neo-burlesque is both nostalgic and campy. Whereas many of Lili's peers twirled their tassels out of financial necessity, the neo-burlesque dancers tend to be educated women in their twenties and thirties who aren't performing as a primary source of income. Today's burlesque dancers often use their routines to make a statement. They use their dance, lyrics, and comedy to speak out on gay and lesbian concerns, war, race, and a host of other political and social issues. "It's almost like sugarcoating something," said Baldwin.[4] "You're taking a heavy political point, but it's wrapped in rhinestones and music and a pretty girl."

Neo-burlesque also challenges the notion of what constitutes a pretty girl. The full-figured, zaftig burlesque dancers gave way to lithe, lean bodies more typical of the high-end showgirls, which gave way to the toned, athletic strippers of the seventies and eighties. But the neo-burlesque dancers feature women of all body types—soft and round, tall and thin, short and athletic. There are no impresarios like Florenz Ziegfeld or Harold Minsky dictating the specific beauty ideal.

Many argue that whether or not a neo-burlesque routine includes politically edged commentary, this new form accepts all body types, challenges stereotypes about what is sexy and beautiful, and overall empowers women. Whether the neo-burlesque movement managed to put a feminist spin on the strip continues to be debated. Regardless, the changes from burlesque to neo-burlesque, from Lili St. Cyr to Vivienne VaVoom, highlight the transformation in Americans' views on sex and women.

When Lili was born in 1917, women's lives looked drastically different. At home, housework remained arduous; vacuum cleaners were too cumbersome or expensive for most, indoor plumbing was rare, and many still washed laundry by hand or in large hand-cranked tubs. Women worked outside the home, but only 10 percent kept their jobs after marriage. Few practiced medicine or law. Contraception and abortion were illegal. Childbirth remained dangerous; during World War I, more American women died from childbirth than men from battle.

In the course of Lili's life, all of that—and so much more—changed. During the eight decades of her life women gained the right to vote, to choose contraception, and to have an abortion. She witnessed the founding of Planned Parenthood, the National Organization for Women, the first women's studies programs at colleges, and *Ms.* magazine. She watched as Alfred Kinsey's reports on sexuality, Hugh Hefner's *Playboy*, and Betty Friedan's *The Feminine Mystique* sparked debate about sex and gender. In her life, the first birth control clinics, rape crisis centers, and HIV/AIDS clinics opened. She saw the invention of the bikini, the birth control pill, and tampons. In her lifetime, Betty Crocker first appeared on grocery store shelves, Miss America earned her first crown, Amelia Earhart flew across the Atlantic Ocean, Barbie debuted, and Sally Ride orbited the earth. Title VII of the Civil Rights Act prohibited sex discrimination at work, Title IX of the Education Amendments opened up school sports programs to women, and women were admitted to the U.S. Military Academies. Women won their first Pulitzer Prize, Nobel Peace Prize, and Purple Heart. They became FBI agents, rabbis, ambassadors, Major

League Baseball scouts, members of Congress, airline pilots, Indy 500 drivers, Olympic marathon runners, and Surgeon General of the United States for the first time.[5]

The national mythology encourages Americans to be independent, achievement-oriented go-getters. For much of the twentieth century, economic forces and cultural ideology whipsawed women between this imperative and the view that women should be dependent, passive, nurturing. Lili and the women of her era cobbled together some compromise between the two as best they could. As *America's Women* author Gail Collins pointed out: "The history of American women is about the fight for freedom, but it's less a war against oppressive men than a struggle to straighten out the perpetually mixed message about women's role that was accepted by almost everybody of both genders."[6]

Ultimately, women won the right to choose: the choice to marry or not, the choice between home and career, the choice to bear children or not. Women may still attack each other for the choices the other makes, but all have the right to choose the life they lead, the path they take. Striptease remains one path still hotly debated. Are women limited or liberated by striptease? Are they empowered by their sexuality or victimized as nothing more than an object of desire? The answer is never easy when it comes to sex. And it is far too easy to pigeonhole women into one category or another.

In November 1999, a few months after Lili's death, *The (Montreal) Gazette* asked readers to vote on the hundred most notable Montrealers. The newspaper compiled a list of several hundred suggestions, which included Lili even though she was an American. One reader responded angrily, writing: "The photos you chose to represent the selection of women as top Montrealers demonstrates a view of females in our society representative of the last century and not the millennium. I certainly do not want to go into the new millennium with a Madonna (Marguerite Bourgeoys) and a whore (Lili St. Cyr) as representative of what women aspire to in terms of role models. It has never been easy being a feminist, and it is certainly discouraging at times like this when I question if we have made any headway at all. . . . You have shown a poor, if not contemptuous, view of women . . ."[7]

Despite this reader's complaints, Lili landed in the number forty-three spot, ahead of *Gazette* founder Fleury Mesplet (number eight-four), prime minister John Abbott (number seventy-six), and actor Donald Sutherland (number fifty-two). More interesting is the *Gazette* reader's need to classify women as Madonna or whore. No woman falls that simply into such categories. Lili was neither Madonna nor whore, neither saint nor sinner, neither exploited pinup nor scheming gold-digger. She was neither mentally shallow nor intellectually subversive, neither socially unimportant nor dangerously vital. Just as striptease presents women in all of the contradictory ways society wants women to be—virginal, lusty, pure, dirty—so Lili offered conflicting images. The woman hidden behind the sex symbol was more complex than any one label suggests; the dancer was not just the hip-swiveling dance.

That complexity is relevant when considering whether Lili was freed or limited by striptease, for in her case she was both. From the beginning, she straddled two worlds: one of glamour, adventure, and caprice; the other of disillusion and disappointment. As a child she studied the first world in the movies, but lived in the other. As a young woman she practiced living the life she dreamed about aboard the steam liners, but was forced to return home because of World War II. As a dancer, she dazzled on stage, but as a stripper she had trouble transitioning to other things. She was glorified for her appeal, yet stigmatized as if she were a prostitute. Striptease liberated her financially, as she literally pulled herself up by her bra strap and G-string. Yet, in depending solely on her appearance, she limited herself later in life. In the end, Lili made the best life she could out of the choices she believed were available to her.

She was born into a poor family, abandoned by her parents, and raised by her grandmother, but she overcame the obstacles of her childhood and used her ambition, beauty, and charm to escape her small-town life. She practiced the art of seduction on rich, older men aboard the steam liners that traveled between the United States and Europe. She perfected the art of the tease on the stages of seamy burlesque theaters, upscale cabarets, and hole-in-the-wall nightclubs. She became the top striptease dancer after World War II. She shimmied across the country's swankiest nightclubs in front of audiences that included Frank Sinatra, Ronald Reagan, and Humphrey Bogart. Her sex appeal rivaled that of Lana Turner and Ava Gardner and inspired Marilyn Monroe. Photos of her in various states of undress covered hundreds of magazines. She danced through several Hollywood movies, including Howard Hughes' *Son of Sinbad* and

Norman Mailer's *The Naked and the Dead*. And she took down six figures a year for taking it off.

Lili became a star not by portraying Cinderella—fairy-tale characters more suited to Disney than burlesque remained rare portrayals for her—but by playing femme fatales and sirens. She reinterpreted the stories of women like Carmen and Salome, who used their beauty and erotic dances to control men. And she created her own characters that gave audiences a voyeuristic glimpse into her character's world. In one, Lili played a mannequin come to life. In another, she starred as a tormented woman who commits suicide. In her most famous, she prepared for a date and audiences watched as she bathed, dressed, and primped before-hand. Onstage and off she starred as a seductress—a woman who used her physical appeal, dance moves, sexpertise, and charisma to enchant men and live outside the traditional feminine sphere.

Lili's generation of striptease dancers called themselves ecdysiasts, H. L. Mencken's coinage reflecting the scientific word for molting or shed-ding. They not only shed their clothes, but also the acceptable, conven-tional norms. In the culmination of a century of boundary-pressing activity, they shed any last remnants of Victorian purity. With a tug at their G-string, they helped unravel the apron strings that had long bound women. Lili lived her life in a manner that went against the status quo. Her widespread appeal made her more popular than any other striptease dancer of her era and splashed her image across countless newspapers and magazines, while her outrageous comments raised eyebrows and blood pressure. And both made her a regular focal point in the debate about striptease and sex.

As Lili herself acknowledged to a reporter before her interview with Mike Wallace, she was not a crusader. In fact, her motives were primarily selfish—to make money and to live the good life. However, the very man-ner she chose to reach those goals challenged traditional gender roles, wrested control over her own sexuality, and broadened the scope of sexual possibilities for other women.

Lili starred not just as a striptease dancer, but also as a twentieth-cen-tury seductress. Seductresses are often dismissed as blonde bimbos, gold-diggers, or vamps, but while far from perfect, they are also about more than sex, more than simply talented at bewitching men. "Seductresses were mistresses of misrule, carnival queens who cast off repressive shackles and declared a public holiday," wrote Betsy Prioleau in *Seductress: Women Who Ravished the World and Their Lost Art of Love*.[8] "Far from sellouts to patriarchy . . . they subvert and sabotage it. They menace male domination. Since antiquity they've roiled the waters and upset the hierarchy."

A seductress uses her erotic nature, her shimmering allure, and her brain to further her own cause. She lives with a captivating vitality and joie de vivre that is near-impossible to refuse or ignore. And she uses these skills, her feminine wiles, to stretch the boundaries of what's acceptable for women. As Prioleau wrote, "The art of love . . . is consistent with the highest principles of feminism. It promotes self-development, autonomy, and liberation and expands our options."[9]

Lili St. Cyr spent her life imagining and presenting this art of love. And as a seductress and striptease dancer, she became part of the twentieth-century debate about sex and gender. Throughout the century, Americans struggled with the tension between the puritanical ethic—sex as sin—and a new message: sex as the ultimate expression of romantic love. Americans danced with and around sexuality, first by shaking off Victorian ideals and exploring sex outside of reproduction, then by publicly celebrating chastity while being teased by women on stage and in the pages of girlie magazines, and then finally by shaking free of the cult of virginity and embracing sexual liberation. Burlesque, replete with innuendo and flashes of flesh, helped introduce the country to overt sexuality and made the discussion and selling of sex more acceptable, and as one of burlesque's most popular stars, Lili helped usher in these changes. As a powerful seductress, she inspired other great sirens, from Marilyn Monroe to Madonna.

At the same time, Lili also struggled with the push and pull surrounding notions of sex. She lived outside the traditional feminine domain by highlighting her very femininity. She seduced millions through her performances, yet found love elusive. She echoed the need to belong to someone even as she chafed at the role. She worked so hard to perfect her acts, and at times seemed to love her work so much, that she sacrificed relationships for it. Yet by the late fifties she publicly questioned her profession. She made her living selling sex, but turned up her nose at the ubiquitous commercialization that followed and that she helped enable. Secure in her sexuality, she dared to be provocative before it was acceptable. She used her beauty as currency and famously said, "I broke hearts and emptied pocketbooks. Sex is currency. What is the use of being beautiful if you can't profit from it."[10] She herself, however, ended up destitute.

Lili was riddled with flaws, plagued by bouts of insecurity, and filled with self-destructive passions. Ultimately she bought into the myth that seniors could not be seductresses; that beauty remained integral to success, happiness, and power. And her finale lacked the happily-ever-after outcome of her fairy-tale inspiration, Cinderella.

These flaws and doubts led Lili to isolate herself completely in the hope that she would be remembered for the beautiful, ahead-of-her-time siren that she was. Instead, she was forgotten. As she grew older, she turned down interviews, refused fans requests, and rebuffed friends' attempts to visit. After more than twenty-five years of seclusion, her name dimmed from the marquee in the public's mind. Now, if she is remembered at all, it is most often as the answer to a trivia question—she is the woman Susan Sarandon's character Janet blessed in the cult film *The Rocky Horror Picture Show.*

More than Lili's self-imposed seclusion, it was her career as a stripper that cast her to the dusty corners of history. Whereas the men of burlesque—Phil Silvers, Abbott and Costello, Jackie Gleason—were celebrated outside of that bawdy world, the women rarely were. The public maintained a contradictory attitude toward the striptease dancer, as Lili and the women of burlesque represented the supreme contradiction for women. The audience projected its wants, needs, loves, or desires on the dancer, but beneath the fantasy lived a real woman. She teased the eye and libido, but remained untouchable. She was at once a heavenly sexual goddess and earthly woman, appealing and abhorrent, glorified and stigmatized. And so the stripper holds no one place in the public mind or the social order. It is often just easier to ignore and forget her.

Ignoring or forgetting Lili and the women of burlesque, however, ignores and forgets an interesting piece of women's history and a fun, flirty piece of our sexual history. Despite Lili's own complications, paradoxes, and flaws, she challenged traditional gender roles, seized control over her own sexuality, and broadened the range of sexual possibilities for other women. At her zenith, the culture celebrated women's hair color—blonde—and the shape of their bodies—hourglass—and defined women by their roles in the lives of men. Lili used these notions to her benefit. She shook her blonde curls, shimmied her hourglass figure, played up her femininity onstage, and earned a fortune and her independence by turn-ing the very idea on its head.

The contradictions in Lili's life and character do not detract from the essence of who she was. Rather, it is within those contradictions that the spirit of her character can be found. They are the same conflicts and incongruities with which most women have long struggled. The difference is in how Lili St. Cyr pieced together those paradoxes—she seduced the world with them. And as philosopher Jean Baudrillard observed, "Seduction foils all systems of power."[11]

Endnotes

FOREWORD

1. *Seductress* by Betsy Prioleau (Viking, 2003).
2. Ibid.
3. "St. Cyr won fame with strip show," *The (Montreal) Gazette*, February 2, 1999.

CHAPTER ONE

1. From *Ma Vie de Stripteaseuse* by Lili St. Cyr and Matthew Tombers (Les Editions Quebecor, 1982); translated by John C. Bucholz for the author. Future citations within this section noted as MVS.
2. Wisconsin Historical Society.
3. "Tells of Early History of Port Edwards," *Wisconsin Rapids Tribune*, February 17, 1921.
4. Author interview with Coy Giambone.
5. Details of Alice's life are compiled from various census records, city directories, marriage records, death certificate, and family history provided by Ellie Hiatt and Kristine Plasch. Interviews with Coy Giambone, Bruce Peseau, Ellie Hiatt, Kristine Plash, Robert Cornett, Curtis Marx, and other family members.
6. Author interview with Ellie Hiatt.
7. Author interview with Kris Plasch.
8. When Marie was Lili St. Cyr, she would tell fans and reporters she had been born Willis Marie. Apparently the Willis was for her uncle William, but her birth certificate lists her middle name as Frances, the feminine version of her two grandfathers' names.
9. "Orderly Registration of Most of Eligibles Is Anticipated Here," *The Minneapolis Morning Tribune*, June 5, 1917.
10. Stats on Camp Lewis from *Making Men Moral* by Nancy K. Bristow (New York University Press, 1996); Information on Van Schaack's war records from military personnel files.
11. *American Beauty* by Lois W. Banner (Alfred A. Knopf, 1983).
12. This estimate is based on a questionnaire given to over 13,000 men at four bases and was reported in "Venereal Disease and the AEF" by Donald Smythe in *Prologue* (National Archives and Records Administration publication), 1994. *Making Men Moral* by Nancy K. Bristow (New York University Press, 1996).

13. *America's Women* by Gail Collins (HarperCollins, 2003).
14. Ibid.
15. *Intimate Matters* by John D'Emilio and Estelle Freedman (Harper and Row, 1988).
16. *Great Moments in Sex* by Cheryl Riley (Three River Press, 1999).
17. History of Pasadena come from interviews with Sue Mossman of Pasadena Heritage and *Pasadena: Crown of the Valley* by Ann Scheid (Windsor Publications, 1986); Information on Chippewa tribe come from *A Native American Encyclopedia* by Barry M. Pritzker (Oxford University Press, 2000).
18. Pasadena Building Permits.
19. *Pasadena: Crown of the Valley* by Ann Scheid (Windsor Publications, 1986).
20. Family genealogy and history culled from various sources including birth certificates, census records, and city directory listings.
21. MVS.
22. MVS.
23. "Missing fathers," *Psychology Today*, April 1987.
24. MVS.
25. *Mariga* by Carola Peck (The Hannon Press, 1997)
26. E-mail from Patrick Guinness to author
27. MVS.
28. MVS.
29. MVS.
30. *Mariga* by Carola Peck (The Hannon Press, 1997).
31. Ibid.
32. *The Entertainment Machine* by Robert Toll (Oxford University Press, 1982).
33. History of burlesque from *Striptease: The Untold History of the Girlie Show* by Rachel Shteir (Oxford University Press, 2004); *Horrible Prettiness: Burlesque and American Culture* by Robert C. Allen (University of North Carolina Press, 1991); and *Minsky's Burlesque* by Morton Minsky and Milt Machlin (Arbor House Publishing Company, 1986).
34. *Curtains* by Kenneth Tynan (Kingsport Press, 1961).
35. "The Great Garbo," *Life*, January 10, 1955.
36. *Popcorn Venus: Women, Movies & The American Dream* by Marjorie Rosen (Coward, McCann & Geoghegan, 1973).
37. MVS.
38. "Milne Business Grows From Bikes to Royalty," *Pasadena Star News*, February 26, 1961.
39. Author interview with Jane Milne Lopez
40. "Milne Business Grows From Bikes to Royalty," *Pasadena Star News*, February 26, 1961.
41. Author interview with speedway racing from historian John Chaplin.
42. MVS.
43. *Marriage, a History* by Stephanie Coontz (Viking Penguin, 2005).
44. *In And Out of Vogue* by Grace Mirabella (Doubleday, 1995).

45. Ibid.

46. *Movie Made America* by Robert Sklar (Random House, 1975).

47. MVS.

48. *Marriage, a History* by Stephanie Coontz (Viking Penguin, 2005); Poll conducted by the Gallup Organization, May 18–May 23, 1936.

49. "Milne Business Grows From Bikes to Royalty," *Pasadena Star News*, February 26, 1961.

50. Author interview with Jane Milne Lopez.

51. MVS.

52. MVS.

53. Author interview with Jane Milne Lopez.

54. MVS.

55. Author interview with Sandy Hicks.

56. Author interview with Jane Milne Lopez.

57. MVS.

58. *And Men My Fuel* by Lili St. Cyr (Novel Books, 1965).

59. Ibid.

60. Author interview with Mike Brown.

61. MVS.

62. Marie and Maxwell's movements determined from various ship manifests.

63. Author interview with Giles Croft.

64. Author interview with Edward Croft.

CHAPTER TWO

1. *City of Nets* by Otto Friedrich (Perennial Library, 1986).

2. *Hollywood Confidential* by Jeffrey Feinman (Playboy Press, 1976).

3. "You call that a blockbuster," *National Post* (Ontario), August 13, 2002.

4. *America's Women* by Gail Collins (HarperCollins, 2003).

5. *Los Angeles City of Dreams* by Harry Carr (D. Appleton-Century Company, 1935).

6. *Hollywood Confidential* by Jeffrey Feinman (Playboy Press, 1976).

7. *The Body Merchant: The Story of Earl Carroll* by Ken Murray (Ward Ritchie Press, 1976).

8. *Blondes Brunettes and Bullets* by Nils T. Granlund (Van Rees Press, 1957).

9. *The English Godfather* by Graham Nown (Hollen Street Press, 1987).

10. *The Encyclopedia of Vaudeville* by Anthony Slide (Greenwood Press, 1994).

11. "Memoirs of a Broadway Drum-Beater" by Abel Green, the *New York Times*, February 10, 1957.

12. "St Cyr Dresses for Women; Men Not Interested in Clothes," *Los Angeles* Times, June 21, 1953.

13. "Schoolgirl, 17 and Blonde, Chosen as Miss California," *Los Angeles* Times, August 12, 1940. Shirley Patterson was not the only Miss California that year. Two other women were also awarded the title in two other competitions. After much debate, Rosemary LaPlanche represented California in the Miss America

competition. She did not win, but returned the following year and became Miss America. After Rosemary's win, the rules were changed so that contestants could only compete once for the title.

14. "N.T.G. Girl Show Opens," *Los Angeles* Times, August 15, 1940.

15. From *Ma Vie de Stripteaseuse* by Lili St. Cyr and Matthew Tombers (Les Editions Quebecor, 1982); translated by John C. Bucholz for the author. Future citations within this section noted as MVS.

16. *Blondes Brunettes and Bullets* by Nils T. Granlund (Van Rees Press, 1957).

17. Author interview with Jean Forray.

18. *Yvonne: An Autobiography* by Yvonne De Carlo with Doug Warren (St. Martin's Press, 1987).

19. "Florentine Gardens," *Variety*, May 15, 1940.

20. *Minsky's Burlesque* by Morton Minsky and Milt Machlin (Arbor House Publishing, 1986).

21. "Burlesque—If You're Interested," *Variety*, January 6, 1937.

22. *The Century of Sex* by James R. Petersen (Grove Press, 1999).

23. *Minsky's Burlesque* by Morton Minsky and Milt Machlin (Arbor House Publishing, 1986).

24. "Rumpus in City Hall," *The New York Times*, March 22, 1942.

25. *Blondes Brunettes and Bullets* by Nils T. Granlund (Van Rees Press, 1957).

26. Louella Parsons columns from December 19, 1940 and December 26, 1940; MVS.

27. MVS

28. *And Men My Fuel* by Lili St. Cyr (Novel Books, 1965).

29. Ibid.

30. "Along Broadway" by Walter Winchell, *The Zanesville Signal*, July 29, 1959.

31. *Yvonne An Autobiography* by Yvonne De Carlo with Doug Warren (St. Martin's Press, 1987).

32. *Hollywood Confidential* by Jeffrey Feinman (Playboy Press, 1976).

33. MVS.

34. *Popcorn Venus: Women, Movies & the American Dream* by Marjorie Rosen (Coward, McCann & Geoghegan, 1973).

35. Info on Duncan Sisters from various news clippings including "Rosetta Duncan, Stage Star, Dies," *New York Times*, December 5, 1959 and Vivian Duncan obituary, *Washington Post*, September 22, 1986.

36. MVS.

37. "Queen of the Strippers: Lili St. Cyr," *Modern Man*, January 1952.

38. MVS.

39. "Thoroughly modern Lillie Langtry had the beauty and fame of a supermodel," *The Observer*, March 21, 1999; "Jersey girl," *The Independent*, October 11, 2003.

40. *Mae West, An Icon in Black and White* by Jill Watts (Oxford University Press, 2001).

41. Ibid.

42. Ibid.

43. "S.F. in a State of Emergency: Civilian Defense Council Takes Necessary Steps to Protect Life and Property," *San Francisco Chronicle*, December 8, 1941.

44. "Let's Go to a Show!" *San Francisco Examiner*, December 11, 1941.

45. MVS.

46. "Stripping away the veil of history from San Diego burlesque house," by Welton Jones, *San Diego Union-Tribune*, October 16, 1994.

47. Ibid.

48. San Diego Historical Society Oral History Program, An Interview with Bob Johnston, May 17, 1980.

49. Biography of Lili St. Cyr, Library of the Academy of Motion Picture Arts and Sciences.

50. Author interview with Katherine Flores.

51. *Striptease from Gaslight to Spotlight* by Jessica Glasscock (Harry N. Abrams, Inc., 2003).

52. Author interview with Katherine Flores.

53. San Diego Historical Society Oral History Program, Jane Cafarra Oral History, nd.

54. Stewart and Ford's service from "Ask the Globe," *Boston Globe*, December 16, 1990; Mitchum's service from "Robert Mitchum, a Hollywood maverick, dead at 79" in the *Vancouver Sun*, July 2, 1997.

55. *City of Nets* by Otto Friedrich (Harper & Row, 1986).

56. Gene Kelly, *Dance* magazine, April 1996; *City of Nets* by Otto Friedrich (Harper & Row, 1986).

57. "It Could Only Happen in Hollywood" by Lee Mortimer, *Daily Mirror*, January 9, 1947.

58. "Dead husband alive; 19-year union annulled," *Los Angeles Times*, June 4, 1943.

59. *Striptease: The Untold History of the Girlie Show* by Rachel Shteir (Oxford University Press, 2004).

60. "How to Tame a Wolf" by Lili St. Cyr, *Cabaret*, September 1955.

61. *Striptease: The Untold History of the Girlie Show* by Rachel Shteir (Oxford University Press, 2004).

62. *America's Women* by Gail Collins (HarperCollins, 2003).

63. *My Ears Are Bent* by Joseph Mitchell (Pantheon Books, 1938).

64. "Lili's Sincere, Wanting It Clear She Doesn't Strip, She Dresses," *Los Angeles Times*, May 15, 1953.

65. "Queen of the Strippers," *Modern Man*, January 1952.

66. MVS.

67. "Jazz quintet takes us back to West 52nd St.," *The Charleston Gazette*, January 31, 2005.

68. *Striptease: The Untold History of the Girlie Show* by Rachel Shteir (Oxford University Press, 2004).

69. *Honey: The Life and Loves of Lenny's Shady Lady* by Honey Bruce (Playboy Press, 1976).

70. MVS.

71. "Stripteasing: A Sex-Oriented Occupation" by James K. Skipper Jr. and Charles H. McCaghy in *Studies in the Sociology of Sex* (Meredith Corporation, 1971).

72. *Horrible Prettiness* by Robert C. Allen (University of North Carolina Press, 1991).

73. *Behind the G-String: An Exploration of the Stripper's Image, Her Person and Her Meaning* by David A. Scott (McFarland & Company, 1996).

74. Author interview with Betty Rowland.

75. Author interview with Liz Renay.

76. *And Men My Fuel* by Lili St. Cyr (Novel Books, 1965).

77. Ibid.

78. *Burlesque: Legendary Stars of the Stage* by Jane Briggeman, (Collectors Press, 2004).

79. *And Men My Fuel* by Lili St. Cyr (Novel Books, 1965).

80. "Leon & Eddie's, New York," *Billboard*, February 9, 1946.

81. *And Men My Fuel* by Lili St. Cyr (Novel Books, 1965.)

82. Ibid.

83. Letters provided to author by Pedro Serramalera.

84. "Man About Boston," *Boston Daily Record*, May 8, 1946.

85. "Wolf Woman," *Police Gazette*, June 1946.

86. Author interview with Kiva.

87. "Night Club Reviews," *Variety*, January 12, 1944.

CHAPTER THREE

1. Figures on city's gambling/brothel industry and quote from "Hot times in the old town: Montreal draws on long history of joie de vivre" by Juan Rodriguez in *The (Montreal) Gazette*, March 15, 2003.

2. "Night Club," *MacLean's*, October 15, 1944.

3. "How Plante and Drapeau Licked the Montreal Underworld," *MacLean's*, December 1, 1954.

4. "Night Club," *MacLean's*, October 15, 1944.

5. From *Ma Vie de Stripteaseuse* by Lili St. Cyr and Matthew Tombers (Les Editions Quebecor, 1982); translated by John C. Bucholz for the author. Future citations within this section noted as MVS.

6. *Montreal Confidential* by Al Palmer (New Stand Library Pocket Edition, 1950).

7. MVS.

8. September 21, 1948 Al Palmer column from column Concordia University Archives collection; The $32 would be the Canadian conversion.

9. Author interview with Vic Vogel.

10. Author interview with Brian MacDonald.

11. Author interview with Joe Mancini.

12. Author interview with Vic Vogel.

13. Ibid.

14. Author interview with Brian MacDonald.

15. Ibid.

16. MVS.

17. Bresciano's relationship with Cotroni confirmed in author interview with Cotroni's nephew; Lili's quotes on Maurice from MVS.

18. MVS.

19. MVS.

20. Author interview with Vic Vogel.

21. Author interview with Joe Mancini.

22. MVS.

23. "La Verte Sur Lili St Cyr" from Centre de Recherché Lionel-Groulx, translated by John C. Bucholz for the author.

24. *Montreal Confidential* by Al Palmer (New Stand Library Pocket Edition, 1950).

25. *Montreal Daily Star,* May 5, 1945.

26. The *(Montreal) Gazette,* May 1, 1948 and May 4, 1948 Al Palmer column from Concordia University Archives.

27. *Deep Waters: The Ottawa River and Canada's Nuclear Adventure* by Kim Krenz (McGill-Queen's University Press, 2004).

28. Author interview with Kim Krenz.

29. *City Unique* by William Weintraub (McClelland & Stewart, 1996).

30. MVS.

31. *Montreal Confidential* by Al Palmer (New Stand Library Pocket Edition, 1950).

32. Al Capp's *Wolf Gal,* No. 1 (Toby Press).

33. Al Capp's *Wolf Gal,* No. 2 (Toby Press).

34. Ibid.

35. "Lili St. Cyr Tells: The Kind of Man I Like," *Sir!,* May 1954.

36. Paul Valentine background culled from clippings in the New York Public Library's Jerome Robbins Collection and Valentine's official biography in the Academy Library.

37. MVS.

38. "Officer tells of strip tease," *Los Angeles Times,* April 15, 1948.

39. "Dancer Headlines Show," *Los Angeles Times,* June 11, 1948.

40. *Norma Jean: My Secret Life with Marilyn Monroe* by Ted Jordan (William Morrow, 1989).

41. Author interview with Gloria Romanoff.

42. *Requiem for Marilyn* by Bruno Bernard (Kensal Press, 1986).

43. Author interview with James Haspiel.

44. "Lili St. Cyr 'Interprets' at Gardens," *Los Angeles Times,* March 3, 1948.

45. MVS.

46. MVS.

47. *City Unique* by William Weintraub (McClelland & Stewart, 1996).

48. Author interview with Doris Quinn Godfrey.

49. *The History of the Detroit Red Wings* by Paul R. Greenland (Turning Leaf Publications, 1997).

50. Ibid.

51. *Montreal Confidential* by Al Palmer (New Stand Library Pocket Edition, 1950).

52. *Swinging in Paradise* by John Gilmore (Vehicule Press, 1988).

53. MVS.
54. Author interview with Jamee Carangello.
55. Author interview with Jimmy Orlando's second wife who asked to remain anonymous.
56. *And Men My Fuel* by Lili St. Cyr (Novel Books, 1965).
57. Author interview with Jamee Carangello.
58. Author interview with William Weintraub.
59. Author interview with Joe Mancini.
60. "King of Grunt & Groan" *Time,* June 24, 1957.
61. MVS.
62. "Love and times of Lili St. Cyr," *Montreal Mirror,* November 4, 2004 and author interview with Kristian Gavenor.
63. Author interview with Doris Quinn Godfrey.
64. Letter to the Athletic Commission from Frank Selke, managing director of the Canadian Arena Company dated December 8, 1961 and provided to author by Doris Quinn Godfrey.
65. Author interview with showgirl.
66. Author interview with Doris Quinn Godfrey.
67. *Behind the G-String* by David A. Scott (McFarland & Company, 1996).
68. *Low Man on a Totem Pole* by H. Allen Smith (Country Life Press, 1941).
69. Author interview with Doris Quinn Godfrey.
70. MVS.
71. Author interview with the showgirl.
72. Author interview with Jamee Carangello.
73. *And Men My Fuel* by Lili St. Cyr (Novel Books, 1965).
74. MVS.
75. MVS.
76. *And Men My Fuel* by Lili St. Cyr (Novel Books, 1965).
77. MVS.
78. Author interview with Bruce Gordon.
79. Author interview with Frank Aletter.
80. Dorothy Kilgallen column, *Lowell Sun,* March 18, 1955.
81. Author interview with Roberta Ralph.
82. Author interview with Claire Shull.
83. Author interview with Marsha Schoen.
84. Author interview with Roberta Ralph.
85. Author interview with Bob Canny.
86. Dorothy Kilgallen column, *Lowell Sun,* March 18, 1955.
87. "Memories of Montreal's Skin Queen," *The Globe and Mail,* February 3, 1999.
88. *And Men My Fuel* by Lili St. Cyr (Novel Books, 1965).

Chapter Four
1. *McCall's,* April 1954.
2. Statistics on marriage and birthrate from *America's Women* by Gail Collins

(HarperCollins, 2003) and *Marriage: A History* by Stephanie Coontz (Viking, 2005).

3. *The Feminine Mystique* by Betty Friedan (Dell Publishing, 1983).
4. *Marriage: A History* by Stephanie Coontz (Viking, 2005).
5. *America's Women* by Gail Collins (HarperCollins, 2003).
6. *Marriage: A History* by Stephanie Coontz (Viking, 2005).
7. "Talk with a toy king," *Reader's Digest*, January 1955.
8. "The little king," *Time*, December 12, 1955.
9. Background on Marx and family from *Fortune* magazine, January 1946; "Talk with a toy king," *Reader's Digest*, Jan. 1955; "The little king," *Time*, December 12, 1955; and *The Hunger of Eve* by Barbara Marx Hubbard (Island Pacific, 1989).
10. Author interview with Patricia Ellsberg.
11. Author interview with Curtis Marx.
12. Author interview with Armando Orsini.
13. Author interview with Curtis Marx.
14. "Actress Quits Wedded Life," *L.A. Times*, July 8, 1948.
15. Author interview with Vic Vogel.
16. "Could this be (blush) burlesque," *Washington Post*, October 11, 1972.
17. *Minsky's Burlesque* by Morton Minsky (Arbor House Publishing, 1986).
18. Author interview with Joan Carter.
19. "'Round Town," *Miami Daily News*, October 14, 1950.
20. "Burlesque," *Real*, June 1966.
21. Ibid.
22. "Wants to be Best Stripper in the World," *Fort Pierce News Tribune*, October 8, 1953.
23. Fidler in Hollywood column, *Nevada State Journal*, November 26, 1950.
24. Author interview with Joan Carter.
25. Author interview with Betty Rowland.
26. From *Ma Vie de Stripteaseuse* by Lili St. Cyr and Matthew Tombers (Les Editions Quebecor, 1982); translated by John C. Bucholz for the author. Future citations within this section noted as MVS.
27. Bob Hope joke and tranquilizer date from *The Century of Sex* by James R. Petersen (Grove Press, 1999).
28. *The Fifties* by David Halberstam (Ballantine Books, 1994).
29. "Why Young Mothers Feel Trapped," *Redbook*, September 1960.
30. MVS.
31. Author interview with Armando Orsini.
32. MVS.
33. Author interview with Armando Orsini.
34. *America's Cities of Sin* (Lion Books, 1951).
35. "How Plante and Drapeau Licked the Montreal Underworld," *MacLean's* magazine, December 1, 1954.
36. Ibid.
37. "Lili St Cyr et la moralite publique," *Le Devoir*, June 7, 1951, translated by John C. Bucholz for the author.

38. Letter from Committee on Public Morality to City Hall.

39. "Her Dance 'In Order' Say Police, the *(Montreal) Gazette*, June 13, 1951.

40. "Montreal 'Morals' Group Hits Stripper St. Cyr," *Variety*, June 13, 1951.

41. "Montreal Cops Haul St. Cyr to Court," *Variety*, June 20, 1951.

42. Ibid.

43. "Exotic Lili St. Cyr Looks on Demurely as Court Rules Her Dances Neither 'Immoral, Indecent or Obscene,'" *The (Montreal) Herald*, June 28, 1951.

44. "Lack of Evidence Frees Shapely Lili of Charges Her Stage Dance Obscene," the *(Montreal) Gazette*, June 28, 1951.

45. "Exotic Lili St. Cyr Looks on Demurely As Court Rules Her Dances Neither 'Immoral, Indecent, or Obscene,'" *The (Montreal) Herald*, June 28, 1951.

46. "Bravo Lili! Bravo Lili! Bravo Lili!," *Commerce Montreal*, June 18, 1951, transcribed by John C. Bucholz for the author.

47. "Margie Hart from Missouri strips for 40 cents as poor man's Garbo," *Life*, June 24, 1940.

48. *The Century of Sex* by James R. Petersen (Grove Press, 1999).

49. *Estes Kefauver: A Biography* by Charles L. Fontenay (University of Tennessee Press, 1980).

50. *Holy Land: A Suburban Memoir* by D. J. Waldie (St. Martin's Griffin, 1997).

51. *Nevada State Journal*, March 4, 1950. Walter Winchell's column.

52. "Clark County Official Literally Stops Show," *Reno Evening Gazette*, September 17, 1951.

53. St. Cyr Dresses for Women; Men Not Interested in Clothes," *Los Angeles Times*, June 21, 1953.

CHAPTER FIVE

1. Herman Hover's unpublished memoir provided to author by Sheila Weller, Hover's niece and author of *Dancing at Ciro's*.

2. *Dancing at Ciro's* by Sheila Weller (St. Martin's Press, 2003).

3. Herman Hover's unpublished memoir provided to author by Sheila Weller, Hover's niece and author of *Dancing at Ciro's*.

4. Ibid.

5. "The Stripper on the Strip," *Ciro's*, Spring 1952.

6. Herman Hover's unpublished memoir provided to author by Sheila Weller, Hover's niece and author of *Dancing at Ciro's*.

7. Hedda Hopper column, *Los Angeles Times*, March 7, 1951.

8. Author interview with Reggie Drew.

9. "Ciro's Sensation," *Night and Day* magazine, July 1951.

10. "Ban Strips But They Like 'Em," *Billboard*, April 7, 1951.

11. Author interview with Reggie Drew.

12. "Justice'd like to see Lili, too!" *The Mirror*, October 22, 1951.

13. "Elevation of the Arts," *Dixon (Illinois) Evening Telegraph*, October 23, 1951.

14. *Dancing at Ciro's* by Sheila Weller (St. Martin's Press, 2003).

15. *The Jerry Giesler Story* by Jerry Giesler (Simon and Schuster, 1960).

16. Ibid.

17. Ibid.

18. "Lili St. Cyr faces indecent show hearing, denies guilt," *L.A. Herald Express*, October 22, 1951.

19. "Lili St. Cyr wins delay in strip tease hearing," *L.A. Times*, October 23, 1951.

20. "Offer made in defense of art," *L.A. Herald Express*, December 4, 1951.

21. *The Jerry Giesler Story* by Jerry Giesler (Simon and Schuster, 1960).

22. Ibid.

23. "Bumpity-Bump-Bump battle over Lili's bump," *L.A. Herald Express*, December 5, 1951.

24. "Tells Lili's Silver Tub," *L.A. Herald & Express*, December 6, 1951.

25. "Lili St. Cyr didn't bump Ciro's operator says," *Los Angeles Times*, December 7, 1951; "What is a 'Bump'? Ciro's owner grinds out answer," *L.A. Herald & Express*, December 7, 1951.

26. Ibid.

27. "Lili St. Cyr didn't bump Ciro's operator says," *Los Angeles Times*, December 7, 1951.

28. "Tells Lili's silver tub," *L.A. Herald & Express*, December 6, 1951.

29. "Lili bares expenses to jury," *L.A. Herald & Express*, December 7, 1951.

30. Ibid.

31. "Bubble dancer withholds her evidence, rests lewdness case," *Dixon (Illinois) Evening Telegraph*, December 8, 1951; "Lili St. Cyr does her act in court—clothed," *San Francisco Chronicle*, December 8, 1951; "Lili St. Cyr takes stand to defend performance," Los Angeles *Times*, December 8, 1951.

32. "Lili St. Cyr takes stand to defend performance," Los Angeles *Times*, December 8, 1951.

33. "Final pleas in trial of Lili St. Cyr," *L.A. Herald Express*, December 10, 1951; "Jury weighs Lili St. Cyr's fate in strip tease case," *L.A. Herald Express*, December 11, 1951; "Jurors listen to summing up in St. Cyr case," Los Angeles *Times*, December 11, 1951.

34. "Final pleas in trial of Lili St. Cyr," *L.A. Herald Express*, December 10, 1951; "Jury weighs Lili St. Cyr's fate in strip tease case," *L.A. Herald Express*, December 11, 1951; "Jurors listen to summing up in St. Cyr case," *Los Angeles* Times, December 11, 1951.

35. "Final pleas in trial of Lili St. Cyr," *L.A. Herald Express*, December 10, 1951; "Jury weighs Lili St. Cyr's fate in strip tease case," *L.A. Herald Express*, December 11, 1951; "Jurors listen to summing up in St. Cyr case," *Los Angeles* Times, December 11, 1951.

36. "Final pleas in trial of Lili St. Cyr," *L.A. Herald Express*, December 10, 1951; "Jury weighs Lili St. Cyr's fate in strip tease case," *L.A. Herald Express*, December 11, 1951; "Jurors listen to summing up in St. Cyr case," *Los Angeles* Times, December 11, 1951.

37. "Final pleas in trial of Lili St. Cyr," *L.A. Herald Express*, December 10, 1951; "Jury weighs Lili St. Cyr's fate in strip tease case," *L.A. Herald Express*, December 11,

1951; "Jurors listen to summing up in St. Cyr case," *Los Angeles* Times, December 11, 1951.

38. "Acquit Lili," *L.A. Herald Express*, December 12, 1951; "Jury rules stripping's art, frees Lili St. Cyr," *L.A. Times*, December 12, 1951; "Jury finds Lili not guilty of any indecent exposure," *San Francisco Chronicle*, December 12, 1951.

39. Virginia MacPherson's Hollywood Report column, *Oxnard Press-Courier*, December 14, 1951.

40. Ibid. December 20, 1951.

41. "College officials hope term end will shut off panty raid craze," *Columbus Citizen*, May 22, 1952.

42. "Lili offers panties, bras to college dorm raiders," *Columbus Citizen*, May 21, 1952.

43. "Capital men ask Lili for panties," *Columbus Citizen*, May 22, 1952.

44. "College authorities taking steps to discourage dormitory raids," *The Coshocton Ohio Tribune*, May 25, 1952.

45. Dorothy Kilgallen column, *New York Journal-American*, February 12, 1952.

46. Interview notes courtesy of Eric Schaefer.

47. Ibid.

48. *Bold! Daring! Shocking! True! A History of Exploitation Films* by Eric Schaefer (Duke University Press, 1999).

49. "Crowd sees films attacked by 2 groups, disappointed," *Oxnard Press Courier*, August 5, 1952.

50. "An excuse to bring on the dancing girls," *New York Times*, July 28, 1955.

51. *Vincent Price: A Daughter's Biography* by Victoria Price (St. Martin's Press, 1999).

52. February 17, 1953 letter to William Feeder, Academy Library's Special Collection on Censorship.

53. From *Ma Vie de Stripteaseuse* by Lili St. Cyr and Matthew Tombers (Les Editions Quebecor, 1982); translated by John C. Bucholz for the author. Future citations within this section noted as MVS.

54. May 25, 1953 letter to William Feeder, Academy Library's Special Collection on Censorship.

55. "Lili St. Cyr likely lead in RKO picture," *Los Angeles Times*, April 25, 1953.

56. "Watching them make pictures," *Hollywood Citizen-News*, May 27, 1953.

57. Erskine Johnson's In Hollywood column, *The Independent Record* (Helena, Montana), July 31, 1953.

58. Bob Thomas' Hollywood News column, *Indiana Evening Gazette*, May 18, 1953.

59. "Watching them make pictures," *Hollywood Citizen-News*, May 27, 1953.

60. MVS.

61. Author interview with Armando Orsini.

62. "My husband doesn't like it," *New York Post*, June 1, 1952.

63. Author interview with Armando Orsini.

64. Ibid.

65. "Lili St. Cyr to shed mate in legal strip routine," *Los Angeles Times*, June 30, 1953.

66. MVS.

67. MVS.

68. *And Men My Fuel* by Lili St. Cyr (Novel Books, 1965).

69. *Dancing at Ciro's* by Sheila Weller (St. Martin's Press, 2003).

CHAPTER SIX

1. *Las Vegas: The Great American Playground* by Robert D. McCracken (University of Nevada Press, 1996).

2. *Fly on the Wall* by Dick Odessky (Huntington Press Publishing, 1999).

3. Ibid.

4. Author interview with Betsy Hammes.

5. "Las Vegas keeps the wheels turning," *New York Times*, October 19, 1958.

6. "Lili pays off old debt here," *Las Vegas Sun*, October 16, 1952.

7. "Joe E. Lewis draws laughter at Las Vegas, *Washington Post*, September 7, 1955.

8. *Cult Vegas* by Mike Weatherford (Huntington Press, 2001).

9. "Stars receive fantastic pay from casinos," *Washington Post*, May 21, 1953.

10. "Once upon a time in Las Vegas," *Nevada* magazine, May/June 1986.

11. *The Lady Is a Vamp* by Tempest Storm (Peachtree Publishers, 1987).

12. Author interview with Mildred Katleman.

13. Ibid.

14. From *Ma Vie de Stripteaseuse* by Lili St. Cyr and Matthew Tombers (Les Editions Quebecor, 1982); translated by John C. Bucholz for the author. Future citations within this section noted as MVS.

15. "She Works Hard for her money" by Joanne L. Goodwin in *The Grit Beneath the Glitter* (University of California Press, 2002).

16. *Las Vegas: City Without Clocks* by Ed Reid (Prentice-Hall, 1961).

17. "Minsky's Hideaway," *Newsweek*, November 8, 1954.

18. "She Works Hard for her money" by Joanne L. Goodwin in *The Grit Beneath the Glitter* (University of California Press, 2002).

19. Author interview with Armando Orsini

20. "Minsky's Hideaway," *Newsweek*, November 8, 1954

21. MVS.

22. "How to Tame a Wolf" by Lili St. Cyr, *Cabaret*, September 1955

23. MVS.

24. *Norma Jean: My Secret Life with Marilyn Monroe* by Ted Jordan (William Morrow and Company, 1989).

25. MVS.

26. "Lili St. Cyr to wed nephew of Ted Lewis," *The Bridgeport Telegram*, October 1, 1954.

27. "Lili sacrificing marriage for fiancée's movie career, she says," *Las Vegas Sun*, October 5, 1954.

28. "Wedding off again for stripper St. Cyr," *The Bridgeport Telegram*, October 4, 1954.

29. "Lili St. Cyr says wedding canceled to help Jordan," *Hollywood Citizen-News*, October 4, 1954.

30. *A Short History of Las Vegas* by Barbara Land and Myrick Land (University of

Nevada Press, 1999).

31. "Stripper St. Cyr weds in 22 yards of chiffon," *L.A. Herald Express*, February 22, 1955.

32. Dorothy Kilgallen column, *Lowell Sun*, March 1, 1955.

33. Author interview with Mildred Katleman.

34. "They pay to wear the pants," *Confidential* magazine, July 1953.

35. "Tips on Tables," *Washington Daily News*, October 11, 1955.

36. Notes on Re-Review of *Son of Sinbad* in Academy Library's Special Collection on Censorship.

37. "Sinbad son falls flat on his fez," *Los Angeles Times*, June 2, 1955.

38. "Memphis bans 'Son of Sinbad,'" *Washington Post*, April 6, 1954.

39. Remarks from Legion of Decency, Academy Library's Special Collection on Censorship.

40. Interview notes courtesy of Eric Schaeffer.

41. MVS.

42. Interview notes courtesy of Eric Schaeffer.

43. Ibid.

44. *The Autograph Collector's Magazine*, 1988.

45. MVS.

46. Interview notes courtesy of Eric Schaeffer.

47. *Intimate Matters: A History of Sexuality in America* by John D'Emilio and Estelle B. Freedman (Harper & Row, 1988) and *Great Moments in Sex* by Cheryl Riley (Three Rivers Press, 1999).

48. *Striptease: The Untold History of the Girlie Show* by Rachel Shteir (Oxford University Press, 2004).

49. "My 10 Favorite Men," *Top Secret* magazine, nd, UNLV Minsky collection.

50. Ibid.

51. *Striptease: The Untold History of the Girlie Show* by Rachel Shteir (Oxford University Press, 2004).

52. *And Men My Fuel* by Lili St. Cyr (Novel Books, 1965).

53. "Talk of the Town," *Las Vegas Sun*, August 18, 1953.

54. *And Men My Fuel* by Lili St. Cyr (Novel Books, 1965).

55. Author interview with Ben Friedman.

56. "Lili is center of fist fight," *Nevada State Journal*, August 26, 1956.

57. Author interview with Ben Friedman.

58. *Norma Jean* by Ted Jordan (William Morrow, 1989).

59. MVS.

CHAPTER SEVEN

1. *Encyclopedia of American Cultural and Intellectual History* (Charles Scribner's Sons, 2001).

2. "Production Cost More Money," nd, UNLV Minsky collection.

3. "Could this be (blush) burlesque?," *Washington Post*, October 11, 1972.

4. "Producer tells how he picks showgirl beauties," nd, UNLV Minsky collection.

5. "Old-time burlesque survives and takes off with new zip," *Chicago Tribune*, July 3, 1977.

6. *Striptease: The Untold History of the Girlie Show* by Rachel Shteir (Oxford University Press, 2004).

7. *A Pictorial History of Burlesque From A to Z* (Sherbourne Press, 1964).

8. "Burlesque," *Real* magazine, June 1966.

9. *Striptease: The Untold History of the Girlie Show* by Rachel Shteir (Oxford University Press, 2004).

10. "Live begins for Harold," *Sir Knight* Vol. 1, No. 5.

11. From *Ma Vie de Stripteaseuse* by Lili St. Cyr and Matthew Tombers (Les Editions Quebecor, 1982); translated by John C. Bucholz for the author. Future citations within this section noted as MVS.

12. *Hollywood at Sunset* by Charles Higham (Saturday Review Press, 1972).

13. "The Scandalmonger," *Vanity Fair*, April 2003.

14. *Striptease: The Untold History of the Girlie Show* by Rachel Shteir (Oxford University Press, 2004).

15. "The truth behind the Roman Orgy," *Hush-Hush*, May 1959.

16. "When Lili St. Cyr tried suicide," *Confidential*, January 1956.

17. "The Scandalmonger," *Vanity Fair*, April 2003.

18. *The Purple Decades* by Tom Wolfe (Farrar, Straus and Giroux, 1982).

19. *Striptease: The Untold History of the Girlie Show* by Rachel Shteir (Oxford University Press, 2004).

20. *Minsky's Burlesque* by Morton Minsky (Arbor House, 1986).

21. Author interview with Paul Gregory.

22. February 4, 1958 letter to RKO Studios, Academy Library Special Collection on Censorship.

23. Ibid.

24. "The Naked and the Dead war film at Randolph," Temple University Paley Library, Urban Archives.

25. "The Screen: Face of War," *New York Times*, August 7, 1958.

26. "War Novels Flat on Film," *Washington Post*, September 6, 1958.

27. The *Naked and the Dead* listing, AFI catalog.

28. *How I Made a Hundred Movies in Hollywood and Never Lost a Dime* by Roger Corman (Dell Publishing, 1990).

29. Ibid.

30. "Lili St. Cyr drops the towel for foreign showing only," UPI story, September 7, 1958, Temple University Urban Archives Nudity Collection.

31. Ibid.

32. Ibid.

33. Ibid.

34. MVS.

35. "You name it, she's done it," *Variety*, May 18, 1983.

36. *And Men My Fuel* by Lili St. Cyr (Novel Books, 1965).

37. "Around the Dials: Wallace to interview Lili St. Cyr, but nobody knows why," *The*

Evening Bulletin, October 5, 1957; from Temple University Urban Archives Nudity Collection.

38. Dorothy Kilgallen column, *Washington Post*, February 28, 1956.
39. Quotes and descriptions from videotape of the interview provided by Mike Wallace's office, transcribed by David Andrukonis.
40. "Stars dodge the Mike Wallace Interview to avoid being tagged 'it' in public," *Los Angeles Times*, December 1, 1957.
41. *The Feminine Mystique* by Betty Friedan (Laurel Book, 1983).
42. *Homeward Bound* by Elaine Tyler May (Basic Books, 1988).
43. "You name it, she's done it," *Variety*, May 18, 1983.
44. MVS.
45. MVS.
46. "Lili St. Cyr reported in suicide try" and "Pills fell Lili St. Cyr" from Temple University Urban Archives Nudity Collection; "Lili St. Cyr out of danger after swallowing pills," *Los Angeles Times*, November 1, 1958.
47. "Lili St. Cyr's Fantastic Flirt with Suicide," *Hush-Hush*, May, 1959.
48. MVS.

CHAPTER EIGHT

1. *Woman and the New Race* by Margaret Sanger (Brentano's, 1920).
2. Background and statistics on the Pill from *A Century of Women* by Deborah G. Felder (Citadel Press, 1999) and *Marriage, a History* by Stephanie Coontz (Viking, 2005).
3. "The pill: how it changed our lives," *Ladies Home Journal*, June 1990.
4. *The Century of Sex* by James R. Petersen (Grove Press, 1999).
5. "The Pill," by Loretta Lynn (Coal Miners Music, 1973).
6. *Marriage, a History* by Stephanie Coontz (Viking, 2005).
7. *Where the Girls Are* by Susan Douglas, (Times Books, 1994).
8. Ibid.
9. "The moral disarmament of Betty Coed," *Esquire*, September 1962.
10. "G-strings and top bananas," *Argosy*, July 1960.
11. *Burlesque: Legendary Stars of the Stage* by Jane Briggeman (Collectors Press, 2004).
12. "2D burlesque show in downtown bow," *New York Times*, December 12, 1963.
13. "G-strings and top bananas," *Argosy*, July 1960.
14. *Burlesque: Legendary Stars of the Stage* by Jane Briggeman (Collectors Press, 2004).
15. *Praise, Vilification & Sexual Innuendo* by Abby Wasserman (Chronicle Books, 1993).
16. "Exotica," *The Gent* magazine, nd, UNLV Minsky collection.
17. Ibid.
18. Ibid.
19. "Burlesque is a Bore for Lili," *San Francisco Chronicle*, nd.
20. "Fade-out on a Hollywood glamour story," *New York Times*, January 26, 1958.

21. Ibid.

22. "Windmill death dramatic chapter in Rancho Fire," *Las Vegas Sun*, June 18, 1960.

23. *Horrible Prettiness* by Robert C. Allen (University of North Carolina Press, 1991).

24. "Ken Murray, Lili St. Cyr set for Mapes," *Nevada State Journal*, June 2, 1961.

25. *Runaway Girl*, Something Weird Video (1993).

26. "Strippers an Unhappy Lot, Lili Discovers," *Runaway Girl* publicity materials, USC Cinema-Television Library.

27. "Burlesque is a Bore for Lili," *San Francisco Chronicle*, nd.

28. *Variety* obituary, July 8, 1997.

29. Author interview with Gloria Zomar.

30. *Richard Boone* by David Rothel (Empire Publishing, 2000).

31. Author interview with Helen Frazee.

32. *And Men My Fuel* by Lili St. Cyr (Novel Books, 1965).

33. *Striptease: The Untold History of the Girlie Show* by Rachel Shteir (Oxford University Press, 2004).

34. "An evening with Lili," *Los Angeles Herald Examiner*, June 8, 1965.

35. "Burlesque is a Bore for Lili," *San Francisco Chronicle*, nd.

36. Author interview with Gloria Zomar.

37. Author interview with Helen Frazee.

38. Author interview with Gloria Zomar.

39. *And Men My Fuel* by Lili St. Cyr (Novel Books, 1965).

40. "Lili St. Cyr divorce no. 6," *Tri City Herald*, July 9, 1964.

41. "Strip queen Lili sheds number 6," *Los Angeles Herald-Examiner*.

42. "Lili St. Cyr sheds no. 6, 'not through,'" *Los Angeles Times*, July 9, 1964.

43. Author interview with Gloria Zomar.

44. From *Ma Vie de Stripteaseuse* by Lili St. Cyr and Matthew Tombers (Les Editions Quebecor, 1982); translated by John C. Bucholz for the author. Future citations within this section noted as MVS.

45. Author interview with Gloria Zomar.

46. *Marriage, a History* by Stephanie Coontz (Viking, 2005).

47. MVS.

48. *And Men My Fuel* by Lili St. Cyr (Novel Books, 1965).

49. *Bare: One Women, Dancing, Sex, and Power* by Elizabeth Eaves (Alfred A. Knopf, 2002).

50. *And Men My Fuel* by Lili St. Cyr (Novel Books, 1965).

CHAPTER NINE

1. *The Entertainment Machine* by Robert C. Toll (Oxford University Press, 1982).

2. Details on how movies changed from *The Entertainment Machine* by Robert C. Toll (Oxford University Press, 1982).

3. *The Century of Sex* by James R. Petersen (Grove Press, 1999); *Great Moments in Sex* by Cheryl Riley (Three Rivers Press, 1999).

4. *The Century of Sex* by James R. Petersen (Grove Press, 1999).

5. Ibid.
6. *Striptease: The Untold History of the Girlie Show* by Rachel Shteir (Oxford University Press, 2004)
7. *Burlesque: Legendary Stars of the Stage* by Jane Briggeman (Collector's Press, 2004).
8. "Naughty-Naughty opens Moulin Rouge, *Los Angeles Herald-Examiner*, June 5, 1964.
9. "Singing the Bourbon St. Blues," *Los Angeles Times*, January 24, 1965.
10. "Burlesque is back off gay white way," *Washington Post*, January 12, 1966.
11. From *Ma Vie de Stripteaseuse* by Lili St. Cyr and Matthew Tombers (Les Editions Quebecor, 1982); translated by John C. Bucholz for the author. Future citations within this section noted as MVS.
12. "La Belle Lili back in town," *Montreal Star*, March 20, 1965.
13. Ibid.
14. "Paving the way to oblivion," *The (Montreal) Gazette*, June 24, 2002.
15. "Lili St-Cyr: 'Montreal est Severe pour les Streap-Teaseuse," *Nouvelles Illustrees*, April 3, 1965; translated by John C. Bucholz for the author.
16. MVS.
17. Author interview with Doris Quinn Godfrey.
18. MVS.
19. Author interview with Doris Quinn Godfrey.
20. Author interview with Jimmy Orlando's wife from the time.
21. Author interview with Jamee Carangello.
22. "Ourtown," (Montreal) *Gazette*, February 11, 1967.
23. "'La Belle Lili' Back in Town," *Montreal Star*, March 20, 1965.
24. "St. Cyr won fame with strip show," *The(Montreal) Gazette*, February 2, 1999.
25. "Lili, all dressed, pleads not guilty," *Montreal Star*, February 21, 1967.
26. "Lili back at work taking them off," From Alan Hustak, dated February 22, 1967.
27. "Lili order arrested—well maybe," March 22, 1967 from Alan Hustak.
28. Author interview with Jamee Carangello.
29. Author interview with Doris Quinn Godfrey.
30. Author interview with Jimmy Orlando's wife from the time.
31. *Carnival Strippers* by Susan Meiselas (Farrar, Straus, Giroux, 1976).
32. *Girl Show: Into the Canvas World of Bump and Grind* by A.W. Stencil (ECW Press, 1999).
33. *Carnival Strippers* by Susan Meiselas (Farrar, Straus, Giroux, 1976).
34. Ibid.
35. Ibid.
36. "Burlesque show at Melodyland," *Los Angeles Times*, November 30, 1967.
37. "Revue shows why burlesque died," *San Francisco Examiner*, November 15, 1967.
38. "La Belle Lili," (Montreal) *Gazette*, February 11, 1967.
39. "Bravo Burlesque has standing room only," From Temple University Paly Library, Urban Archives, Nudity Collection. Dated July 18, 1967.
40. *Where the Girls Are* by Susan Douglas (Random House, 1995).

41. *America's Women* by Gail Collins (HarperCollins, 2003).

42. "Could this be (blush) burlesque?" *Washington Post*, October 11, 1972.

43. *Behind the G-String* by David A. Scott (McFarland & Company, 2003).

44. *Bare* by Elisabeth Eaves (Alfred A. Knopf, 2002).

45. "Striptease: The Art of Spectacle and Transgression," *Journal of Popular Culture*, Summer 2000.

46. "At top of the best (un)dressed list—superstars of stripping," *New York Times*, May 23, 1967.

47. "Stripteasing: A Sex-Oriented Occupation," in *Studies in the Sociology of Sex* (Meredith Corporation, 1971).

48. "Burlesque," *Real* magazine, June 1966.

49. *Striptease: The Untold History of the Girlie Show* by Rachel Shteir (Oxford University Press, 2004).

50. "Stripteasing: A Sex-Oriented Occupation," in *Studies in the Sociology of Sex* (Meredith Corporation, 1971).

51. "My 10 Favorite Men," *Top Secret* magazine, nd, UNLV Minsky collection.

52. "Lili St. Cyr: There're two things in life—work and sex," *San Francisco Examiner & Chronicle*, September 20, 1970.

53. "Past and Present Glory of Burlesque Theater," Transcript from Weekend Edition, March 1, 2003.

54. "Stormy weather," *American Theatre*, April 2003.

55. *Striptease: The Untold History of the Girlie Show* by Rachel Shteir (Oxford University Press, 2004).

56. "Stormy weather," *American Theatre*, April 2003.

57. *Striptease: From Gaslight to Spotlight* by Jessica Glasscock (Harry N. Abrams, Inc, 2003).

58. "Lili St. Cyr: There're two things in life—work and sex," *San Francisco Examiner & Chronicle*, September 20, 1970.

59. *Blondes Brunettes and Bullets* by Nils T. Granlund (Van Rees Press, 1957).

CHAPTER TEN

1. "Hollywood news," *Indiana Evening Gazette*, May 18, 1953.

2. *And Men My Fuel* by Lili St. Cyr (Novel Books, 1965).

3. Photocopy of lingerie ads provided by author Rudolph Grey.

4. Author interview with Babette Ory.

5. Quotes from Lili's letters from author's personal collection.

6. Author interview with Bob Bethia.

7. Ibid.

8. Ibid.

9. Ibid.

10. Ibid.

11. Ibid.

12. *The Autograph Collector's Magazine*, 1988.

13. *Whatever Became Of . . .* by Richard Lamparski, (Bantam Books, 1974).

14. Author interview with Bob Bethia.
15. "That blonde the cops called on was Lili St. Cyr," *Uncensored* magazine, February 1957.
16. Author interview with Bob Bethia.
17. "No more divas anymore," *Sunday Tribune*, July 6, 2003.
18. *Popcorn Venus: Women, Movies & the American Dream* by Marjorie Rosen (Coward, McCann & Geoghegan, 1973).
19. Author interview with Andrea Hedrick.
20. Ibid.
21. Ibid.
22. Ibid.
23. "The kind of men I like," *Sir!*, May 1954.
24. Author interview with Andrea Hedrick.
25. Ibid.
26. Ibid.
27. Ibid.
28. "Lili St. Cyr: There're two things in life—work and sex," *San Francisco Examiner & Chronicle*, September 20, 1970.
29. Author interview with Andrea Hedrick.
30. FBI file obtained by author; *Hanford Sentinel* obituary information sheet sent by Odell Funeral Home.
31. Author interview with Kris Plasch.
32. Author interview with Andrea Hedrick.
33. Ibid.
34. Ibid.
35. Quotes from Lili's letters from author's personal collection.
36. Author interview with Andrea Hedrick.
37. *A Century of Women* by Deborah G. Felder (Citadel Press, 1999).
38. Ibid.
39. *And Men My Fuel* by Lili St. Cyr (Novel Books, 1965).
40. Author interview with Andrea Hedrick.
41. *Marriage, a History* by Stephanie Coontz (Viking, 2005).
42. Ibid.
43. Author interview with Andrea Hedrick.
44. Author interview with Dr. W.
45. Ibid.
46. Author interview with Babette Ory.
47. From *Ma Vie de Stripteaseuse* by Lili St. Cyr and Matthew Tombers (Les Editions Quebecor, 1982); translated by John C. Bucholz for the author.
48. *Trainspotting*, 1999.
49. Author interview with Andrea Hedrick.
50. Ibid.
51. Ibid.

CHAPTER ELEVEN

1. "The Gossip Column," *Washington Post*, October 24, 1982.
2. *American Beauty* by Lois W. Banner (Alfred A. Knopf, 1983).
3. *Norma Jean: My Secret Life with Marilyn Monroe* by Ted Jordan (William Morrow, 1989).
4. "Actor claims discovery of Marilyn Monroe's red diary," UPI, August 19, 1982.
5. Untitled article, UPI, August 20, 1982.
6. "Actor admits he never had Monroe diary," Associated Press, August 20, 1982.
7. Los Angeles County District Attorney Bureau of Investigation report by Al Tomich, August 20, 1982.
8. Los Angeles County District Attorney Bureau of Investigation report by Al Tomich, September 30, 1982.
9. "Names and Faces," *Boston Globe*, August 26, 1982.
10. "Los Angeles Inquiry on Marilyn Monroe Rules Out Murder," *New York Times*, December 28, 1982.
11. Untitled article, *Variety*, December 30, 1982, from the Academy Library's files on Ted Jordan.
12. *Goddess: The Secret Lives of Marilyn Monroe* by Anthony Summers (Onyx Books, 1986).
13. "'Norma Jean' tells story of an affair," *Los Angeles Times*, November 18, 1989.
14. Author interview with Ernie Volkman.
15. Ibid.
16. "Inside New York," *Newsday*, May 2, 1989.
17. Author interview with James Haspiel.
18. Author interview with Anthony Summers.
19. Author interview with James Haspiel.
20. *Requiem for Marilyn* by Bruno Bernard (Kensal Press, 1986).
21. Author interview with Liz Renay.
22. Author interview with Armando Orsini.
23. Author interview with Ben Friedman.
24. Author interview with Mildred Katleman.
25. Author interview with Ernie Volkman.
26. Author interview with Ben Friedman.
27. "Marilyn revealed," *Playboy*, June 2005.
28. "OC man recalls his Norma Jean," *Orange County Register*, November 7, 1989.
29. *And Men My Fuel* by Lili St. Cyr (Novel Books, 1965).

CHAPTER TWELVE

1. *Eat Pray Love* by Elizabeth Gilbert (Viking, 2006).
2. Author interview with Augusto Lodi.
3. Author interview with Armando Orsini.
4. Author interview with Betty Rowland.
5. Author interview with Bob Bethia.
6. Ibid.

7. Ibid.

8. Author interview with Kash.

9. Ibid.

10. Ibid.

11. Ibid.

12. Ibid.

13. Ibid.

14. Author interview with Dr. W.

15. Author interview with Kash.

16. Author interview with Armando Orsini.

17. Author interview with Aland Hustak.

18. Author interview with Andrea Hedrick.

19. Author interview with Dr. W.

20. "Ah! cette Lili St. Cyr que les Montréalais ont tant aimée!," *La Presse*, February 4, 1999, translated by Lisa Sumner.

21. Author interview with Armando Orsini.

22. "St. Cyr won fame with strip show," *The (Montreal) Gazette*, February 2, 1999.

23. "Obituary: Lili St. Cyr," *The Guardian*, March 2, 1999.

24. Author interview with Bob Bethia.

25. Author interview with Andrea Hedrick.

26. Author interview with Irene Terheggen.

27. *Rouge Pulp* by Dorothy Barresi (University of Pittsburgh Press, 2002).

EPILOGUE

1. "Naughty takes off," *Washington Post*, November 30, 2003.

2. "Stripping Down to the Roots," *Time*, May 20, 2002.

3. Author interview with Michelle Baldwin for "Burlesque Comeback Tries to Dance with Feminism," *Women's News*, December 7, 2004.

4. Ibid.

5. From *A Century of Women* by Deborah G. Felder (Citadel Press, 1999) and *America's Women* by Gail Collins (William Morrow, 2003).

6. *America's Women* by Gail Collins (William Morrow, 2003).

7. "Women insulted by Top 100 List," *The (Montreal) Gazette*, November 17, 1999.

8. *Seductress* by Betsy Prioleau (Viking, 2003).

9. Ibid.

10. "St. Cyr won fame with strip show," *The (Montreal) Gazette*, February 2, 1999.

11. Ibid.

Index